THE RISE OF MODERN RELIGIOUS IDEAS IN AMERICA

– Editorial Director –

SYDNEY E. AHLSTROM, American Studies Program, Yale University

EDWARD CALDWELL MOORE

An Outline of the History of Christian Thought Since Kant

Reprint Edition
with a New Introduction

THE REGINA PRESS

Reprint Edition 1975

THE REGINA PRESS
7 Midland Avenue
Hicksville, New York 11801

Library of Congress Catalog Number: 74-78286
International Standard Book Number: 0-88271-022-2

This volume is reprinted according to the standards established in 1972 by the Rare Book Libraries' Conference on Facsimiles.

Manufactured in the United States of America.

INTRODUCTION TO THE REPRINT EDITION
by Sydney E. Ahlstrom,
American Studies Program,
Yale University

EDWARD CALDWELL MOORE (1857-1943) joined the Harvard Divinity School faculty in 1901 and in the course of his teaching career made the history of Christian thought since the time of Immanuel Kant a field of his own. In the course of his teaching he came to see the nineteenth century as a period when major forces and trends created *new* problems in a far more drastic way than the Reformation had done. When a new series of "Studies in Theology" was projected for publication, he was thus a natural choice. And it can be said that not only does his contribution equal the excellence maintained by the series but that his volume has stood the test of time better than most, though there has been an immense volume of scholarly research on nineteenth-century thought since 1912 when this work was first published. Even so there are very few such works that match Moore's ability to organize his material, describe the major thinkers, and draw untendentious conclusions as to their significance.

This is not to say that Moore was neutral on the main issue in question (whether or not post-Kantian developments in Western thought were good or bad) or on the innumerable other particular issues with which he had to deal. Moore did not lament the scientific, scholarly, literary, and aesthetic changes that had taken place. He was basically a grateful legatee of what he regarded as an extraordinarily profound series of movements and counter-movements. He has appropriated the work of Kant, Schleiermacher, Ritschl, and the many other greater or lesser figures who people his book. He dedicates the volume to Adolf Harnack as did Arthur Cushman McGiffert who wrote the preceding volume in this series, on *Protestant Thought Before Kant.* Like so many scholars of this period, he took Harnack's prodigious studies as a standard by which to measure his own.

The times in which this reprinted volume appears have also been deeply disturbed and challenged by the problems which science, scholarship, technological advance, and a disorienting degree of social change have created. Yet because many if not all of these problems are extensions of those which this book treats, students of all sorts and conditions should find this a helpful and illuminating account. Whether they are in academic institutions or not they will be grateful for a book that is succinct, orderly, lucid, and interesting.

Edward Caldwell Moore was born in West Chester, Pennsylvania. He received his B.A. from Marietta College and then went on to Union Theological Seminary in New York, graduating in 1884. From 1884 to 1886, he studied and attended lectures at the universities of Berlin, Göttingen, and Giessen in Germany. (He later received an honorary doctorate from the last named.) On returning to the United States, he served for three years as a Presbyterian minister in Yonkers, New York. He then became minister of the Central Congregational Church of Providence, Rhode Island, until he joined the Harvard faculty as Parkman Professor of Theology, in 1901. While in Providence he received his PhD. from Brown University. In 1915 Moore also became Plumber Professor of Christian Morals, Preacher to the University, and chairman of the Board of Preachers at Harvard University. He retired in 1929. Aside from research and writing in his chief field of interest, he also wrote two historical works on Christian missions and various reports for the American Board for Foreign Missions, whose activities he did much to advance. His last major work, published in his retirement was *The Nature of Religion*, (1939), which was based on course lectures delivered during his years as a teacher. It ranges widely over the field of religion as an introductory course might do, treating many aspects of Christian history and theology, the philosophy of religion, and the history of religions. It was based on wide reading and much traveling in various parts of the world. It documents his indebtedness to the great nineteenth-century revolution in Western religion but lacks the verve and precision of his *Outline of the History of Christian Thought Since Kant*. E. C. Moore has always been overshadowed by the eminence of his brother, George Foot Moore, a colleague at Harvard, who is remembered as one of America's finest scholars of Judaism. But his historical work nevertheless warrants the extension of its influence that this edition may provide.

AN OUTLINE OF THE HISTORY OF
CHRISTIAN THOUGHT SINCE KANT

AN OUTLINE OF THE
HISTORY OF CHRISTIAN
THOUGHT SINCE KANT

BY

EDWARD CALDWELL MOORE

PARKMAN PROFESSOR OF THEOLOGY IN HARVARD UNIVERSITY

NEW YORK
CHARLES SCRIBNER'S SONS
1920

PREFATORY NOTE

It is hoped that this book may serve as an outline for a larger work, in which the judgments here expressed may be supported in detail. Especially, the author desires to treat the literature of the social question and of the modernist movement with a fulness which has not been possible within the limits of this sketch. The philosophy of religion and the history of religions should have place, as also that estimate of the essence of Christianity which is suggested by the contact of Christianity with the living religions of the Orient.

PASQUE ISLAND, MASS.,
July 28, 1911.

CONTENTS

CHAPTER I

CHAPTER II

CHAPTER III

CHAPTER IV

CHAPTER V

CHAPTER VI

AN OUTLINE OF THE HISTORY OF
CHRISTIAN THOUGHT SINCE KANT

AN OUTLINE OF THE HISTORY OF CHRISTIAN THOUGHT SINCE KANT

CHAPTER I

A.—INTRODUCTION

THE Protestant Reformation marked an era both in life and thought for the modern world. It ushered in a revolution in Europe. It established distinctions and initiated tendencies which are still significant. These distinctions have been significant not for Europe alone. They have had influence also upon those continents which since the Reformation have come under the dominion of Europeans. Yet few would now regard the Reformation as epoch-making in the sense in which that pre-eminence has been claimed. No one now esteems that it separates the modern from the mediæval and ancient world in the manner once supposed. The perspective of history makes it evident that large areas of life and thought remained then untouched by the new spirit. Assumptions which had their origin in feudal or even in classical culture continued unquestioned. More than this, impulses in rational life and in the interpretation of religion, which showed themselves with clearness in one and another of the reformers themselves, were lost sight of, if not actually repudiated, by their successors. It is possible to view many things in the intellectual and religious life of the nineteenth century, even some which Protestants have passionately reprobated, as but the taking up again of clues which the reformers had let fall, the carrying out of purposes of their movement which were partly hidden from themselves.

A

Men have asserted that the Renaissance inaugurated a period of paganism. They have gloried that there supervened upon this paganism the religious revival which the Reformation was. Even these men will, however, not deny that it was the intellectual rejuvenation which made the religious reformation possible or, at all events, effective. Nor can it be denied that after the Reformation, in the Protestant communions the intellectual element was thrust into the background. The practical and devotional prevailed. Humanism was for a time shut out. There was more room for it in the Roman Church than among Protestants. Again, the Renaissance itself had been not so much an era of discovery of a new intellectual and spiritual world. It had been, rather, the rediscovery of valid principles of life in an ancient culture and civilisation. That thorough-going review of the principles at the basis of all relations of the life of man, which once seemed possible to Renaissance and Reformation, was postponed to a much later date. When it did take place, it was under far different auspices.

There is a remarkable unity in the history of Protestant thought in the period from the Reformation to the end of the eighteenth century. There is a still more surprising unity of Protestant thought in this period with the thought of the mediæval and ancient Church. The basis and methods are the same. Upon many points the conclusions are identical. There was nothing of which the Protestant scholastics were more proud than of their agreement with the Fathers of the early Church. They did not perceive in how large degree they were at one with Christian thinkers of the Roman communion as well. Few seem to have realised how largely Catholic in principle Protestant thought has been. The fundamental principles at the basis of the reasoning have been the same. The notions of revelation and inspiration were identical. The idea of authority was common to both, only the instance in which that authority is lodged was different. The thoughts of God and man, of the world, of creation, of providence and prayer, of the nature and means of salvation, are similar. Newman was right in discovering

that from the first he had thought, only and always, in
what he called Catholic terms. It was veiled from him that
many of those who ardently opposed him thought in those
same terms.

It is impossible to write upon the theme which this book
sets itself without using the terms Catholic and Protestant in
the conventional sense. The words stand for certain historic
magnitudes. It is equally impossible to conceal from ourselves how misleading the language often is. The line between
that which has been happily called the religion of authority and
the religion of the spirit does not run between Catholic and
Protestant. It runs through the middle of many Protestant
bodies, through the border only of some, and who will say
that the Roman Church knows nothing of this contrast ?
The sole use of recurrence here to the historic distinction is
to emphasise the fact that this distinction stands for less
than has commonly been supposed. In a large way the
history of Christian thought, from earliest times to the end
of the eighteenth century, presents a very striking unity.

In contrast with this, that modern reflection which has
taken the phenomenon known as religion and, specifically,
that historic form of religion known as Christianity, as its
object, has indeed also slowly revealed the fact that it is in
possession of certain principles. Furthermore, these principles, as they have emerged, have been felt to be new and
distinctive principles. They are essentially modern principles. They are the principles which, taken together,
differentiate the thinker of the nineteenth century from all
who have ever been before him. They are principles which
unite all thinkers at the end of the nineteenth and the
beginning of the twentieth centuries, in practically every
portion of the world, as they think of all subjects except
religion. It comes more and more to be felt that these
principles must be reckoned with in our thought concerning
religion as well.

One of these principles is, for example, that of dealing in
true critical fashion with problems of history and literature.
Long before the end of the age of rationalism, this principle

had been applied to literature and history, other than those called sacred. The thorough-going application of this scientific method to the literatures and history of the Old and New Testaments is almost wholly an achievement of the nineteenth century. It has completely altered the view of revelation and inspiration. The altered view of the nature of the documents of revelation has had immeasurable consequences for dogma.

Another of these elements is the new view of nature and of man's relation to nature. Certain notable discoveries in physics and astronomy had proved possible of combination with traditional religion, as in the case of Newton. Or again, they had proved impossible of combination with any religion, as in the case of Laplace. The review of the religious and Christian problem in the light of the ever-increasing volume of scientific discoveries—this is the new thing in the period which we have undertaken to describe. A theory of nature as a totality, in which man, not merely as physical, but even also as social and moral and religious being, has place in a series which suggests no break, has affected the doctrines of God and of man in a way which neither those who revered nor those who repudiated religion, at the beginning of the nineteenth century could have imagined.

Another leading principle grows out of Kant's distinction of two worlds and two orders of reason. That distinction issued in a new theory of knowledge. It laid a new foundation for an idealistic construing of the universe. In one way it was the answer of a profoundly religious nature to the triviality and effrontery into which the great rationalistic movement had run out. By it the philosopher gave standing forever to much that pietists and mystics in every age had felt to be true, yet had never been able to prove by any method which the ordered reasoning of man had provided. Religion as feeling regained its place. Ethics was set once more in the light of the eternal. The soul of man became the object of a scientific study.

There have been thus indicated three, at least, of the larger factors which enter into an interpretation of Christianity which may fairly be said to be new in the nineteenth century. They are new in a sense in which the intellectual elements entering into the reconsideration of Christianity in the age of the Reformation were not new. They are characteristic of the nineteenth century. They would naturally issue in an interpretation of Christianity in the general context of the life and thought of that century. The philosophical revolution inaugurated by Kant, with the general drift toward monism in the interpretation of the universe, separates from their forebears men who have lived since Kant, by a greater interval than that which divided Kant from Plato. The evolutionary view of nature, as developed from Schelling and Comte through Darwin to Bergson, divides men now living from the contemporaries of Kant in his youthful studies of nature, as those men were not divided from the followers of Aristotle.

Of purpose, the phrase Christian thought has been inter-preted as thought concerning Christianity. The problem which this book essays is that of an outline of the history of the thought which has been devoted, during this period of marvellous progress, to that particular object in conscious-ness and history which is known as Christianity. Christi-anity, as object of the philosophical, critical, and scientific reflection of the age—this it is which we propose to consider. Our religion as affected in its interpretation by principles of thought which are already widespread, and bid fair to become universal among educated men—this it is which in this little volume we aim to discuss. The term religious thought has not always had this significance. Philosophy of religion has signified, often, a philosophising of which religion was, so to say, the atmosphere. We cannot wonder if, in these circumstances, to the minds of some, the atmo-sphere has seemed to hinder clearness of vision. The whole subject of the philosophy of religion has within the last few decades undergone a revival, since it has been accepted that the aim is not to philosophise upon things in general in a religious spirit. On the contrary, the aim is to consider religion itself, with the best aid which current philosophy

and science afford. In this sense only can we give the study
of religion and Christianity a place among the sciences.

It remains true, now as always, that the majority, at all
events, of those who have thought profoundly concerning
Christianity will be found to have been Christian men.
Religion is a form of consciousness. It will be those who
have had experience to which that consciousness corresponds,
whose judgments can be supposed to have weight. That
remark is true, for example, of æsthetic matters as well.
To be a good judge of music one must have musical feeling
and experience. To speak with any deeper reasonableness
concerning faith, one must have faith. To think profoundly
concerning Christianity one needs to have had the Christian
experience. But this is very different from saying that to
speak worthily of the Christian religion, one must needs have
made his own the statements of religion which men of a former
generation may have found serviceable. The distinction
between religion itself, on the one hand, and the expression of religion in doctrines and rites, or the application
of religion through institutions, on the other hand, is
in itself one of the great achievements of the nineteenth
century. It is one which separates us from Christian men
in previous centuries as markedly as does any other. It is
a simple implication of the Kantian theory of knowledge.
The evidence for its validity has come through the application of historical criticism to all the creeds. Mystics of
all ages have seen the truth from far. The fact that we may
assume the prevalence of this distinction among Christian men,
and lay it at the basis of the discussion we propose, is assuredly
one of the gains which the nineteenth century has to record.

It follows that not all of the thinkers with whom we have
to deal will have been, in their own time, of the number of
avowedly Christian men. Some who have greatly furthered
movements which in the end proved fruitful for Christian
thought, have been men who were in their own time alienated
from professed and official religion. In the retrospect we
must often feel that their opposition to that which they took
to be religion was justifiable. Yet their identification of that

with religion itself, and their frank declaration of what they called their own irreligion, was often a mistake. It was a mistake to which both they and their opponents in due proportion contributed. A still larger class of those with whom we have to do have indeed asserted for themselves a personal adherence to Christianity. But their identification with Christianity, or with a particular Christian Church, has been often bitterly denied by those who bore official responsibility in the Church. The heresy of one generation is the orthodoxy of the next. There is something perverse in Gottfried Arnold's maxim, that the true Church, in any age, is to be found with those who have just been excommunicated from the actual Church. However, the maxim points in the direction of a truth. By far the larger part of those with whom we have to do have had acknowledged relation to the Christian tradition and institution. They were Christians and, at the same time, true children of the intellectual life of their own age. They esteemed it not merely their privilege, but also their duty, to endeavour to ponder anew the religious and Christian problem, and to state that which they thought in a manner congruous with the thoughts which the men of the age would naturally have concerning other themes.

It has been to most of these men axiomatic that doctrine has only relative truth. Doctrine is but a composite of the content of the religious consciousness with materials which the intellect of a given man or age or nation in the total view of life affords. As such, doctrine is necessary and inevitable for all those who in any measure live the life of the mind. But the condition of doctrine is its mobile, its fluid and changing character. It is the combination of a more or less stable and characteristic experience, with a reflection which, exactly in proportion as it is genuine, is transformed from age to age, is modified by qualities of race and, in the last analysis, differs with individual men. Dogma is that portion of doctrine which has been elevated by decree of ecclesiastical authority, or even only by common consent, into an absoluteness which is altogether foreign to its nature. It is that part of doctrine concerning which men have forgotten that it had a history, and have decided that it shall have no more. In its very notion dogma confounds a statement of truth, which must of necessity be human, with the truth itself, which is divine. In its identification of statement and truth it demands credence instead of faith. Men have confounded doctrine and dogma; they have been taught so to do. They have felt the history of Christian doctrine to be an unfruitful and uninteresting theme. But the history of Christian thought would seek to set forth the series of interpretations put, by successive generations, upon the greatest of all human experiences, the experience of the communion of men with God. These interpretations ray out at all edges into the general intellectual life of the age. They draw one whole set of their formative impulses from the general intellectual life of the age. It is this relation of the progress of doctrine to the general history of thought in the nineteenth century, which the writer designed to emphasise in choosing the title of this work.

As was indicated in the closing paragraphs of the preceding volume of this series, the issue of the age of rationalism had been for the cause of religion on the whole a distressing one. The majority of those who were resolved to follow reason were agreed in abjuring religion. That they had, as it seems to us, but a meagre understanding of what religion is, made little difference in their conclusion. Bishop Butler complains in his *Analogy* that religion was in his time hardly considered a subject for discussion among reasonable men. Schleiermacher in the very title of his *Discourses* makes it plain that in Germany the situation was not different. If the reasonable eschewed religion, pietists in Germany, evangelicals in England, the men of the great revivals in America, many of them, took up a corresponding position as towards the life of reason, especially toward the use of reason in religion. The sinister cast which the word rationalism bears in much of the popular speech is evidence of this fact. To many minds it appeared as if one could not be an adherent both of reason and of faith. That was a contradiction which Kant, first of all in his own experience, and then through his system of thought, did much to transcend. The deliverance which he wrought has been compared to the deliverance which Luther in his time achieved for those who had been in bondage to scholasticism in the Roman Church. Although Kant has been dead a hundred years, both the defence of religion and the assertion of the right of reason are still, with many, on the ancient lines. There is no such strife between rationality and belief as has been supposed. But the confidence of that fact is still far from being shared by all Christians at the beginning of the twentieth century. The course in reinterpretation and readjustment of Christianity, which that calm conviction would imply, is still far from being the one taken by all of those who bear the Christian name. If it is permissible in the writing of a book like this to have an aim besides that of the most objective delineation, the author may perhaps be permitted to say that he writes with the earnest hope that in some measure he may contribute also to the establishment of an understanding upon which so much both for the Church and the world depends.

We should say a word at this point as to the general relation of religion and philosophy. We realise the evil which Kant first in clearness pointed out. It was the evil of an apprehension which made the study of religion a department of metaphysics. The tendency of that apprehension was to do but scant justice to the historical content of Christianity. Religion is an historical phenomenon. Especially is this true of Christianity. It is a fact, or rather, a vast complex of facts. It is a positive religion. It is connected with personalities, above all with one transcendent personality, that of Jesus. It sprang out of another religion which had already emerged into the light of world-history. It has been associated for two thousand years with portions of the race which have made achievements in culture and left record of those achievements. It is the function of speculation to interpret this phenomenon. When speculation is tempted to spin by its own processes something which it would set beside this historic magnitude or put in place of it, and still call that Christianity, we must disallow the

claim. It was the licence of its speculative endeavour, and
the identification of these endeavours with Christianity,
which finally discredited Hegelianism with religious men.
Nor can it be denied that theologians themselves have been
sinners in this respect. The disposition to regard Christianity
as a revealed and divinely authoritative metaphysic began
early and continued long. When theologians also set out
to interpret Christianity and end in offering us a substitute,
which, if it were acknowledged as absolute truth, would do
away with Christianity as historic fact, as little can we allow
the claim.

Again, Christianity exists not merely as a matter of history.
It exists also as a fact in living consciousness. It is the
function of psychology to investigate that consciousness.
We must say that, accurately speaking, there is no such thing
as Christian philosophy. There are philosophies, good or bad,
current or obsolete. These are Christian only in being
applied to the history of Christianity and the content of the
Christian consciousness. There is, strictly speaking, no such
thing as Christian consciousness. There is the human con
sciousness, operating with and operated upon by the impulse
of Christianity. It is the great human experience from which
we single out for investigation that part which is concerned
with religion, and call that the religious experience. It is
essential, therefore, that those general investigations of
human consciousness and experience, as such, which are
being carried on all about us, should be reckoned with, if
our Christian life and thought are not altogether to fall out
of touch with advancing knowledge. For this reason we have
misgiving about the position of some followers of Ritschl.
Their opinion, pushed to its limit, seems to mean that we
have nothing to do with philosophy, or with the advance of
science. Religion is a feeling of which he alone who possesses it can give account. He alone who has it can appreciate
such an account when given. We acknowledge that religion
is in part a feeling. But that feeling must have rational
justification. It must also have rational guidance if it is
to be saved from degenerating into fanaticism.

To say that we have nothing to do with philosophy ends in our having to do with a bad philosophy. In that case we have a philosophy with which we operate without having investigated it, instead of having one with which we operate because we have investigated it. The philosophy of which we are aware we have. The philosophy of which we are not aware has us. No doubt, we may have religion without philosophy, but we cannot formulate it even in the rudest way to ourselves, we cannot communicate it in any way whatsoever to others, except in the terms of a philosophy. In the general sense in which every man has a philosophy, this is merely the deposit of the regnant notions of the time. It may be amended or superseded, and our theology with it. Yet while it lasts it is our one possible vehicle of expression. It is the interpreter and the critique of what we have experienced. It is not open to a man to retreat within himself and say, I am a Christian, I feel thus, I think so, these thoughts are the content of Christianity. The consequence of that position is that we make the religious experience to be no part of the normal human experience. If we contend that the being a Christian is the great human experience, that the religious life is the true human life, we must pursue the opposite course. We must make the religious life coherent with all the other phases and elements of life. If we would contend that religious thought is the truest and deepest thought, we must begin at this very point. We must make it conform absolutely to the laws of all other thought. To contend for its isolation, as an area by itself and a process subject only to its own laws, is to court the judgment of men, that in its zeal to be Christian it has ceased to be thought.

Our most profitable mode of procedure would seem to be this. We shall seek to follow, as we may, those few main movements of thought marking the nineteenth century which have immediate bearing upon our theme. We shall try to register the effect which these movements have had upon religious conceptions. It will not be possible at any point to do more than to select typical examples. Perhaps the true method is that we should go back to the beginnings

of each one of these movements. We should mark the
emergence of a few great ideas. It is the emergence of an
idea which is dramatically interesting. It is the moment of
emergence in which that which is characteristic appears.
Our subject is far too complicated to permit that the ramifications of these influences should be followed in detail.
Modifications, subtractions, additions, the reader must make
for himself.

These main movements of thought are, as has been said,
three in number. We shall take them in their chronological
order. There is first the philosophical revolution which
is commonly associated with the name of Kant. If we
were to seek with arbitrary exactitude to fix a date for the
beginning of this movement, this might be the year of the
publication of his first great work, *Kritik der reinen Vernunft*, in 1781.[1] Kant was indeed himself, both intellectually and spiritually, the product of tendencies which had
long been gathering strength. He was the exponent of ideas
which in fragmentary way had been expressed by others, but
he gathered into himself in amazing fashion the impulses
of his age. Out from some portion of his works lead almost
all the paths which philosophical thinkers since his time have
trod. One cannot say even of his work, *Die Religion innerhalb
der Grenzen der blossen Vernunft*, 1793, that it is the sole
source, or even the greatest source, of his influence upon
religious thinking. But from the body of his work as a whole,
there came a new theory of knowledge which has changed
completely the notion of revelation. There came also a view
of the universe as an ideal unity which, especially as elaborated by Fichte, Schelling and Hegel, has radically altered
the traditional ideas of God, of man, of nature and of their
relations, the one to the other.

We shall have then, secondly, to note the historical and
critical movement. It is the effort to apply consistently and
without fear the maxims of historical and literary criticism

---

[1] In the text the titles of books which are discussed are given for the first
time in the language in which they are written. Books which are merely
alluded to are mentioned in English.

to the documents of the Old and New Testaments. With still greater arbitrariness, and yet with appreciation of the significance of Strauss' endeavour, we might set as the date of the full impact of this movement upon cherished religious convictions, that of the publication of his *Leben Jesu,* 1835. This movement has supported with abundant evidence the insight of the philosophers as to the nature of revelation. It has shown that that which we actually have in the Scriptures is just that which Kant, with his reverence for the freedom of the human mind, had indicated that we must have, if revelation is to be believed in at all. With this changed view has come an altered attitude toward many statements which devout men had held that they must accept as true, because these were found in Scripture. With this changed view the whole history, whether of the Jewish people or of Jesus and the origins of the Christian Church, has been set in a new light.

In the third place, we shall have to deal with the influence of the sciences of nature and of society, as these have been developed throughout the whole course of the nineteenth century. If one must have a date for an outstanding event in this portion of the history, perhaps that of the publication of Darwin's *Origin of Species,* 1859, would serve as well as any other. The principles of these sciences have come to underlie in a great measure all the reflection of cultivated men in our time. In amazing degree they have percolated, through elementary instruction, through popular literature, and through the newspapers, to the masses of mankind. They are recognised as the basis of a triumphant material civilisation, which has made everything pertaining to the inner and spiritual life seem remote. Through the social sciences there has come an impulse to the transfer of emphasis from the individual to society, the disposition to see everything in its social bearing, to do everything in the light of its social antecedents and of its social consequences. Here again we have to note the profoundest influence upon religious conceptions. The very notion connected with the words redemption and salvation appears to have been changed.

In the case of each of these particular movements the church, as the organ of Christianity, has passed through a period of antagonism to these influences, of fear of their consequences, of resistance to their progress. In large portions of the church at the present moment the protest is renewed. The substance of these modern teachings, which yet seem to be the very warp and woof of the intellectual life of the modern man, is repudiated and denounced. It is held to imperil the salvation of the soul. It is pronounced impossible of combination with belief in a divinely revealed truth concerning the universe and a saving faith for men. In other churches, and outside the churches, the forms in which men hold their Christianity have been in large mersure adjusted to the results of these great movements of thought. They have, as these men themselves believe, been immensely strengthened and made sure by those very influences which were once esteemed dangerous.

In connection with this indication of the nature of our materials, we have sought to say something of the time of emergence of the salient elements. It may be in point also to give some intimation of the place of their origins, that is to say, of the participation of the various nationalities in this common task of the modern Christian world. That international quality of scholarship which seems to us natural, is a thing of very recent date. That a discovery should within a reasonable interval become the property of all educated men, that scholars of one nation should profit by that which the learned of another land have done, appears to us a thing to be assumed. It has not always been so, especially not in matters of religious truth. The Roman Church and the Latin language gave to mediæval Christian thought a certain international character. Again the Renaissance and Reformation had a certain world-wide quality. The relations of the English Church in the reigns of the last Tudors to Germany, Switzerland and France are not to be forgotten. But the life of the Protestant national churches in the eighteenth century shows little of this trait. The barriers of language counted for something. The pro-

vincialism of national churches and denominational pre-
dilections counted for more.

In the philosophical movement we must begin with the
Germans. The movement of English thought known as
deism was a distinct forerunner of the rationalist movement,
within the particular area of the discussion of religion.
However, it ran into the sand. The rationalist movement,
considered in its other aspects, never attained in England
in the eighteenth century the proportions which it assumed
in France and Germany. In France that movement ran its
full course, both among the learned and, equally, as a radical
and revolutionary influence among the unlearned. It had
momentous practical consequences. In no sphere was it
more radical than in that of religion. Not in vain had
Voltaire for years cried, ' *Écrasez l'infâme,*' and Rousseau
preached that the youth would all be wise and pure, if only
the kind of education which he had had in the religious
schools were made impossible. There was for many minds
no alternative between clericalism and atheism. Quite
logically, therefore, after the downfall of the Republic and of
the Empire there set in a great reaction. Still it was simply
a reversion to the absolute religion of the Roman Catholic
Church as set forth by the Jesuit party. There was no real
transcending of the rationalist movement in France in the
interest of religion. There has been no great constructive
movement in religious thought in France in the nineteenth
century. There is relatively little literature of our subject
in the French language until recent years.

In Germany, on the other hand, the rationalist movement
had always had over against it the great foil and counterpoise
of the pietist movement. Rationalism ran a much soberer
course than in France. It was never a revolutionary and
destructive movement as in France. It was not a dilettante
and aristocratic movement as deism had been in England.
It was far more creative and constructive than elsewhere.
Here also before the end of the century it had run its course.
Yet here the men who transcended the rationalist movement
and shaped the spiritual revival in the beginning of the

nineteenth century were men who had themselves been trained in the bosom of the rationalist movement. They had appropriated the benefits of it. They did not represent a violent reaction against it, but a natural and inevitable progress within and beyond it. This it was which gave to the Germans their leadership at the beginning of the nineteenth century in the sphere of the intellectual life. It is worthy of note that the great heroes of the intellectual life in Germany, in the period of which we speak, were most of them deeply interested in the problem of religion. The first man to bring to England the leaven of this new spirit, and therewith to transcend the old philosophical standpoint of Locke and Hume, was Coleridge with his *Aids to Reflection*, published in 1825. But even after this impulse of Coleridge the movement remained in England a sporadic and uncertain one. It had nothing of the volume and consecutiveness which belonged to it in Germany.

Coleridge left among his literary remains a work published in 1840 under the title of *Confessions of an Enquiring Spirit*. What is here written is largely upon the basis of intuition and forecast like that of Reimarus and Lessing a half-century earlier in Germany. Strauss and others were already at work in Germany upon the problem of the New Testament, Vatke and Reuss upon that of the Old. This was a different kind of labour, and destined to have immeasurably greater significance. George Eliot's maiden literary labour was the translation into English of Strauss' first edition. But the results of that criticism were only slowly appropriated by the English. The ostensible results were at first radical and subversive in the extreme. They were fiercely repudiated in Strauss' own country. Yet in the main there was acknowledgment of the correctness of the principle for which Strauss had stood. Hardly before the decade of the sixties was that method accepted in England in any wider way, and hardly before the decade of the seventies in America. Renan was the first to set forth, in 1863, the historical and critical problem in the new spirit, in a way that the wide public which read French understood.

When we come to speak of the scientific movement it is not easy to say where the leadership lay. Many Englishmen were in the first rank of investigators and accumulators of material. The first attempt at a systematisation of the results of the modern sciences was that of Auguste Comte in his *Philosophie Positive*. This philosophy, however, under its name of Positivism, exerted a far greater influence, both in Comte's time and subsequently, in England than it did in France. Herbert Spencer, after the middle of the decade of the sixties, essayed to do something of the sort which Comte had attempted. He had far greater advantages for the solution of the problem. Comte's foil in all of his discussions of religion was the Catholicism of the south of France. None the less, the religion which in his later years he created, bears striking resemblance to that which in his earlier years he had sought to destroy. Spencer's attitude toward religion was in his earlier work one of more pronounced antagonism or, at least, of more complete agnosticism than in later days he found requisite to the maintenance of his scientific freedom and conscientiousness. Both of these men represent the effort to construe the world, including man, from the point of view of the natural and also of the social sciences, and to define the place of religion in that view of the world which is thus set forth. The fact that there had been no such philosophical readjustment in Great Britain as in Germany, made the acceptance of the evolutionary theory of the universe, which more and more the sciences enforced, slower and more difficult. The period of resistance on the part of those interested in religion extended far into the decade of the seventies.

A word may be added concerning America. The early settlers had been proud of their connection with the English universities. An extraordinary number of them, in Massachusetts at least, had been Cambridge men. Yet a tradition of learning was later developed, which was not without the traits of isolation natural in the circumstances. The residence, for a time, even of a man like Berkeley in this country, altered that but little. The clergy remained in singular

degree the educated and highly influential class.   The
churches had developed, in consonance with their Puritan
character, a theology and philosophy so portentous in their
conclusions, that we can without difficulty understand the reaction which was brought about. Wesleyanism had modified
it in some portions of the country, but intensified it in others.
Deism apparently had had no great influence. When the
rationalist movement of the old world began to make itself felt,
it was at first largely through the influence of France.   The
religious life of the country at the beginning of the nineteenth
century was at a low ebb.   Men like Belsham and Priestley
were known as apostles of a freer spirit in the treatment of
the problem of religion.   Priestley came to Pennsylvania in
his exile.   In the large, however, one may say that the New
England liberal movement, which came by and by to be
called Unitarian, was as truly American as was the orthodoxy
to which it was opposed.   Channing reminds one often of
Schleiermacher.   There is no evidence that he had learned
from Schleiermacher.   The liberal movement by its very
impetuosity gave a new lease of life to an orthodoxy which,
without that antagonism, would sooner have waned.   The
great revivals, which were a benediction to the life of the
country, were thought to have closer relation to the theology
of those who participated in them than they had.   The
breach between the liberal and conservative tendencies of
religious thought in this country came at a time when the
philosophical reconstruction was already well under way in
Europe.   The debate continued until long after the biblical-
critical movement was in progress.   The controversy was
conducted upon both sides in practically total ignorance of
these facts.   There are traces upon both sides of that insight
which makes the mystic a discoverer in religion, before the
logic known to him will sustain the conclusion which he draws.
There will always be interest in the literature of a discussion
conducted by reverent and, in their own way, learned and
original men.   Yet there is a pathos about the sturdy originality of good men expended upon a problem which had been
already solved.   The men in either camp proceeded from

assumptions which are now impossible to the men of both. It was not until after the Civil War that American students of theology began in numbers to study in Germany. It is a much more recent thing that one may assume the immediate reading of foreign books, or boast of current contribution from American scholars to the labour of the world's thought upon these themes.

We should make a great mistake if we supposed that the progress has been an unceasing forward movement. Quite the contrary, in every aspect of it the life of the early part of the nineteenth century presents the spectacle of a great reaction. The resurgence of old ideas and forces seems almost incredible. In the political world we are wont to attribute this fact to the disillusionment which the French Revolution had wrought, and the suffering which the Napoleonic Empire had entailed. The reaction in the world of thought, and particularly of religious thought, was, moreover, as marked as that in the world of deeds. The Roman Church profited by this swing of the pendulum in the minds of men as much as did the absolute State. Almost the first act of Pius VII. after his return to Rome in 1814, was the revival of the Society of Jesus, which had been after long agony in 1773 dissolved by the papacy itself. 'Altar and throne' became the watchword of an ardent attempt at restoration of all of that which millions had given their lives to do away. All too easily, one who writes in sympathy with that which is conventionally called progress may give the impression that our period is one in which movement has been all in one direction. That is far from being true. One whose very ideal of progress is that of movement in directions opposite to those we have described may well say that the nineteenth century has had its gifts for him as well. The life of mankind is too complex that one should write of it with one exclusive standard as to loss and gain. And whatever be one's standard the facts cannot be ignored.

The France of the thirties and the forties saw a liberal movement within the Roman Church. The names of Lamennais, of Lacordaire, of Montalembert and Ozanam, the title

l'Avenir occur to men's minds at once. Perhaps there has
never been in France a party more truly Catholic, more
devout, refined and tolerant, more fitted to heal the breach
between the cultivated and the Church. However, before
the Second Empire, an end had been made of that. It
cannot be said that the French Church exactly favoured
the infallibility. It certainly did not stand against the decree
as in the old days it would have done. The decree of infallibility is itself the greatest witness of the steady progress
of reaction in the Roman Church. That action, theoretically
at least, does away with even that measure of popular constitution in the Church to which the end of the Middle Age
had held fast without wavering, which the mightiest of popes
had not been able to abolish and the Council of Trent had
not dared earnestly to debate. Whether the decree of 1870
is viewed in the light of the *Syllabus of Errors* of 1864, and
again of the *Encyclical* of 1907, or whether the encyclicals are
viewed in the light of the decree, the fact remains that a
power has been given to the Curia against what has come to
be called Modernism such as Innocent never wielded against
the heresies of his day. Meantime, so hostile are exactly
those peoples among whom Roman Catholicism has had full
sway, that it would almost appear that the hope of the Roman
Church is in those countries in which, in the sequence of the
Reformation, a religious tolerance obtains, which the Roman
Church would have done everything in its power to prevent.

Again, we should deceive ourselves if we supposed that
the reaction had been felt only in Roman Catholic lands.
A minister of Prussia forbade Kant to speak concerning
religion.   The Prussia of Frederick William III. and of
Frederick William IV. was almost as reactionary as if Metter-
nich had ruled in Berlin as well as in Vienna. The history
of the censorship of the press and of the repression of free
thought in Germany until the year 1848 is a sad chapter.
The ruling influences in the Lutheran Church in that era,
practically throughout Germany, were reactionary. The
universities did indeed in large measure retain their ancient
freedom. But the church in which Hengstenberg could be

a leader, and in which staunch seventeenth-century Lutheranism could be effectively sustained, was almost doomed to
further that alienation between the life of piety and the life
of learning which is so much to be deplored. In the Church
the conservatives have to this moment largely triumphed.
In the theological faculties of the universities the liberals
in the main have held their own. The fact that both Church
and faculties are functionaries of the State is often cited as
sure in the end to bring about a solution of this unhappy
state of things. For such a solution, it must be owned, we
wait.

The England of the period after 1815 had indeed no such
cause for reaction as obtained in France or even in Germany.
The nation having had its Revolution in the seventeenth century escaped that of the eighteenth. Still the country was
exhausted in the conflict against Napoleon. Commercial,
industrial and social problems agitated it. The Church
slumbered. For a time the liberal thought of England
found utterance mainly through the poets. By the decade
of the thirties movement had begun. The opinions of the
Noetics in Oriel College, Oxford, now seem distinctly mild.
They were sufficient to awaken Newman and Pusey, Froude,
Keble, and the rest. Then followed the most significant
ecclesiastical movement which the Church of England in the
nineteenth century has seen, the Oxford or Tractarian movement, as it has been called. There was conscious recurrence
of a mind like that of Newman to the Catholic position. He
had never been able to conceive religion in any other terms
than those of dogma, or the Christian assurance on any other
basis than that of external authority. Nothing could be
franker than the antagonism of the movement, from its inception, to the liberal spirit of the age. By inner logic
Newman found himself at last in the Roman Church. Yet
the Anglo-Catholic movement is to-day overwhelmingly in
the ascendant in the English Church. The Broad Churchmen
of the middle of the century have had few successors. It is
the High Church which stands over against the great mass
of the dissenting churches which, taken in the large, can

hardly be said to be theologically more liberal than itself. It is the High Church which has showed Franciscanlike devotion in the problems of social readjustment which England to-day presents.   It has shown in some part of its constituency a power of assimilation of new philosophical, critical and scientific views, which makes all comparison of it with the Roman Church misleading.   And yet it remains in its own consciousness Catholic to the core.

In America also the vigour of onset of the liberalising forces at the beginning of the century tended to provoke reaction.   The alarm with which the defection of so considerable a portion of the Puritan Church was viewed gave coherence to the opposition.   There were those who devoutly held that the hope of religion lay in its further liberalisation. Equally there were those who deeply felt that the deliverance lay in resistance to liberalisation.   One of the concrete effects of the division of the churches was the separation of the education of the clergy from the universities, the entrusting it to isolated theological schools under denominational control.   The system has done less harm than might have been expected.   Yet at present there would appear to be a general movement of recurrence to the elder tradition. The maintenance of the religious life is to some extent a matter of nurture and observances, of religious habit and practice.   This truth is one which liberals, in their emphasis upon liberty and the individual, are always in danger of overlooking.   The great revivals of religion in this century, like those of the century previous, have been connected with a form of religious thought pronouncedly pietistic.   The building up of religious institutions in the new regions of the West, and the participation of the churches of the country in missions, wear predominantly this cast.   Antecedently, one might have said that the lack of ecclesiastical cohesion among the Christians of the land, the ease with which a small group might split off for the furtherance of its own particular view, would tend to liberalisation.   It is doubtful whether this is true.   Isolation is not necessarily a condition of progress.   The emphasis upon trivial differences becomes rather a condition of their permanence. The middle of the nineteenth century in the United States was a period of intense denominationalism. That is synonymous with a period of the stagnation of Christian thought. The religion of a people absorbed in the practical is likely to be one which they at least suppose to be a practical religion. In one age the most practical thing will appear to men to be to escape hell, in another to further socialism. The need of adjustment of religion to the great intellectual life of the world comes with contact with that life. What strikes one in the survey of the religious thought of the country, by and large, for a century and a quarter, is not so much that it has been reactionary, as that it has been stationary. Almost every other aspect of the life of our country, including even that of religious life as distinguished from religious thought, has gone ahead by leaps and bounds. This it is which in a measure has created the tension which we feel.

B.—THE BACKGROUND

Deism

In England before the end of the Civil War a movement for the rationalisation of religion had begun to make itself felt. It was in full force in the time of the Revolution of 1688. It had not altogether spent itself by the middle of the eighteenth century. The movement has borne the name of Deism. In so far as it had one watchword, this came to be ' natural religion.' The antithesis had in mind was that to revealed religion, as this had been set forth in the tradition of the Church, and particularly under the bibliolatry of the Puritans. It is a witness to the liberty of speech enjoyed by Englishmen in that day and to their interest in religion, that such a movement could have arisen largely among laymen who were often men of rank. It is an honour to the English race that, in the period of the rising might of the rational spirit throughout the western world, men should have sought at once to utilise that force for the restatement of religion. Yet one may say quite simply that this undertaking of the deists was premature. The time was not ripe for the endeavour. The rationalist movement itself needed greater breadth and deeper understanding of itself. Above all, it needed the salutary correction of opposing principles before it could avail for this delicate and difficult task. Religion is the most conservative of human interests. Rationalism would be successful in establishing a new interpretation of religion only after it had been successful in many other fields. The arguments of the deists were never successfully refuted. On the contrary, the striking thing is that their opponents, the militant divines and writers of numberless volumes of ' Evidences for Christianity,' had come to the same rational basis with the deists. They referred even the most subtle questions to the pure reason, as no one now would do. The deistical movement was not really defeated. It largely compelled its opponents to adopt its methods. It left a deposit which is more nearly rated at its worth at the present than it was in its own time. But it ceased to command confidence, or even interest. Samuel Johnson said, as to the publication of Bolingbroke's work by his executor, three years after the author's death : ' It was a rusty old blunderbuss, which he need not have been afraid to discharge himself, instead of leaving a half-crown to a Scotchman to let it off after his death.'

It is a great mistake, however, in describing the influence of rationalism upon Christian thought to deal mainly with deism. English deism made itself felt in France, as one may see in the case of Voltaire. Kant was at one time deeply moved by some English writers who would be assigned to this class. In a sense Kant showed traces of the deistical view to the last. The centre of the rationalistic movement had, however, long since passed from England to the Continent. The religious problem was no longer its central problem. We quite fail to appreciate what the nineteenth century owes to the eighteenth and to the rationalist movement in general, unless we view this latter in a far larger way.

Rationalism

In 1784 Kant wrote a tractate entitled, *Was ist Auf-klärung?* He said · 'Aufklärung is the advance of man beyond the stage of voluntary immaturity. By immaturity is meant a man's inability to use his understanding except under the guidance of another. The immaturity is voluntary when the cause is not want of intelligence but of resolution. *Sapere aude!* " Dare to use thine own understanding," is therefore the motto of free thought. If it be asked, " Do we live in a free-thinking age ? " the answer is, " No, but we live in an age of free thought." As things are at present, men in general are very far from possessing, or even from being able to acquire, the power of making a sure and right use of their own understanding without the guidance of others. On the other hand, we have clear indications that the field now lies, nevertheless, open before them, to which they can freely make their way and that the hindrances to general freedom of thought are gradually becoming less.' And again he says : ' If we wish to insure the true use of the under-standing by a method which is universally valid, we must first critically examine the laws which are involved in the very nature of the understanding itself. For the knowledge of a truth which is valid for everyone is possible only when based on laws which are involved in the nature of the human mind, as such, and have not been imported into it from without through facts of experience, which must always be accidental and conditional.'

There speaks, of course, the prophet of the new age which was to transcend the old rationalist movement. Men had come to harp in complacency upon reason. They had never inquired into the nature and laws of action of the reason itself. Kant, though in fullest sympathy with its fundamental principles, was yet aware of the excesses and weaknesses in which the rationalist movement was running out. No man was ever more truly a child of rationalism. No man has ever written, to whom the human reason was more divine and inviolable. Yet no man ever had greater reserves within himself which rationalism, as it had been, had never touched. It was he, therefore, who could lay the foundations for a new and nobler philosophy for the future. The word *Aufklärung*, which the speech of the Fatherland furnished him, is a better word than ours. It is a better word than the French *l'Illuminisme*, the Enlightenment. Still we are apparently committed to the term Rationalism, although it is not an altogether fortunate designation which the English-speaking race has given to a tendency practically universal in the thinking of Europe, from about 1650 to the beginning of the nineteenth century. Historically, the rationalistic movement was the necessary preliminary for the modern period of European civilisation, as distinguished from the ecclesiastically and theologically determined culture which had prevailed up to that time. It marks the great cleft between the ancient and mediæval world of culture on the one hand and the modern world on the other. The Reformation had but pushed ajar the door to the modern world and then seemed in surprise and fear about to close it again. The thread of the Renaissance was taken up again only in the Enlightenment. The stream flowed underground which was yet to fertilise the modern world.

We are here mainly concerned to note the breadth and universality of the movement. It was a transformation of culture, a change in the principles underlying civilisation, in all departments of life. It had indeed, as one of its most general traits, the antagonism to ecclesiastical and theological authority. Whatever it was doing, it was never without a sidelong glance at religion. That was because the alleged divine right of churches and states was the one might which it seemed everywhere necessary to break. The conflict with ecclesiasticism, however, was taken up also by Pietism, the other great spiritual force of the age. This was in spite of the fact that the pietists' view of religion was the opposite of the rationalist view. Rationalism was characterised by thorough-going antagonism to supernaturalism with all its consequences. This arose from its zeal for the natural and the human, in a day when all men, defenders and assailants of religion alike, accepted the dictum that what **was** human could not be divine, the divine must necessarily be the opposite of the human. In reality this general trait of opposition to religion deceives us. It is superficial. In large part the rationalists were willing to leave the question of religion on one side if the ecclesiastics would let them alone. This is true in spite of the fact that the pot-house rationalism of Germany and France in the eighteenth century found tho main butt of its ridicule in the priesthood and the Church. On its sober side, in the studies of scholars, in the bureaux of statesmen, in the laboratories of discoverers, it found more solid work. It accomplished results which that other trivial aspect must not hide from us.

Troeltsch first in our own day has given us a satisfactory account of the vast achievement of the movement in every department of human life.[1] It annihilated the theological notion of the State. In the period after the Thirty Years' War men began to question what had been the purpose of it all. Diplomacy freed itself from Jesuitical and papal notions. It turned preponderantly to commercial and economic aims. A secular view of the purpose of God in history began to prevail in all classes of society. The Grand Monarque was ready to proclaim the divine right of the State which was himself. Still, not until the period of his dotage did that claim bear any relation to what even he would have called religion. Publicists, both Catholic and Protestant, sought to recur to the *lex naturæ* in contradistinction with the old *lex divina*. The natural rights of man, the rights of the people, the rationally conditioned rights of the State, a natural, prudential, utilitarian morality interested men. One of the consequences of this theory of the State was a complete alteration in the thought of the relation of State and Church. The nature of the Church itself as an empirical institution in the midst of human society was subjected to the same criticism with the State. Men saw the Church in a new light. As the State was viewed as a kind of contract in men's social

[1] Troeltsch, Art. 'Aufklärung' in Herzog-Hauck, *Realencyclopädie*, 3 Aufl., Bd. ii., s. 225 f.

interest, so the Church was regarded as but a voluntary association to care for their religious interests. It was to be judged according to the practical success with which it performed this function.

Then also, in the economic and social field the rational spirit made itself felt. Commerce and the growth of colonies, the extension of the middle class, the redistribution of wealth, the growth of cities, the dependence in relations of trade of one nation upon another, all these things shook the ancient organisation of society. The industrial system grew up upon the basis of a naturalistic theory of all economic relations. Unlimited freedom in labour and in the use of capital were claimed. There came a great revolution in public opinion upon all matters of morals. The ferocity of religious wars, the cruelty of religious persecutions, the bigotry and abusiveness of religious controversies, the casuistry of the confessional, these all, which, only a generation earlier, had been taken by long-suffering humanity as if they had been matters of course, were now viewed with contrition by the more exalted spirits and with contempt and embitterment by the rest. Men said, if religion can give us no better morality than this, it is high time we looked to the natural basis of morality. Natural morality came to be the phrase ever on the lips of the leading spirits. Too frequently they had come to look askance at the morality of those who alleged a supernatural sanction for that which they at least enjoined upon others. We come in this field also, as in the others, upon the assertion of the human as nobler and more beautiful than that which had by the theologians been alleged to be divine. The assertion came indeed to be made in ribald and blasphemous forms, but it was not without a great measure of provocation.

Then there was the altered view of nature which came through the scientific discoveries of the age. Bacon, Copernicus, Kepler, Galileo, Gassendi, Newton, are the fathers of the modern sciences. These are the men who brought new worlds to our knowledge and new methods to our use. That the sun does not move about the earth, that the earth is but a speck in space, that heaven cannot be above nor hell beneath, these are thoughts which have consequences. Instead of the old deductive method, that of the mediæval Aristotelianism, which had been worse than fruitless in the study of nature, men now set out with a great enthusiasm to study facts, and to observe their laws. Modern optics, acoustics, chemistry, geology, zoology, psychology and medicine, took their rises within the period of which we speak. The influence was indescribable. Newton might maintain his own simple piety side by side, so to say, with his character, as a scientific man, though even he did not escape the accusation of being a Unitarian. In the resistance which official religion offered at every step to the advance of the sciences, it is small wonder if natures less placid found the maintenance of their ancestral faith too difficult. Natural science was deistic with Locke and Voltaire, it was pantheistic in the antique sense with Shaftesbury, it was pantheistic-mystical with Spinoza, spiritualistic with Descartes, theistic with Leibnitz, materialistic with the men of the Encyclopædia. It was orthodox with nobody. The miracle as traditionally defined became impossible. At all events it became the millstone around the neck of the apologists. The movement went to an extreme. All the evils of excess upon this side from which we since have suffered were forecast. They were in a measure called out by the evils and errors which had so long reigned upon the other side.

Again, in the field of the writing of history and of the critique of ancient literatures, the principles of rational criticism were worked out and applied in all seriousness. Then these maxims began to be applied, sometimes timidly and sometimes in scorn and shallowness, to the sacred history and literature as well. To claim, as the defenders of the faith were fain to do, that this one department of history was exempt, was only to tempt historians to say that this was equivalent to confession that we have not here to do with history at all.

Nor can we overlook the fact that the seventeenth and eighteenth centuries witnessed a great philosophical revival. Here again it is the rationalist principle which is everywhere at work. The observations upon nature, the new feeling concerning man, the vast complex of facts and impulses which we have been able in these few words to suggest, demanded a new philosophical treatment. The philosophy which now took its rise was no longer the servant of theology. It was, at most, the friend, and even possibly the enemy, of theology. Before the end of the rationalist period it was the master of theology, though often wholly indifferent to theology, exactly because of its sense of mastery. The great philosophers of the eighteenth century, Hume, Berkeley, and Kant, belong with a part only of their work and tendency to the rationalist movement. Still their work rested upon that which had already been done by Spinoza and Malebranche, by Hobbes and Leibnitz, by Descartes and Bayle, by Locke and Wolff, by Voltaire and the Encyclopædists. With all of the contrasts among these men there are common elements. There is an ever-increasing antipathy to the thought of original sin and of supernatural revelation, there is the confidence of human reason, the trust in the will of man, the enthusiasm for the simple, the natural, the intelligible and practical, the hatred of what was scholastic and, above all, the repudiation of authority.

All these elements led, toward the end of the period, to the effort at the construction of a really rational theology. Leibnitz and Lessing both worked at that problem. However, not until after the labours of Kant was it possible to utilise the results of the rationalist movement for the reconstruction of theology. If evidence for this statement were wanting, it could be abundantly given from the work of Herder. He was younger than Kant, yet the latter seems to have exerted but slight influence upon him. He earnestly desired to reinterpret Christianity in the new light of his time, yet perhaps no part of his work is so futile.

Pietism

Allusion has been made to pietism. We have no need to set forth its own achievements. We must recur to it merely as one of the influences which made the transition from the century of rationalism to bear, in Germany, an aspect different from that which it bore in any other land. Pietism had at first much in common with rationalism. It shared with the latter its opposition to the whole administration of religion established by the State, its antagonism to the social distinctions which prevailed, its individualism, its emphasis upon the practical. It was part of a general religious reaction against ecclesiasticism, as were also Jansenism in France, and Methodism in England, and the Whitefieldian revival in America. But, through the character of Spener, and through the peculiarity of German social relations, it gained an influence over the educated classes, such as Methodism never had in England, nor, on the whole, the Great Awakening in America. In virtue of this, German pietism was able, among influential persons, to present victorious opposition to the merely secular tendencies of the rationalistic movement. In no small measure it breathed into that movement a religious quality which in other lands was utterly lacking. It gave to it an ethical seriousness from which in other places it had too often set itself free.

In England there had followed upon the age of the great religious conflict one of astounding ebb of spiritual interest. Men turned with all energy to the political and economic interests of a wholly modern civilisation. They retained, after a short period of friction, a smug and latitudinarian orthodoxy, which Methodism did little to change. In France not only was the Huguenot Church annihilated, but the Jansenist movement was savagely suppressed. The tyranny of the Bourbon State and the corruption of the Gallican Church which was so deeply identified with it caused the rationalist movement to bear the trait of a passionate opposition to religion. In the time of Pascal, Jansenism had a moment when it bade fair to be to France what pietism was to Germany. Later, in the anguish and isolation of the conflict the movement lost its poise and intellectual quality. In Germany, even after the temporary alliance of pietism and rationalism against the Church had been transcended, and the length and breadth of their mutual

antagonism had been revealed, there remained a deep mutual
respect and salutary interaction. Obscurantists and senti-
mentalists might denounce rationalism. Vulgar ranters like
Dippel and Barth might defame religion. That had little
weight as compared with the fact that Klopstock, Hamann
and Herder, Jacobi, Goethe and Jean Paul, had all passed
at some time under the influence of pietism. Lessing
learned from the Moravians the undogmatic essence of religion. Schleiermacher was bred among the devoted followers
of Zinzendorf. Even the radicalism of Kant retained from
the teaching of his pietistic youth the stringency of its ethic,
the sense of the radical evil of human nature and of the
categorical imperative of duty. It would be hard to find
anything to surpass his testimony to the purity of character
and spirit of his parents, or the beauty of the home life in
which he was bred. Such facts as these made themselves felt
both in the philosophy and in the poetry of the age. The
rationalist movement itself came to have an ethical and
spiritual trait. The triviality, the morbidness and superstition of pietism received their just condemnation. But
among the leaders of the nation in every walk of life were
some who felt the drawing to deal with ethical and religious
problems in the untrammelled fashion which the century
had taught.

We may be permitted to try to show the meaning of pietism
by a concrete example. No one can read the correspondence
between the youthful Schleiermacher and his loving but
mistaken father, or again, the lifelong correspondence of
Schleiermacher with his sister, without receiving, if he has any
religion of his own, a touching impression of what the pietistic
religion meant. The father had long before, unknown to
the son, passed through the torments of the rational assault
upon a faith which was sacred to him. He had preached,
through years, in the misery of contradiction with himself.
He had rescued his drowning soul in the ark of the most
intolerant confessional orthodoxy. In the crisis of his son's
life he pitiably concealed these facts. They should have
been the bond of sympathy. The son, a sorrowful little

motherless boy, was sent to the Moravian school at Niesky,
and then to Barby. He was to escape the contamination
of the universities, and the woes through which his father had
passed. Even there the spirit of the age pursued him. The
precocious lad, in his loneliness, raised every question which
the race was wrestling with. He long concealed these facts,
dreading to wound the man he so revered. Then in a burst
of filial candour, he threw himself upon his father's mercy,
only to be abused and measurelessly condemned. He had
his way. He resorted to Halle, turned his back on sacred
things, worked in titanic fashion at everything but the problem of religion. At least he kept his life clean and his soul
sensitive among the flagrantly immoral who were all about
him, even in the pietists' own university. He laid the foundations for his future philosophical construction. He bathed
in the sentiments and sympathies, poetic, artistic and humani-
tarian, of the romanticist movement. In his early Berlin
period he was almost swept from his feet by its flood. He
rescued himself, however, by his rationalism and romanticism
into a breadth and power of faith which made him the
prophet of the new age. By him, for a generation, men
like-minded saved their souls. As one reads, one realises that
it was the pietists' religion which saved him, and which, in
another sense, he saved. His recollections of his instruction
among the Herrnhuter are full of beauty and pathos. His
sister never advanced a step upon the long road which he
travelled. Yet his sympathy with her remained unimpaired.
The two poles of the life of the age are visible here. The
episode, full of exquisite personal charm, is a veritable
miniature of the first fifty years of the movement which
we have to record. No one did for England or for France
what Schleiermacher had done for the Fatherland.

Æsthetic Idealism

Besides pietism, the Germany of the end of the eighteenth
century possessed still another foil and counterpoise to its
decadent rationalism. This was the so-called æsthetic-

idealistic movement, which shades off into romanticism.
The debt of Schleiermacher to that movement has been
already hinted at. It was the revolt of those who had this
in common with the pietists, that they hated and despised
the outworn rationalism. They thought they wanted no
religion. It is open to us to say that they misunderstood
religion. It was this misunderstanding which Schleiermacher sought to bring home to them. What religion
they understood, ecclesiasticism, Roman or Lutheran,
or again, the banalities and fanaticisms of middle-class
pietism, they despised. Their war with rationalism was
not because it had deprived men of religion. It had been
equally destructive of another side of the life of feeling, the
æsthetic. Their war was not on behalf of the good, it was in
the name of the beautiful. Rationalism had starved the soul,
it had minimised and derided feeling. It had suppressed
emotion. It had been fatal to art. It was barren of poetry.
It had had no sympathy with history and no understanding
of history. It had reduced everything to the process by
which two and two make four. The pietists said that the
frenzy for reason had made men oblivious of the element of
the divine. The æsthetic idealists said that it had been fatal
to the element of the human. From this point of view their
movement has been called the new humanism. The glamour
of life was gone, they said. Mystery had vanished. And
mystery is the womb of every art. Rationalism had been
absolutely uncreative, only and always destructive. Rousseau had earlier uttered this wail in France, and had greatly
influenced certain minds in Germany. Shelley and Keats
were saying something of the sort in England. Even as to
Wordsworth, it may be an open question if his religion was not
mainly romanticism. All these men used language which had
been conventionally associated with religion, to describe this
other emotion.

Rationalism had ended in proving deadly to ideals. This
was true. But men forgot for the moment how glorious an
ideal it had once been to be rational and to assert the
rationality of the universe. Still the time had come when,

in Germany at all events, the great cry was, 'back to the ideal.' It is curious that men always cry 'back' when they mean 'forward.' For it was not the old idealism, either religious or æsthetic, which they were seeking. It was a new one in which the sober fruits of rationalism should find place. Still, for the moment, as we have seen, the air was full of the cry, 'back to the State by divine right, back to the Church, back to the Middle Age, back to the beauty of classical anti-quity.' The poetry, the romance, the artistic criticism of this movement set themselves free at a stroke from theo-logical bondage and from the externality of conventional ethics. It shook off the dust of the doctrinaires. It ridi-culed the petty utilitarianism which had been the vogue. It had such an horizon as men had never dreamed before. It owed that horizon to the rationalism it despised. From its new elevation it surveyed all the great elements of the life of man. It saw morals and religion, language and society, along with art and itself, as the free and unconscious product through the ages, of the vitality of the human spirit. It must be said that it neither solved nor put away the ancient questions. Especially through its one-sided æstheticism it veiled that element of dualism in the world which Kant clearly saw, and we now see again, after a century which has sometimes leaned to easy pantheism. However, it led to a study of the human soul and of all its activities, which came closer to living nature than anything which the world had yet seen.

To this group of æsthetic idealists belong, not to mention lesser names, Lessing and Hamann and Winckelmann, but above all Herder and Goethe. Herder was surely the finest spirit among the elder contemporaries of Goethe. Bitterly hostile to the rationalists, he had been moved by Rousseau to enthusiasm for the free creative life of the human spirit. With Lessing he felt the worth of every art in and for itself, and the greatness of life in its own fulfilment. He sets out from the analysis of the poetic and artistic powers, the appreciation of which seemed to him to be the key to the understanding of the spiritual world. Then first he approaches the analysis of the ethical and religious feeling. All the knowledge and insight thus gained he gathers together into a history of the spiritual life of mankind. This life of the human spirit comes forth everywhere from nature, is bound to nature. It constitutes one whole with a nature which the devout soul calls God, and apprehends within itself as the secret of all that it is and does. Even in the period in which he had become passionately Christian, Herder never was able to attain to a scientific establishing of his Christianity, or to any sense of the specific aim of its development. He felt himself to be separated from Kant by an impassable gulf. All the sharp antinomies among which Kant moved, contrasts of that which is sensuous with that which is reasonable, of experience with pure conception, of substance and form in thought, of nature and freedom, of inclination and duty, seemed to Herder grossly exaggerated, if not absolutely false. Sometimes Herder speaks as if the end of life were simply the happiness which a man gets out of the use of all his powers and out of the mere fact of existence. Deeper is Kant's contention, that the true aim of life can be only moral culture, even independent of happiness, or rather one must find his noblest happiness in that moral culture.

At a period in his life when Herder had undergone conversion to court orthodoxy at Bückeburg and threatened to throw away that for which his life had stood, he was greatly helped by Goethe. The identification of Herder with Christianity continued to be more deep and direct than that of Goethe ever became. Yet Goethe has also his measure of significance for our theme. If he steadied Herder in his religious experience, he steadied others in their poetical emotionalism and artistic sentimentality, which were fast becoming vices of the time. The classic repose of his spirit, his apparently unconscious illustration of the ancient maxim, 'nothing too much,' was the more remarkable, because there were few influences in the whole gamut of human life to which he did not sooner or later surrender himself, few experiences which he did not seek, few areas of thought upon which he did not enter. Systems and theories were never much to his mind. A fact, even if it were inexplicable, interested him much more. To the evolution of formal thought in his age he held himself receptive rather than directing. He kept, to the last, his own manner of brooding and creating, within the limits of a poetic impressionableness which instinctively viewed the material world and the life of the soul in substantially similar fashion. There is something almost humorous in the way in which he eagerly appropriated the results of the philosophising of his time, in so far as he could use these to sustain his own positions, and caustically rejected those which he could not thus use. He soon got by heart the negative lessons of Voltaire and found, to use the words which he puts into the mouth of Faust, that while it freed him from his superstitions, at the same time it made the world empty and dismal beyond endurance. In the mechanical philosophy which presented itself in the *Système de la Nature* as a positive substitute for his lost faith, he found only that which filled his poet's soul with horror. 'It appeared to us,' he says, 'so grey, so cimmerian and so dead that we shuddered at it as at a ghost. We thought it the very quintessence of old age. All was said to be necessary, and therefore there was no God. Why not a necessity for a God to take its place among the other necessities!' On the other hand, the ordinary teleological theology, with its external architect of the world and its externally determined designs, could not seem to Goethe more satisfactory than the mechanical philosophy. He joined for a time in Rousseau's cry for the return to nature. But Goethe was far too well balanced not to perceive that such a cry may be the expression of a very artificial and sophisticated state of mind. It begins indeed in the desire to throw off that which is really oppressive. It ends in a fretful and reckless revolt against the most necessary conditions of human life. Goethe lived long enough to see in France that dissolution of all authority, whether of State or Church, for which Rousseau had pined. He saw it result in the return of a portion of mankind to what we now believe to have been their primitive state, a state in which they were 'red in tooth and claw.'

It was not that paradisaic state of love and innocence, which, curiously enough, both Rousseau and the theologians seem to have imagined was the primitive state.

The thought of the discipline and renunciation of our lower nature in order to the realisation of a higher nature of mankind is written upon the very face of the second part of *Faust*. Certain passages in *Dichtung und Wahrheit* are even more familiar. ' Our physical as well as our social life, morality, custom, knowledge of the world, philosophy, religion, even many an accidental occurrence in our daily life, all tell us that we must renounce.' ' Renunciation, once for all, in view of the eternal,' that was the lesson which he said made him feel an atmosphere of peace breathed upon him. He perceived the supreme moral significance of certain Christian ideas, especially that of the atonement as he interpreted it. ' It is altogether strange to me,' he writes to Jacobi, ' that I, an old heathen, should see the cross planted in my own garden, and hear Christ's blood preached without its offending me.'

Goethe's quarrel with Christianity was due to two causes. In the first place, it was due to his viewing Christianity as mainly, if not exclusively, a religion of the other world, as it has been called, a religion whose God is not the principle of all life and nature and for which nature and life are not divine. In the second place, it was due to the prominence of the negative or ascetic element in Christianity as commonly presented, to the fact that in that presentation the law of self-sacrifice bore no relation to the law of self-realisation. In both of these respects he would have found himself much more at home with the apprehension of Christianity which we have inherited from the nineteenth century. The programme of charity which he outlines in the *Wanderjahre* as a substitute for religion would be taken to-day, so far as it goes, as a rather moderate expression of the very spirit of the Christian religion.

CHAPTER II

IDEALISTIC PHILOSOPHY

THE causes which we have named, religious and æsthetic, as well as purely speculative, led to such a revision of philosophical principles in Germany as took place in no other land. The new idealistic philosophy, as it took shape primarily at the hands of Kant, completed the dissolution of the old rationalism. It laid the foundation for the speculative thought of the western world for the century which was to come. The answers which æstheticism and pietism gave to rationalism were incomplete. They consisted largely in calling attention to that which rationalism had overlooked. Kant's idealism, however, met the intellectual movement on its own grounds. It triumphed over it with its own weapons. The others set feeling over against thought. He taught men a new method in thinking. The others put emotion over against reason. He criticised in drastic fashion the use which had been made of reason. He inquired into the nature of reason. He vindicated the reasonableness of some truths which men had indeed felt to be indefeasibly true, but which they had not been able to establish by reasoning.

KANT

Immanuel Kant was born in 1724 in Königsberg, possibly of remoter Scottish ancestry. His father was a saddler, as Melanchthon's had been an armourer and Wolff's a tanner. His native city with its university was the scene of his whole life and labour. He was never outside of Prussia except for a brief interval when Königsberg belonged to Russia. He was a German professor of the old style. Studying, teaching, writing books, these were his whole existence. He was the fourth of nine children of a devoted pietist household. Two of his sisters served in the houses of friends. The consistorial-rath opened the way to the university. An uncle aided him to publish his first books. His earlier interest was in the natural sciences. He was slow in coming to promotion. Only after 1770 was he full professor of logic and metaphysics. In 1781 he published the first of the books upon which rests his world-wide fame. Nevertheless, he lived to see the triumph of his philosophy in most of the German universities. His subjects are abstruse, his style involved. It never occurred to him to make the treatment of his themes easier by use of the imagination. He had but a modicum of that quality. He was hostile to the pride of intellect often manifested by petty rationalists. He was almost equally hostile to excessive enthusiasm in religion. The note of his life, apart from his intellectual power, was his ethical seriousness. He was in conflict with ecclesiastical personages and out of sympathy with much of institutional religion. None the less, he was in his own way one of the most religious of men. His brief conflict with Wöllner's government was the only instance in which his peace and public honour were disturbed. He never married. He died in Königsberg in 1804. He had been for ten years so much enfeebled that his death was a merciful release.

Kant used the word ' critique ' so often that his philosophy has been called the 'critical philosophy.' The word therefore needs an explanation. Kant himself distinguished two types of philosophy, which he called the dogmatic and critical types. The essence of a dogmatic philosophy is that it makes belief to rest upon knowledge. Its endeavour is to demonstrate that which is believed. It brings out as its foil the characteristically sceptical philosophy. This esteems that the proofs advanced in the interest of belief are inadequate. The belief itself is therefore an illusion. The essence of a critical philosophy, on the other hand, consists in this, that it makes a distinction between the functions of knowing and believing

It distinguishes between the perception of that which is in accordance with natural law and the understanding of the moral meaning of things.[1] Kant thus uses his word critique in accordance with the strict etymological meaning of the root. He seeks to make a clear separation between the provinces of belief and knowledge, and thus to find an adjustment of their claims. Of an object of belief we may indeed say that we know it. Yet we must make clear to ourselves that we know it in a different sense from that in which we know physical fact. Faith, since it does not spring from the pure reason, cannot indeed, as the old dogmatisms, both philosophical and theological, have united in asserting, be demonstrated by the reason. Equally it cannot, as scepticism has declared, be overthrown by the pure reason.

The ancient positive dogmatism had been the idealistic philosophy of Plato and Aristotle. The old negative dogmatism had been the materialism of the Epicureans. To Plato the world was the realisation of ideas. Ideas, spiritual entities, were the counterparts and necessary antecedents of the natural objects and actual facts of life. To the Epicureans, on the other hand, there are only material bodies and natural laws. There are no ideas or purposes. In the footsteps of the former moved all the scholastics of the Middle Age, and again, even Locke and Leibnitz in their so-called 'natural theology.' In the footsteps of the latter moved the men who had made materialism and scepticism to be the dominant philosophy of France in the latter half of the eighteenth century. The aim of Kant was to resolve this age-long contradiction. Free, unprejudiced investigation of the facts and laws of the phenomenal world can never touch the foundations of faith. Natural science can lead to the knowledge only of the realm of the laws of things. It cannot give us the inner moral sense of those things. To speak of the purposes of nature as men had done was absurd. Natural theology, as men had talked of it, was impossible. What science can give is a knowledge of the facts about us in the world, of the growth of the cosmos, of

[1] Paulsen, *Kant*, s. 2.

the development of life, of the course of history, all viewed
as necessary sequences of cause and effect.

On the other hand, with the idealists, Kant is fully per-
suaded that there is a meaning in things and that we can
know it. There is a sense in life. With immediate certainty
we set moral good as the absolute aim in life. This is done,
however, not through the pure reason or by scientific thinking, but primarily through the will, or as Kant prefers to
call it, the practical reason. What he means by the practical
reason is the intelligence, the will and the affections operating
together; that is to say, the whole man, and not merely
his intellect, directed to those problems upon which, in sympathy and moral reaction, the whole man must be directed
and upon which the pure reason, the mere faculty of ratio-
cination, does not adequately operate. In the practical
reason the will is the central thing. The will is that faculty
of man to which moral magnitudes appeal. It is with moral
magnitudes that the will is primarily concerned. The pure
reason may operate without the will and the affections.
The will, as a source of knowledge, never works without the
intelligence and the affections. But it is the will which alone
judges according to the predicates good and evil. The pure
reason judges according to the predicates true and false. It
is the practical reason which ventures the credence that
moral worth is the supreme worth in life. It then confirms
this ventured credence in a manifold experience that yields a
certainty with which no certainty of objects given in the
senses is for a moment to be compared. We know that which
we have believed. We know it as well as that two and two
make four. Still we do not know it in the same way. Nor
can we bring knowledge of it to others save through an act
of freedom on their part, which is parallel to the original act
of freedom on our own part.

How can these two modes of thought stand related the
one to the other ? Kant's answer is that they correspond to
the distinction between two worlds, the world of sense and
the transcendental or supersensible world. The pure and the
practical reason are the faculties of man for dealing with

these two worlds respectively, the phenomenal and the noumenal. The world which is the object of scientific investigation is not the actuality itself. This is true in spite of the fact that to the common man the material and sensible is always, as he would say, the real. On the contrary, in Kant's opinion the material world is only the presentation to our senses of something deeper, of which our senses are no judge. The reality lies behind this sensible presentation and appearance. The world of religious belief is the world of this transcendent reality. The spirit of man, which is not pure reason only, but moral will as well, recognises itself also as part of this reality. It expresses the essence of that mysterious reality in terms of its own essence. Its own essence as free spirit is the highest aspect of reality of which it is aware. It may be unconscious of the symbolic nature of its language in describing that which is higher than anything which we know, by the highest which we do know. Yet, granting that, and supposing that it is not a contradiction to attempt a description of the transcendent at all, there is no description which carries us so far.

This series of ideas was perhaps that which gave to Kant's philosophy its immediate and immense effect upon the minds of men wearied with the endless strife and insoluble contradiction of the dogmatic and sceptical spirits. We may disagree with much else in the Kantian system. Even here we may say that we have not two reasons, but only two functionings of one. We have not two worlds. The philosophical myth of two worlds has no better standing than the religious myth of two worlds. We have two characteristic aspects of one and the same world. These perfectly interpenetrate the one the other, if we may help ourselves with the language of space. Each is everywhere present. Furthermore, these actions of reason and aspects of world shade into one another by imperceptible degrees. Almost all functionings of reason have something of the qualities of both. However, when all is said, it was of greatest worth to have had these two opposite poles of thought brought clearly to mind. The dogmatists, in the interest of faith, were resisting at every step the progress of the sciences, feeling that that progress was inimical to faith. The devotees of science were saying that its processes were of universal validity, its conclusions irresistible, the gradual dissolution of faith was certain. Kant made plain that neither party had the right to such conclusions. Each was attempting to apply the processes appropriate to one form of rational activity within the sphere which belonged to the other. Nothing but confusion could result. The religious man has no reason to be jealous of the advance of the sciences. The interests of faith itself are furthered by such investigation. Illusions as to fact which have been mistakenly identified with faith are thus done away. Nevertheless, its own eternal right is assured to faith. With it lies the interpretation of the facts of nature and of history, whatsoever these facts may be found to be. With the practical reason is the interpretation of these facts according to their moral worth, a worth of which the pure reason knows nothing and scientific investigation reveals nothing.

Here was a deliverance not unlike that which the Reformation had brought. The mingling of Aristotelianism and religion in the scholastic theology Luther had assailed. Instead of assent to human dogmas Luther had the immediate assurance of the heart that God was on his side. And what is that but a judgment of the practical reason, the response of the heart in man to the spiritual universe? It is given in experience. It is not mediated by argument. It cannot be destroyed by syllogism. It needs no confirmation from science. It is capable of combination with any of the changing interpretations which science may put upon the outward universe. The Reformation had, however, not held fast to its great truth. It had gone back to the old scholastic position. It had rested faith in an essentially rationalistic manner upon supposed facts in nature and alleged events of history in connection with the revelation. It had thus jeopardised the whole content of faith, should these supposed facts of nature or events in history be at any time disproved. Men had made faith to rest upon statements of Scripture, alleging such and such facts and events. They did not recognise these as the naïve and childlike assumptions concerning nature and history which the authors of Scripture would naturally have. When, therefore, these statements began with the progress of the sciences to be disproved, the defenders of the faith presented always the feeble spectacle of being driven from one form of evidence to another, as the old were in turn destroyed. The assumption was rife at the end of the eighteenth century that Christianity was discredited in the minds of all free and reasonable men. Its tenets were incompatible with that which enlightened men infallibly knew to be true. It could be no long time until the hollowness and sham would be patent to all. Even the interested and the ignorant would be compelled to give it up. Of course, the invincibly devout in every nation felt of instinct that this was not true. They felt that there is an inexpugnable truth of religion. Still that was merely an intuition of their hearts. They were right. But they were unable to prove that they were right, or even to get a hearing with many of the cultivated of their age. To Kant we owe the debt, that he put an end to this state of things. He made the real evidence for religion that of the moral sense, of the conscience and hearts of men themselves. The real ground of religious conviction is the religious experience. He thus set free both science and religion from an embarrassment under which both laboured, and by which both had been injured.

Kant parted company with the empirical philosophy which had held that all knowledge arises from without, comes from experienced sensations, is essentially perception. This theory had not been able to explain the fact that human experience always conforms to certain laws. On the other hand, the philosophy of so-called innate ideas had sought to derive all knowledge from the constitution of the mind itself. It left out of consideration the dependence of the mind upon experience. It tended to confound the creations of its own speculation with reality, or rather, to claim correspondence with fact for statements which had no warrant in experience.

There was no limit to which this speculative process might not be pushed.   By this process the mediæval theologians, with all gravity, propounded the most absurd speculations concerning nature.   By this process men made the most astonishing declarations upon the basis, as they supposed, of revelation.   They made allegations concerning history and the religious experience which the most rudimentary knowledge of history or reflection upon consciousness proved to be quite contrary to fact.

Both empiricism and the theory of innate ideas had agreed in regarding all knowledge as something given, from without or from within.   The knowing mind was only a passive recipient of impressions thus imparted to it.   It was as wax under the stylus, *tabula rasa*, clean paper waiting to be written upon.   Kant departed from this radically.   He declared that all cognition rests upon the union of the mind's activity with its receptivity.   The material of thought, or at least some of the materials of thought, must be given us in the multiformity of our perceptions, through what we call experience from the outer world.   On the other hand, the formation of this material into knowledge is the work of the activity of our own minds.   Knowledge is the result of the systematising of experience and of reflection upon it.   This activity of the mind takes place always in accordance with the mind's own laws.   Kant held thus to the absolute dependence of knowledge upon material supplied in experience. He compared himself to Copernicus who had taught men that they themselves revolved about a central fact of the universe.   They had supposed that the facts revolved about them.   The central fact of the intellectual world is experience.   This experience seems to be given us in the forms of time and space and cause.   These are merely forms of the mind's own activity.   It is not possible for us to know ' the thing in itself,' the *Ding-an-sich* in Kant's phrase, which is the external factor in any sensation or perception.   We cannot distinguish that external factor from the contribution to it, as it stands in our perception, which our own minds have made.   If we cannot do that even for ourselves, how much less can we do it for others! It is the subject, the thinking being who says ' I,' which, by means of its characteristic and necessary active processes, in the perception of things under the forms of time and space, converts the chaotic material of knowledge into a regular and ordered world of reasoned experience. In this sense the understanding itself imposes laws, if not upon nature, yet, at least, upon nature as we can ever know it. There is thus in Kant's philosophy a sceptical aspect. Knowledge is limited to phenomena. We cannot by pure reason know anything of the world which lies beyond experience. This thought had been put forth by Locke and Berkeley, and by Hume also, in a different way. But with Kant this scepticism was not the gist of his philosophy. It was urged rather as the basis of the unconditioned character which he proposed to assert for the practical reason. Kant's scepticism is therefore very different from that of Hume. It does not militate against the profoundest religious conviction. Yet it prepared the way for some of the just claims of modern agnosticism.

According to Kant, it is as much the province of the practical reason to lay down laws for action as it is the province of pure reason to determine the conditions of thought, though the practical reason can define only the form of action which shall be in the spirit of duty. It cannot present duty to us as an object of desire. Desire can be only a form of self-love. In the end it reckons with the advantage of having done one's duty. It thus becomes selfish and degraded. The identification of duty and interest was particularly offensive to Kant. He was at war with every form of hedonism. To do one's duty because one expects to reap advantage is not to have done one's duty. The doing of duty in this spirit simply resolves itself into a subtler and more pervasive form of selfishness. He castigates the popular presentation of religion as fostering this same fault. On the other hand, there is a trait of rigorism in Kant, a survival of the ancient dualism, which was not altogether consistent with the implications of his own philosophy. This philosophy afforded, as we have seen, the basis for a monistic view of the universe. But to his mind the natural inclinations of man are opposed to good conscience and sound reason. He had contempt for the shallow optimism of his time, according to which the nature of man was all good, and needed only to be allowed to run its natural course to produce highest ethical results. He does not seem to have penetrated to the root of Rousseau's fallacy, the double sense in which he constantly used the words 'nature' and ' natural.' Otherwise, Kant would have been able to re-pudiate the preposterous doctrine of Rousseau, without him-self falling back upon the doctrine of the radical evil of human nature. In this doctrine he is practically at one with the popular teaching of his own pietistic background, and with Calvinism as it prevailed with many of the religiously-minded of his day. In its extreme statements this latter reminds one of the pagan and oriental dualisms which so long ran parallel to the development of Christian thought and so profoundly influenced it.

Kant's system is not at one with itself at this point. According to him the natural inclinations of men are such as to produce a never-ending struggle between duty and desire. To desire to do a thing made him suspicious that he was not actuated by the pure spirit of duty in doing it. The sense in which man may be in his nature both a child of God, and, at the same time, part of the great complex of nature, was not yet clear either to Kant or to his opponents. His pessimism was a reflection of his moral seriousness. Yet it failed to reckon with that which is yet a glorious fact. One of the chief results of doing one's duty is the gradual escape from the desire to do the contrary. It is the gradual fostering by us, the ultimate dominance in us, of the desire to do that duty. Even to have seen one's duty is the dawning in us of this high desire. In the lowest man there is indeed the super-ficial desire to indulge his passions. There is also the latent longing to be conformed to the good. There is the sense that he fulfils himself then only when he is obedient to the good. One of the great facts of spiritual experience is this gradual, or even sudden, inversion of standard within us. We do really cease to desire the things which are against right reason and conscience. We come to desire the good, even if it shall cost us pain and sacrifice to do it. Paul could write : ' When I would do good, evil is present with me.' But, in the vividness of his identification of his willing self with his better self against his sinning self, he could also write : ' So then it is no more I that do the sin.' *Das radicale Böse* of human nature is less radical than Kant supposed, and ' the categorical imperative ' of duty less externally categorical than he alleged. Still it is the great merit of Kant's philosophy to have brought out with all possible emphasis, not merely as against the optimism of the shallow, but as against the hedonism of soberer people, that our life is a conflict between inclination and duty. The claims of duty are the higher ones. They are mandatory, absolute. We do our duty whether or not we superficially desire to do it. We do our duty whether or not we foresee advantage in having done it. We should do it if we foresaw with clearness disadvantage. We should find our satisfaction in having done it, even at the cost of all our other satisfactions. There is a must which is over and above all our desires. This is what Kant really means by the categorical imperative. Nevertheless, his statement comes in conflict with the principle of freedom, which is one of the most fundamental in his system. The phrases above used only eddy about the one point which is to be held fast. There may be that in the universe which destroys the man who does not conform to it, but in the last analysis he is self-destroyed, that is, he chooses not to conform. If he is saved, it is because he chooses thus to conform. Man would be then most truly man in resisting that which would merely overpower him, even if it were goodness. Of course, there can be no goodness which overpowers. There can be no goodness which is not willed. Nothing can be a motive except through awakening our desire. That which one desires is never wholly external to oneself.

According to Kant, morality becomes religion when that which the former shows to be the end of man is conceived also to be the end of the supreme law-giver, God. Religion is the recognition of our duties as divine commands. The distinction between revealed and natural religion is stated thus: In the former we know a thing to be a divine command before we recognise it as our duty. In the latter we know it to be our duty before we recognise it as a divine command. Religion may be both natural and revealed. Its tenets may be such that man can be conceived as arriving at them by unaided reason. But he would thus have arrived at them at a later period in the evolution of the race. Hence revelation might be salutary or even necessary for certain times and places without being essential at all times or, for that matter, a permanent guarantee of the truth of religion. There is nothing here which is new or original with Kant. This line of reasoning was one by which men since Lessing had helped themselves over certain difficulties. It is cited only to show how Kant, too, failed to transcend his age in some matters, although he so splendidly transcended it in others.

The orthodox had immemorially asserted that revelation imparted information not otherwise attainable, or not then attainable. The rationalists here allege the same. Kant is held fast in this view. Assuredly what revelation imparts is not information of any sort whatsoever, not even information concerning God. What revelation imparts is God himself, through the will and the affection, the practical reason. Revelation is experience, not instruction. The revealers are those who have experienced God, Jesus the foremost among them. They have experienced God, whom then they have manifested as best they could, but far more significantly in what they were than in what they said. There is surely the gravest exaggeration of what is statutory and external in that which Kant says of the relation of ethics and religion. How can we know that to be a command of God, which does not commend itself in our own heart and conscience? The traditionalist would have said, by documents miraculously confirmed. It was not in consonance with his noblest ideas for Kant to say that. On the other hand, that which I perceive to be my duty I, as religious man, feel to be a command of God, whether or not a mandate of God to that effect can be adduced. Whether an alleged revelation from God inculcates such a truth or duty may be incidental. In a sense it is accidental. The content of all historic revelation is conditioned in the circumstances of the man to whom the revelation is addressed. It is clear that the whole matter of revelation is thus apprehended by Kant with more externality than we should have believed. His thought is still essentially archaic and dualistic. He is, therefore, now and then upon the point of denying that such a thing as revelation is possible. The very idea of revelation, in this form, does violence to his fundamental principle of the autonomy of the human reason and will. At many points in his reflection it is transparently clear that nothing can ever come to a man, or be given forth by him, which is not creatively shaped by himself. As regards revelation, however, Kant never frankly took that step. The implications of his own system would have led him to that step. They led to an idea of revelation which was psychologically in harmony with the assumptions of his system, and historically could be conceived as taking place without the interjection of the miraculous in the ordinary sense. If the divine revelation is to be thought as taking place within the human spirit, and in consonance with the laws of all other experience, then the human spirit must itself be conceived as standing in such relation to the divine that the eternal reason may express and reveal itself in the regular course of the mind's own activity. Then the manifold moral and religious ideals of mankind in all history must take their place as integral factors also in the progress of the divine revelation.

When we come to the more specific topics of his religious teaching, freedom, immortality, God, Kant is prompt to assert that these cannot be objects of theoretical knowledge. Insoluble contradictions arise whenever a proof of them is attempted. If an object of faith could be demonstrated it would cease to be an object of faith. It would have been brought down out of the transcendental world. Were God to us an object among other objects, he would cease to be a God. Were the soul a demonstrable object like any other object, it would cease to be the transcendental aspect of

ourselves. Kant makes short work of the so-called proofs for
the existence of God which had done duty in the scholastic
theology. With subtilty, sometimes also with bitter irony,
he shows that they one and all assume that which they set
out to prove. They are theoretically insufficient and practically unnecessary. They have such high-sounding names—
the ontological argument, the cosmological, the physico-
theological—that almost in spite of ourselves we bring a
reverential mood to them. They have been set forth with
solemnity by such redoubtable thinkers that there is something
almost startling in the way that Kant knocks them about.
The fact that the ordinary man among us easily perceives that
Kant was right shows only how the climate of the intellectual world has changed. Freedom, immortality, God, are not
indeed provable. If given at all, they can be given only in
the practical reason. Still they are postulates in the moral
order which makes man the citizen of an intelligible world.
There can be no 'ought' for a being who is necessitated.
We can perceive, and do perceive, that we ought to do a
thing. It follows that we can do it. However, the hindrances
to the realisation of the moral ideal are such that it cannot
be realised in a finite time. Hence the postulate of eternal
life for the individual. Finally, reason demands the realisation
of a supreme good, both a perfect virtue and a corresponding happiness. Man is a final end only as a moral subject.
There must be One who is not only the law-giver, but in
himself also the realisation of the law of the moral world.

Kant's moral argument thus steps out of the line of the
others. It is not a proof at all in the sense in which they
attempted to be proofs. The existence of God appears as a
necessary assumption, if the highest good and value in the
world are to be fulfilled. But the conception and possibility
of realisation of a highest good is itself something which
cannot be concluded with theoretical evidentiality. It is
the object of a belief which in entire freedom is directed to
that end. Kant lays stress upon the fact that among the
practical ideas of reason, that of freedom is the one whose
reality admits most nearly of being proved by the laws of

pure reason, as well as in conduct and experience. Upon an act of freedom, then, belief rests. 'It is the free holding that to be true, which for the fulfilment of a purpose we find necessary.' Now, as object of this 'free holding something to be true,' he sets forth the conception of the highest good in the world, to be realised through freedom. It is clear that before this argument would prove that a God is necessary to the realisation of the moral order, it would have to be shown that there are no adequate forces immanent within society itself for the establishment and fulfilment of that order. As a matter of fact, reflexion in the nineteenth century, devoted as it has been to the evolution of society, has busied itself with hardly anything more than with the study of those immanent elements which make for morality. It is therefore not an external guarantor of morals, such as Kant thought, which is here given. It is the immanent God who is revealed in the history and life of the race, even as also it is the immanent God who is revealed in the consciousness of the individual soul. Even the moral argument, therefore, in the form in which Kant puts it, sounds remote and strange to us. His reasoning strains and creaks almost as if he were still trying to do that which he had just declared could not be done. What remains of significance for us, is this. All the debate about first causes, absolute beings, and the rest, gives us no God such as our souls need. If a man is to find the witness for soul, immortality and God at all, he must find it within himself and in the spiritual history of his fellows. He must venture, in freedom, the belief in these things, and find their corroboration in the contribution which they make to the solution of the mystery of life. One must venture to win them. One must continue to venture, to keep them. If it were not so, they would not be objects of faith.

The source of the radical evil in man is an intelligible act of human freedom not further to be explained. Moral evil is not, as such, transmitted. Moral qualities are inseparable from the responsibility of the person who commits the deeds. Yet this radical disposition to evil is to be changed into a good one, not altogether by a process of moral reformation. There is such a thing as a fundamental revolution of a man's habit of thought, a conscious and voluntary transference of a man's intention to obey, from the superficial and selfish desires which he has followed, to the deep and spiritual ones which he will henceforth allow. There is an epoch in a man's life when he makes the transition. He probably does it under the spell of personal influence, by the power of example, through the beauty of another personality. To Kant salvation was character. It was of and in and by character. To no thinker has the moral participation of a man in the regeneration of his own character been more certain and necessary than to Kant. Yet the change in direction of the will generally comes by an impulse from without. It comes by the impress of a noble personality. It is sustained by enthusiasm for that personality. Kant has therefore a perfectly rational and ethical and vital meaning for the phrase ' new birth.'

For the purpose of this impulse to goodness, nothing is so effective as the contemplation of an historical example of such surpassing moral grandeur as that which we behold in Jesus. For this reason we may look to Jesus as the ideal of goodness presented to us in flesh and blood. Yet the assertion that Jesus' historical personality altogether corresponds with the complete and eternal ethical ideal is one which we have no need to make. We do not possess in our own minds the absolute ideal with which in that assertion we compare him. The ethical ideal of the race is still in process of development. Jesus has been the greatest factor urging forward that development. We ourselves stand at a certain point in that development. We have the ideals which we have because we stand at that point at which we do. The men who come after us will have a worthier ideal than have we. Again, to say that Jesus in his words and conduct expressed in its totality the eternal ethical ideal, would make of his life something different from the real, human life. Every real, human life is lived within certain actual antitheses which call out certain qualities and do not call out others. They demand certain reactions and not others. This is the con-

crete element without which nothing historical can be conceived. To say that Jesus lived in entire conformity to the
ethical ideal so far as we are able to conceive it, and within
the circumstances which his own time and place imposed, is
the most that we can say. But in any case, Kant insists,
the real object of our religious faith is not the historic man,
but the ideal of humanity well-pleasing to God. Since this
ideal is not of our own creation, but is given us in our supersensible nature, it may be conceived as the Son of God come
down from heaven.

The turn of this last phrase is an absolutely characteristic
one, and brings out another quality of Kant's mind in dealing
with the Christian doctrines. They are to him but symbols,
forms into which a variety of meanings may be run. He had
no great appreciation of the historical element in doctrine.
He had no deep sense of the social element and of that for
which Christian institutions stand. We may illustrate with
that which he says concerning Christ's vicarious sacrifice.
Substitution cannot take place in the moral world. Ethical
salvation could not be conferred through such a substitution,
even if this could take place. Still, the conception of the
vicarious suffering of Christ may be taken as a symbolical
expression of the idea that in the pain of self-discipline, of
obedience and patience, the new man in us suffers, as it were
vicariously, for the old. The atonement is a continual ethical
process in the heart of the religious man. It is a grave defect
of Kant's religious philosophy, that it was so absolutely
individualistic. Had he realised more deeply than he did the
social character of religion and the meaning of these doctrines,
not alone as between man and God, but as between man and
man, he surely would have drawn nearer to that interpretation
of the doctrine of the atonement which has come more and
more to prevail. This is the solution which finds in the
atonement of Christ the last and most glorious example of
a universal law of human life and history. That law is that
no redemptive good for men is ever secured without the
suffering and sacrifice of those who seek to confer that good
upon their fellows. Kant was disposed to regard the tradi-

tional forms of Christian doctrine, not as the old rationalism had done, as impositions of a priesthood or inherently absurd. He sought to divest them indeed of that which was speculatively untrue, though he saw in them only symbols of the great moral truths which lie at the heart of religion. The historical spirit of the next fifty years was to teach men a very different way of dealing with these same doctrines.

Kant had said that the primary condition, fundamental not merely to knowledge, but to all connected experience, is the knowing, experiencing, thinking, acting self. It is that which says ' I,' the ego, the permanent subject. But that is not enough. The knowing self demands in turn a knowable world. It must have something outside of itself to which it yet stands related, the object of knowledge. Knowledge is somehow the combination of these two, the result of their co-operation. How have we to think of this co-operation ? Both Hume and Berkeley had ended in scepticism as to the reality of knowledge. Hume was in doubt as to the reality of the subject, Berkeley as to that of the object. Kant dissented from both. He vindicated the undoubted reality of the impression which we have concerning a thing. Yet how far that impression is the reproduction of the thing as it is in itself, we can never perfectly know. What we have in our minds is not the object. It is a notion of that object, although we may be assured that we could have no such notion were there no object. Equally, the notion is what it is because the subject is what it is. We can never get outside the processes of our own thought. We cannot know the thing as it is, the *Ding-an-sich*, in Kant's phrase. We know only that there must be a ' thing in itself.'

FICHTE

Fichte asked, Why ? Why must there be a *Ding-an-sich* ? Why is not that also the result of the activity of the ego ?

Why is not the ego, the thinking subject, all that is, the creator
of the world, according to the laws of thought ?   If so much
is reduced to idea, why not all ?   This was Fichte's rather
forced resolution of the old dualism of thought and thing.
It is not the denial of the reality of things, but the assertion
that their ideal element, that part of them which is not mere
' thing,' the action and subject of the action, is their underlying reality.   According to Kant things exist in a world
beyond us.   Man has no faculty by which he can penetrate
into that world.   Still, the farther we follow Kant in his
analysis the more does the contribution to knowledge from
the side of the mind tend to increase, and the more does the
factor in our impressions from the side of things tend to fade
away.   This basis of impression being wholly unknowable is as
good as non-existent for us.   Yet it never actually disappears.
There would seem to be inevitable a sort of kernel of matter
or prick of sense about which all our thoughts are generated.
Yet this residue is a vanishing quantity.   This seemed to
Fichte to be a self-contradiction and a half-way measure.
Only two positions appeared to him thorough-going and
consequent.   Either one posits as fundamental the thing
itself, matter, independent of any consciousness of it.   So
Spinoza had taught.   Or else one takes consciousness, the
conscious subject, independent of any matter or thing as
fundamental.   This last Fichte claimed to be the real issue of
Kant's thought.   He asserts that from the point of view of the
thing in itself we can never explain knowledge.   We may be
as skilful as possible in placing one thing behind another in
the relation of cause to effect.   It is, however, an unending
series.   It is like the cosmogony of the Eastern people which
fabled that the earth rests upon the back of an elephant.
The elephant stands upon a tortoise.   The question is, upon
what does the tortoise stand ?   So here, we may say, in the
conclusive manner in which men have always said, that God
made the world.   Yet sooner or later we come to the child's
question : Who made God ?   Fichte rightly replied : ' If
God is for us only an object of knowledge, the *Ding-an-sich* at
the end of the series, there is no escape from the answer that

man, the thinker, in thinking God made him.' All the world, including man, is but the reflexion, the revelation in forms of the finite, of an unceasing action of thought of which the ego is the subject. Nothing more paradoxical than this conclusion can be imagined. It seems to make the human subject, the man myself, the creator of the universe, and the universe only that which I happen to think it to be.

This interpretation was at first put upon Fichte's reasoning with such vigour that he was accused of atheism. He was driven from his chair in Jena. Only after several years was he called to a corresponding post in Berlin. Later, in his *Vocation of Man*, he brought his thought to clearness in this form : ' If God be only the object of thought, it remains true that he is then but the creation of man's thought. God is, however, to be understood as subject, as the real subject, the transcendent thinking and knowing subject, indwelling in the world and making the world what it is, indwelling in us and making us what we are. We ourselves are subjects only in so far as we are parts of God. We think and know only in so far as God thinks and knows and acts and lives in us. The world, including ourselves, is but the reflection of the thought of God, who thus only has existence. Neither the world nor we have existence apart from him.'

Johann Gottlieb Fichte was born at Rammenau in 1762. His father was a ribbon weaver. He came of a family distinguished for piety and uprightness. He studied at Jena, and became an instructor there in 1793. He was at first a devout disciple of Kant, but gradually separated himself from his master. There is a humorous tale as to one of his early books which was, through mistake of the publisher, put forth without the author's name. For a brief time it was hailed as a work of Kant—his *Critique of Revelation*. Fichte was a man of high moral enthusiasms, very uncompromising, unable to put himself in the place of an opponent, in incessant strife. The great work of his Jena period was his *Wissenschaftslehre*, 1794. His popular works, *Die Bestimmung des Menschen* and *Anweisung zum seligen Leben*, belong to his Berlin period. The disasters of 1806 drove him out of Berlin.

Amidst the dangers and discouragements of the next few years he wrote his famous *Reden an die deutsche Nation.* He drew up the plan for the founding of the University of Berlin. In 1810 he was called to be rector of the newly established university. He was, perhaps, the chief adviser of Frederick William III. in the laying of the foundations of the university, which was surely a notable venture for those trying years. In the autumn of 1812 and again in 1813, when the hospitals were full of sick and wounded after the Russian and Leipzig campaigns, Fichte and his wife were unceasing in their care of the sufferers. He died of fever contracted in the hospital in January 1814.

According to Fichte, as we have seen, the world of sense is the reflection of our own inner activity. It exists for us as the sphere and material of our duty. The moral order only is divine. We, the finite intelligences, exist only in and through the infinite intelligence. All our life is thus God's life. We are immortal because he is immortal. Our consciousness is his consciousness. Our life and moral force is his, the reflection and manifestation of his being, individuation of the infinite reason which is everywhere present in the finite. In God we see the world also in a new light. There is no longer any nature which is external to ourselves and unrelated to ourselves. There is only God manifesting himself in nature. Even the evil is only a means to good and, therefore, only an apparent evil. We are God's immediate manifestation, being spirit like himself. The world is his mediate manifestation. The world of dead matter, as men have called it, does not exist. God is the reality within the forms of nature and within ourselves, by which alone we have reality. The duty to which a God outside of ourselves could only command us, becomes a privilege to which we need no commandment, but to the fulfilment of which, rather, we are drawn in joy by the forces of our own being. How a man could, even in the immature stages of these thoughts, have been persecuted for atheism, it is not easy to see, although we may admit that his earlier forms of statement were bewildering. When we have his whole thought before us we should say rather that it borders on acosmic pantheism, for which everything is God and the world does not exist.

We have no need to follow Fichte farther. Suffice it to say, with reference to the theory of knowledge, that he had discovered that one could not stand still with Kant. One must either go back toward the position of the old empiricism which assumed the reality of the world exactly as it appeared, or else one must go forward to an idealism more thorough-going than Kant had planned. Of the two paths which, with all the vast advance of the natural sciences, the thought of the nineteenth century might traverse, that of the denial of everything except the mechanism of nature, and that of the assertion that nature is but the organ of spirit and is instinct with reason, Fichte chose the latter and blazed out the path along which all the idealists have followed him. In reference to the philosophy of religion, we must say that, with all the extravagance, the pantheism and mysticism of his phrases, Fichte's great contribution was his breaking down of the old dualism between God and man which was still fundamental to Kant. It was his assertion of the unity of man and God and of the life of God in man. This thought has been appropriated in all of modern theology.

SCHELLING

It was the meagreness of Fichte's treatment of nature which impelled Schelling to what he called his outbreak into reality. Nature will not be dismissed, as simply that which is not I. You cannot say that nature is only the sphere of my self-realisation. Individuals are in their way the children of nature. They are this in respect of their souls as much as of their bodies. Nature was before they were. Nature is, moreover, not alien to intelligence. On the contrary, it is a treasure-house of intelligible forms which demand to be treated as such. It appeared to Schelling, therefore, a truer idealism to work out an intelligible system of nature, exhibiting its essential oneness with personality.

Friedrich Wilhelm Joseph von Schelling was born in 1775

at Leonberg in Württemberg. His father was a clergyman. He was precocious in his intellectual development and much spoiled by vanity. Before he was twenty years old he had published three works upon problems suggested by Fichte. At twenty-three he was extraordinarius at Jena. He had apparently a brilliant career before him. He published his *Erster Entwurf eines Systems der Naturphilosophie*, 1799, and also his *System des transcendentalen Idealismus*, 1800. Even his short residence at Jena was troubled by violent conflicts with his colleagues. It was brought to an end by his marriage with the wife of Augustus von Schlegel, who had been divorced for the purpose. From 1806 to 1841 he lived in Munich in retirement. The long-expected books which were to fulfil his early promise never appeared. Hegel's stricture was just. Schelling had no taste for the prolonged and intense labour which his brilliant early works marked out. He died in 1854, having reached the age of seventy-nine years, of which at least fifty were as melancholy and fruitless as could well be imagined.

The dominating idea of Schelling's philosophy of nature may be said to be the exhibition of nature as the progress of intelligence toward consciousness and personality. Nature is the ego in evolution, personality in the making. All natural objects are visible analogues and counterparts of mind. The intelligence which their structure reveals, men had interpreted as residing in the mind of a maker of the world. Nature had been spoken of as if it were a watch. God was its great artificer. No one asserted that its intelligence and power of development lay within itself. On the contrary, nature is always in the process of advance from lower, less highly organised and less intelligible forms, to those which are more highly organised, more nearly the counterpart of the active intelligence in man himself. The personality of man had been viewed as standing over against nature, this last being thought of as static and permanent. On the contrary, the personality of man, with all of its intelligence and free will, is but the climax and fulfilment of a long succession of intelligible forms in nature, passing upward from the inorganic to the organic, from the unconscious to the conscious, from the non-moral to the moral, as these are at last seen in man.   Of course, it was the life of organic nature which first suggested this notion to Schelling.   An organism is a self-moving, self-producing whole.   It is an idea in process of self-realisation.   What was observed in the organism was then made by Schelling the root idea of universal nature. Nature is in all its parts living, self-moving along the lines of its development, productivity and product both in one. Empirical science may deal with separate products of nature. It may treat them as objects of analysis and investigation. It may even take the whole of nature as an object.   But nature is not mere object.   Philosophy has to treat of the inner life which moves the whole of nature as intelligible productivity, as subject, no longer as object.   Personality has slowly arisen out of nature.   Nature was going through this process of self-development before there were any men to contemplate it.   It would go through this process were there no longer men to contemplate it.

Schelling has here rounded out the theory of absolute idealism which Fichte had carried through in a one-sided way.   He has given us also a wonderful anticipation of certain modern ideas concerning nature, a preparation for the doctrine of evolution, which is a stroke of genius in its way.   He attempted to arrange the realm of unconscious intelligences in an ascending series, which should bridge the gulf between the lowest of natural forms and the fully equipped organism in which self-consciousness, with the intellectual, the emotional, and moral life, at last emerges.   Inadequate material and a fondness for analogies led Schelling into vagaries in following out this scheme.   Nevertheless, it is only in detail that we can look askance at his attempt.   In principle our own conception of the universe is the same.   It is the dynamic view of nature and an application of the principle of evolution in the widest sense.   His errors were those into which a man was bound to fall who undertook to forestall by a sweep of the imagination that which has been the result of the detailed and patient investigation of three generations.   What

Schelling attempted was to take nature as we know it and to exhibit it as in reality a function of intelligence, pointing, through all the gradations of its varied forms, towards its necessary goal in self-conscious personality. Instead, therefore, of our having in nature and personality two things which cannot be brought together, these become members of one great organism of intelligence of which the immanent God is the source and the sustaining power. These ideas constitute Schelling's contribution to an idealistic and, of course, an essentially monistic view of the universe. The unity of man with God, Fichte had asserted. Schelling set forth the oneness of God and nature, and again of man and nature. The circle was complete.

If we have succeeded in conveying a clear idea of the movement of thought from Kant to Hegel, that idea might be stated thus. There are but three possible objects which can engage the thought of man. These are nature and man and God. There is the universe, of which we become aware through experience from our earliest childhood. Then there is man, the man given in self-consciousness, primarily the man myself. In this sense man seems to stand over against nature. Then, as the third possible object of thought, we have God. Upon the thought of God we usually come from the point of view of the category of cause. God is the name which men give to that which lies behind nature and man as the origin and explanation of both. Plato's chief interest was in man. He talked much concerning a God who was somehow the speculative postulate of the spiritual nature in man. Aristotle began a real observation of nature. But the ancient and, still more, the mediæval study of nature was dominated by abstract and theological assumptions. These prevented any real study of that nature in the midst of which man lives, in reaction against which he develops his powers, and to which, on one whole side of his nature, he belongs. Even in respect of that which men reverently took to be thought concerning God, they seem to have been unaware how much of their material was imaginative and poetic symbolism drawn from the experience of man. The traditional idea of revelation proved a disturbing factor. Assuming that revelation gave information concerning God, and not rather the religious experience of communion with God himself, men accepted statements of the documents of revelation as if they had been definitions graciously given from out the realm of the unseen. In reality, they were but fetches from out the world of the known into the world of the unknown.

The point of interest is this :—In all possible combinations in which, throughout the history of thought, these three objects had been set, the one with the others, they had always remained three objects. There was no essential relation of the one to the other. They were like the points of a triangle of which any one stood over against the other two. God stood over against the man whom he had fashioned, man over against the God to whom he was responsible. The consequences for theology are evident. When men wished to describe, for example, Jesus as the Son of God, they laid emphasis upon every quality which he had, or was supposed to have, which was not common to him with other men. They lost sight of that profound interest of religion which has always claimed that, in some sense, all men are sons of God and Jesus was the son of man. Jesus was then only truly honoured as divine when every trait of his humanity was ignored. Similarly, when men spoke of revelation they laid emphasis upon those particulars in which this supposed method of coming by information was unlike all other methods. Knowledge derived directly from God through revelation was in no sense the parallel of knowledge derived by men in any other way. So also God stood over against nature. God was indeed declared to have made nature. He had, however, but given it, so to say, an original impulse. That impulse also it had in some strange way lost or perverted, so that the world, though it had been made by God, was not good. For the most part it moved itself, although God's sovereignty was evidenced in that he could still super-

vene upon it, if he chose.   The supernatural was the realm
of God.   Natural and supernatural were mutually exclusive
terms, just as we saw that divine and human were exclusive
terms.   So also, on the third side of our triangle, man stood
over against nature.   Nature was to primitive men the
realm of caprice, in which they imagined demons, spirits and
the like.   These were antagonistic to men, as also hostile to
God.   Then, when with the advance of reflexion these
spirits, and equally their counterparts, the good genii and
angels, had all died, nature became the realm of iron necessity, of regardless law, of all-destroying force, of cruel and
indifferent fate.   From this men took refuge in the thought
of a compassionate God, though they could not withdraw
themselves or those whom they loved from the inexorable
laws of nature.   They could not see that God always, or even
often, intervened on their behalf.   It cannot be denied that
these ideas prevail to some extent in the popular theology
at the present moment.   Much of our popular religious
language is an inheritance from a time when they universally
prevailed.   The religious intuition even of psalmists and
prophets opposed many of these notions.   The pure religious
intuition of Jesus opposed almost every one of them.   Mystics
in every religion have had, at times, insight into an altogether
different scheme of things.   The philosophy, however, even
of the learned, would, in the main, have supported the views
above described, from the dawn of reflexion almost to our
own time.

It was Kant who first began the resolution of this three-
cornered difficulty.   When he pointed out that into the world,
as we know it, an element of spirit goes, that in it an element
of the ideal inheres, he began a movement which has issued
in modern monism.   He affirmed that that element from
my thought which enters into the world, as I know it, may
be so great that only just a point of matter and a prick of
sense remains.   Fichte said: ' Why do we put it all in so
perverse a way ?   Why reduce the world of matter to just
a point ?   Why is it not taken for what it is, and yet understood to be all alive with God and we able to think of it,

because we are parts of the great thinker God ? ' Still Fichte had busied himself almost wholly with consciousness. Schelling endeavoured to correct that. Nature lives and moves in God, just as truly in one way as does man in another. Men arise out of nature. A circle has been drawn through the points of our triangle. Nature and man are in a new and deeper sense revelations of God. In fact, supplementing one another, they constitute the only possible channels for the manifestation of God. It hardly needs to be said that these thoughts are widely appropriated in our modern world. These once novel speculations of the kings of thought have made their way slowly to all strata of society. Remote and difficult in their first expression in the language of the schools, their implications are to-day on everybody's lips. It is this unitary view of the universe which has made difficult the acceptance of a theology, the understanding of a religion, which are still largely phrased in the language of a philosophy to which these ideas did not belong. There is not an historic creed, there is hardly a greater system of theology, which is not stated in terms of a philosophy and science which no longer reign. Men are asking: ' cannot Christianity be so stated and interpreted that it shall meet the needs of men of the twentieth century, as truly as it met those of men of the first or of the sixteenth ? ' Hegel, the last of this great group of idealistic philosophers whom we shall name, enthusiastically believed in this new interpretation of the faith which was profoundly dear to him. He made important contribution to that interpretation.

HEGEL

Georg Wilhelm Friedrich Hegel was born in Stuttgart in 1770. His father was in the fiscal service of the King of Württemberg. He studied in Tübingen. He was heavy and slow of development, in striking contrast with Schelling. He served as tutor in Bern and Frankfort, and began to lecture in Jena in 1801. He was much overshadowed by Schelling. The victory of Napoleon at Jena in 1806 closed the university

for a time. In 1818 he was called to Fichte's old chair in
Berlin. Never on very good terms with the Prussian Government, he yet showed his large sympathy with life in every
way. After 1820 a school of philosophical thinkers began
to gather about him. His first great book, his *Phenomeno-
logie des Geistes* 1807 (translated, Baillie, London, 1910), was
published at the end of his Jena period. His *Philosophie der
Religion* and *Philosophie der Geschichte* were edited after his
death. They are mainly in the form which his notes took
between 1823 and 1827. He died during an epidemic of
cholera in Berlin in 1831.

Besides his deep interest in history the most striking feature
of Hegel's preliminary training was his profound study of
Christianity. He might almost be said to have turned to
philosophy as a means of formulating the ideas which he had
conceived concerning the development of the religious consciousness, which seemed to him to have been the bearer of all
human culture. No one could fail to see that the idea of the
relation of God and man, of which we have been speaking,
was bound to make itself felt in the interpretation of the
doctrine of the incarnation and of all the dogmas, like that
of the trinity, which are connected with it. Characteristically,
Hegel had pure joy in the speculative aspects of the problem.
If one may speak in all reverence, and, at the same time, not
without a shade of humour, Hegel rejoiced to find himself
able, as he supposed, to rehabilitate the dogma of the trinity,
rationalised in approved fashion. It is as if the dogma had
been a revered form or mould, which was for him indeed
emptied of its original content. He felt bound to fill it anew.
Or to speak more justly, he was really convinced that the new
meaning which he poured into the dogma was the true meaning
which the Church Fathers had been seeking all the while.
In the light of two generations of sober dealing, as historians,
with such problems, we can but view his solution in a manner
very different from that which he indulged. He was even
disposed mildly to censure the professional theologians for
leaving the defence of the doctrine of the trinity to the philosophers. There were then, and have since been, defenders

of the doctrine who have thought that Hegel rendered them great aid. As a matter of fact, despite his own utter serious-ness and reverent desire, his solution was a complete dis-solution of the doctrine and of much else besides. His view would have been fatal, not merely to that particular form of orthodox thought, but, what is much more serious, to the religious meaning for which it stood. Sooner or later men have seen that the whole drift of Hegelianism was to transform religion into intellectualism. One might say that it was exactly this which the ancient metaphysicians, in the classic doctrine of the trinity, had done. They had transformed religion into metaphysics. The matter would not have been remedied by having a modern metaphysician do the same thing in another way.

Hegel was weary of Fichte's endless discussion of the ego and Schelling's of the absolute. It was not the abyss of the unknowable from which things are said to come, or that into which they go, which interested Hegel. It was their process and progress which we can know. It was that part of their movement which is observable within actual experience, with which he was concerned. Now one of the laws of the movement of all things, he said, is that by which every thought suggests, and every force tends directly to produce, its opposite. Nothing stands alone. Everything exists by the balance and friction of opposing tendencies. We have the universal contrasts of heat and cold, of light and darkness, of inward and outward, of static and dynamic, of yes and no. There are two sides to every case, democratic government and absolutism, freedom of religion and authority, the in-dividualistic and the social principles, a materialistic and a spiritual interpretation of the universe. Only things which are dead have ceased to have this tide and alternation. Christ is for living religion now a man, now God, revelation now natural, now supernatural. Religion is the eternal con-flict between reason and faith, morals the struggle of good and evil, God now mysterious and now manifest.

Fichte had said: The essence of the universe is spirit. Hegel said: Yes, but the true notion of spirit is that of the resolution

of contradiction, of the exhibition of opposites as held together in their unity. This is the meaning of the trinity. In
the trinity we have God who wills to manifest himself, Jesus
in whom he is manifest, and the spirit common to them both.
God's existence is not static, it is dynamic. It is motion,
not rest. God is revealer, recipient, and revelation all in one.
The trinity was for Hegel the central doctrine of Christianity.
Popular orthodoxy had drawn near to the assertion of three
Gods. The revolt, however, in asserting the unity of God,
had made of God a meaningless absolute as foundation of
the universe. The orthodox, in respect to the person of
Christ, had always indeed asserted in laboured way that Jesus
was both God and man. Starting from their own abstract
conception of God, and attributing to Jesus the qualities of
that abstraction, they had ended in making of the humanity
of Jesus a perfectly unreal thing. On the other hand, those
who had set out from Jesus's real humanity had been unable
to see that he was anything more than a mere man, as
their phrase was. On their own assumption of the mutual
exclusiveness of the conceptions of God and man, they could
not do otherwise.

Hegel saw clearly that God can be known to us only in
and through manifestation. We can certainly make no
predication as to how God exists, in himself, as men say, and
apart from our knowledge. He exists for our knowledge
only as manifest in nature and man. Man is for Hegel
part of nature and Jesus is the highest point which the
nature of God as manifest in man has reached. In this
sense Hegel sometimes even calls nature the Son of God, and
mankind and Jesus are thought of as parts of this one manifestation of God. If the Scripture asserts, as it seemed to the
framers of the creeds to do, that God manifested himself from
before all worlds in and to a self-conscious personality like
his own, Hegel would answer : But the Scripture is no third
source of knowledge, besides nature and man. Scripture is
only the record of God's revelation of himself in and to men.
If these men framed their profoundest thought in this way,
that is only because they lived in an age when men had all

their thoughts of this sort in a form which we can historically trace. For Platonists and Neoplatonists, such as the makers of the creeds—and some portions of the Scripture show this influence, as well—the divine, the ideal, was always thought of as eternal. It always existed as pure archetype before it ever existed as historic fact. The rabbins had a speculation to the same effect. The divine which exists must have pre-existed. Jesus as Son of God could not be thought of by the ancient world in any terms but these. The divine was static, changelessly perfect. For the modern man the divinest of all things is the mystery of growth. The perfect man is not at the beginning, but far down the immeasurable series of approaches to perfection. The perfection of other men is the work of still other ages, in which this extraordinary and inexplicable moral magnitude which Jesus is, has had its influence, and conferred upon them power to aid them in the fulfilment of God's intent for themselves, which is like that intent for himself which Jesus has fulfilled.

Surely enough has been said to show that what we have here is only the absorption of even the profoundest religious meanings into the vortex of an all-dissolving metaphysical system. The most obvious meaning of the phrase 'Son of God,' its moral and spiritual, its real religious meaning, is dwelt on, here in Hegel, as little as Hegel claimed that the Nicene trinitarians had dwelt upon it. Nothing marks more clearly the distance we have travelled since Hegel than does the general recognition that his attempted solution does not even lie in the right direction. It is an attempt within the same area as that of the Nicene Council and the creeds, namely, the metaphysical area. What is at stake is not the pre-existence or the two natures. Hegel was right in what he said concerning these. The pre-existence cannot be thought of except as ideal. The two natures we assert for every man, only not in such a manner as to destroy unity in the personality. The heart of the dogma is not in these. It is the oneness of God and man, a moral and spiritual oneness, oneness in conduct and consciousness, the presence and realisation of God, who is spirit, in a real man, the divineness of Jesus, in a sense which sees no meaning any longer in the old debate as between his divinity and his deity.

In the light of the new theory of the universe which we have reviewed, it flashes upon us that both defenders and assailants of the doctrine of the incarnation, in the age-long debate, have proceeded from the assumption that God and man are opposites. Men contended for the divineness of Jesus in terms which by definition shut out his true humanity. They asserted the identity of a real man, a true historic personage, with an abstract notion of God which had actually been framed by the denial of all human qualities. Their opponents with a like helplessness merely reversed the situation. To admit the deity of Jesus would have been for them, in all candour and clear-sightedness, absolutely impossible, because the admission would have shut out his true humanity. On the old definitions we cannot wonder that the struggle was a bitter one. Each party was on its own terms right. If God is by definition other than man, and man the opposite of God, then it is not surprising that the attempt to say that Jesus of Nazareth was both, remained mysticism to the one and seemed folly to the other.

Now, within the area of the philosophy which begins with Kant this old antinomy has been resolved. An actual circle of clear relations joins the points of the old hopeless triangle. Men are men because of God indwelling in them, working through them. The phrase ' mere man ' is seen to be a mere phrase. To say that the Nazarene, in some way not genetically to be explained, but which is hidden within the recesses of his own personality, shows forth in incomparable fulness that relation of God and man which is the ideal for us all, seems only to be saying over again what Jesus said when he proclaimed : ' I and My Father are one.' That Jesus actualised, not absolutely in the sense that he stood out of relation to history, but still perfectly within his relation to history, that which in us and for us is potential, the sonship of God—that seems a very simple and intelligible assertion. It certainly makes a large part of the debate of ages seem remote from us. It brings home to us that we live in a new world.

Interesting and fruitful is Hegel's expansion of the idea of redemption beyond that of the individual to that of the whole humanity, and in every aspect of its life. In my relation to the world are given my duties. The renunciation of outward duty makes the inward life barren. The principle which is to transform the world wears an aspect very different from that of stoicism, of asceticism or even of the individualism which has sought soul-salvation. In the midst of unworthiness and helplessness there springs up the consciousness of reconciliation. Man, with all his imperfections, becomes aware that he is the object of the loving purpose of God. Still this redemption of a man is something which is to be worked out, in the individual life and on the stage of universal history. The first step beyond the individual life is that of the Church. It is from within this community of believers that men, in the rule, receive the impulse to the good. The community is, in its idea, a society in which the conquest of evil is already being achieved, where the individual is spared much bitter conflict and loneliness. Nevertheless, so long as this unity of the life of man with God is realised in the Church alone there remains a false and harmful opposition between the Church and the world. Religion is faced by a hostile power to which its principles have no application. The world is denounced as unholy. With this stigma cast upon it, it may be unholy. Yet the retribution falls also upon the Church, in that it becomes artificial, clerical, pharisaical. The end is never that what have been called the standards of the Church shall prevail. The end is that the Church shall be the shrine and centre of an influence by virtue of which the standard of truth and goodness which naturally belongs to any relation of life shall prevail. The distinction between religion and secular life must be abandoned. Nothing is less sacred than a Church set on its own aggrandisement. The relations of family and of the State, of business and social life, are to be restored to the divineness which belongs to them, or rather, the divineness which is inalienable from them is to be recognised. In the laws and customs of a true State, Christianity first penetrates with its

principles the real world.   One sees how large a portion of
these thoughts have been taken up into the programme of
modern social movements.   They are the basis of what men
call a social theology.   A book like Fremantle's *World as the
Subject of Redemption* is their thorough-going exposition in
the English tongue.

We have no cause to pursue the philosophical movement
beyond this point.   Its exponents are not without interest.
Especially is this true of Schopenhauer.   But the deposit
from their work is for our particular purpose not great.
The wonderful impulse had spent itself.   These four brilliant
men stand together, almost as much isolated from the generation which followed them as from that which went before.
The historian of Christian thought in the nineteenth century
cannot overestimate the significance of their personal interest
in religion.

CHAPTER III

THEOLOGICAL RECONSTRUCTION

THE outstanding trait of Kant's reflection upon religion is its supreme interest in morals and conduct. Metaphysician that he was, Kant saw the evil which intellectualism had done to religion. Religion was a profoundly real thing to him in his own life. Religion is a life. It is a system of thought only because life is a whole. It is a system of thought only in the way of deposit from a vivid and vigorous life. A man normally reflects on the conditions and aims of what he does. Religion is conduct. Ends in character are supreme. Religions and the many interpretations of Christianity have been good or bad, according as they ministered to character. So strong was this ethical trait in Kant that it dwarfed all else. He was not himself a man of great breadth or richness of feeling. He was not a man of imagination. His religion was austere, not to say arid. Hegel was before all things an intellectualist. Speculation was the breath of life to him. He had metaphysical genius. He tended to transform in this direction everything which he touched. Religion is thought. He criticised the rationalist movement from the height of vantage which idealism had reached. But as pure intellectualist he would put most rationalists to shame. We owe to this temperament his zeal for an interpretation of the universe ' all in one piece.' Its highest quality would be its abstract truth. His understanding of religion had the glory and the limitations which attend this view.

SCHLEIERMACHER

Between Kant and Hegel came another, Schleiermacher. He too was no mean philosopher. But he was essentially a theologian, the founder of modern theology. He served in the same faculty with Hegel and was overshadowed by him. His influence upon religious thought was less immediate. It has been more permanent. It was characteristically upon the side which Kant and Hegel had neglected. That was the side of feeling. His theology has been called the theology of feeling. He defined religion as feeling. Christianity is for him a specific feeling. Because he made so much of feeling, his name has been made a theological household word by many who appropriated little else of all he had to teach. His warmth and passion, his enthusiasm for Christ, the central place of Christ in his system, made him loved by many who, had they understood him better, might have loved him less. For his real greatness lay, not in the fact that he possessed these qualities alone, but that he possessed them in a singularly beautiful combination with other qualities. The emphasis is, however, correct. He was the prophet of feeling, as Kant had been of ethical religion and Hegel of the intellectuality of faith. The entire Protestant theology of the nineteenth century has felt his influence. The English-speaking race is almost as much his debtor as is his own. The French Huguenots of the revival felt him to be one of themselves. Even to Amiel and Scherer he was a kindred spirit.

It is a true remark of Dilthey that in unusual degree an understanding of the man's personality and career is necessary to the appreciation of his thought. Friedrich Ernst Daniel Schleiermacher was born in 1768 in Breslau, the son of a chaplain in the Reformed Church. He never connected himself officially with the Lutheran Church. We have alluded to an episode broadly characteristic of his youth. He was tutor in the house of one of the landed nobility of Prussia, curate in a country parish, preacher at the Charité in Berlin in 1795, professor extraordinarius at Halle in 1804, preacher at the Church of the Dreifaltigkeit in Berlin in 1807, professor of theology and organiser of that faculty in the newly-founded University of Berlin in 1810. He never gave up his position as pastor and preacher, maintaining this activity along

with his unusual labours as teacher, executive and author.
He died in 1834.   In his earlier years in Berlin he belonged to
the circle of brilliant men and women who made Berlin
famous in those years.   It was a fashionable society composed of persons more or less of the rationalistic school.   Not
a few of them, like the Schlegels, were deeply tinged with
romanticism.   There were also among them Jews of the house
of the elder Mendelssohn.   Morally it was a society not
altogether above reproach.   Its opposition to religion was a
by-word.   An affection of the susceptible youth for a woman
unhappily married brought him to the verge of despair.
It was an affection which his passing pride as romanticist
would have made him think it prudish to discard, while the
deep, underlying elements of his nature made it inconceivable
that he should indulge.   Only in later years did he heal his
wound in a happy married life.

The episode was typical of the experience he was passing
through.   He understood the public with which his first book
dealt.   That book bears the striking title, *Reden über die
Religion, an die Gebildeten unter ihren Verächtern* (translated,
Oman, Oxford, 1893).   His public understood him.   He could
reach them as perhaps no other man could do.   If he had ever
concealed what religion was to him, he now paid the price.
If they had made light of him, he now made war on them.
This meed they could hardly withhold from him, that he
understood most other things quite as well as they, and
religion much better than they.   The rhetorical form is a
fiction.   The addresses were never delivered.   Their tension
and straining after effect is palpable.   They are a cry of pain
on the part of one who sees that assailed which is sacred to
him, of triumph as he feels himself able to repel the assault,
of brooding persuasiveness lest any should fail to be won for
his truth.   He concedes everything.   It is part of his art to
go further than his detractors.   He is so well versed in his
subject that he can do that with consummate mastery,
where they are clumsy or dilettante.   It is but a pale ghost
of religion that he has left.   But he has attained his purpose.
He has vindicated the place of religion in the life of culture.

He has shown the relation of religion to every great thing in civilisation, its affinity with art, its common quality with poetry, its identity with all profound activities of the soul. These all are religion, though their votaries know it not. These are reverence for the highest, dependence on the highest, self-surrender to the highest. No great man ever lived, no great work was ever done, save in an attitude toward the universe, which is identical with that of the religious man toward God. The universe is God. God is the universe. That religionists have obscured this simple truth and denied this grand relation is true, and nothing to the point. The cultivated should be ashamed not to know this. Then, with a sympathy with institutional religion and a knowledge of history in which he stood almost alone, he retracts much that he has yielded, he rebuilds much that he has thrown down, proclaims much which they must now concede. The book was published in 1799. Twenty years later he said sadly that if he were re-writing it, its shafts would be directed against some very different persons, against glib and smug people who boasted the form of godliness, conventional, even fashionable religion-ists and loveless ecclesiastics. Vast and various influences in the Germany of the first two decades of the century had wrought for the revival of religion. Of those influences, not the least had been that of Schleiermacher's book. Among the greatest had been Schleiermacher himself.

The religion of feeling, as advocated in the *Reden,* had left much on the ethical side to be desired. This defect the author sought to remedy in his *Monologen,* published in 1800. The programme of theological studies for the new University of Berlin, *Kurze Darstellung des Theologischen Studiums,* 1811, shows his theological system already in large part matured. His *Der christliche Glaube,* published in 1821, revised three years before his death in 1834, is his monumental work. His *Ethik,* his lectures upon many subjects, numerous volumes of sermons, all published after his death, witness his versatility. His sermons have the rare note which one finds in Robertson and Brooks.

All of the immediacy of religion, its independence of rational

argument, of historical tradition or institutional forms, which
was characteristic of Schleiermacher to his latest day, is
felt in the *Reden*. By it he thrilled the hearts of men as they
have rarely been thrilled. It is not forms and traditions which
create religion. It is religion which creates these. They
cannot exist without it. It may exist without them, though
not so well or so effectively. Religion is the sense of God.
That sense we have, though many call it by another name.
It would be more true to say that that sense has us. It is
inescapable. All who have it are the religious. Those who
hold to dogmas, rites, institutions in such a way as to obscure
and overlay this sense of God, those who hold these as substitute for that sense, are the nearest to being irreligious. Any
form, the most *outré*, bizarre and unconventional, is good,
so only that it helps a man to God. All forms are evil, the
most accredited the most evil, if they come between a man
and God. The pantheism of the thought of God in all of
Schleiermacher's early work is undeniable. He never wholly
put it aside. The personality of God seemed to him a limitation. Language is here only symbolical, a mere expression
from an environment which we know, flung out into the
depths of that we cannot see. If the language of personal
relations helps men in living with their truth—well and
good. It hinders also. For himself he felt that it hindered
more than helped. His definition of religion as the feeling
of dependence upon God, is cited as evidence of the effect
upon him of his contention against the personalness of God.
Religion is also, it is alleged, the sentiment of fellowship
with God. Fellowship implies persons. But to no man was
the fellowship with the soul of his own soul and of all the
universe more real than was that fellowship to Schleiermacher. This was the more true in his maturer years, the
years of the magnificent rounding out of his thought. God
was to him indeed not 'a man in the next street.' What
he says about the problem of the personalness of God is
true. We see, perhaps, more clearly than did he that the
debate is largely about words. Similarly, we may say that
Schleiermacher's passing denial of the immortality of the

soul was directed, in the first instance, against the crass, unsocial and immoral view which has disfigured much of the teaching of religion. His contention was directed toward that losing of oneself in God through ideals and service now, which in more modern phrase we call the entrance upon the immortal life here, the being in eternity now. For a soul so disposed, for a life thus inspired, death is but an episode. For himself he rejoices to declare it one to the issue of which he is indifferent. If he may thus live with God now, he cares little whether or not he shall live by and by.

In his *Monologues* Schleiermacher first sets forth his ethical thought. As it is religion that a man feels himself dependent upon God, so is it the beginning of morality that a man feels his dependence upon his fellows and their dependence on him. Slaves of their own time and circumstance, men live out their lives in superficiality and isolation. They are a prey to their own selfishness. They never come into those relations with their fellows in which the moral ideal can be realised. Man in his isolation from his fellows is nothing and accomplishes nothing. The interests of the whole humanity are his private interests. His own happiness and welfare are not possible to be secured save through his co-operation with others, his work and service for others. The happiness and welfare of others not merely react upon his own. They are in a large sense identical with his own. This oneness of a man with all men is the basis of morality, just as the oneness of man with God is the basis of religion. In both cases the oneness exists whether or not we know it. The contradictions and miseries into which immoral or unmoral conduct plunges us, are the witness of the fact that this inviolable unity of a man with humanity is operative, even if he ignores it. Often it is his ignoring of this relation which brings him through misery to consciousness of it. Man as moral being is but an individuation of humanity, just as, again, as religious being he is but an individuation of God. The goal of the moral life is the absorption of self, the elimination of self, which is at the same time the realisation of self, through the life and service for others. The goal of religion is the elimination of self, the swallowing up of self, in the service of God. In truth, the unity of man with man is at bottom only another form of his unity with God, and the service of humanity is the identical service of God. Other so-called services of God are a means to this, or else an illusion. This parallel of religion and morals is to be set over against other passages, easily to be cited, in which Schleiermacher speaks of passivity and contemplation as the means of the realisation of the unity of man and God, as if the elimination of self meant a sort of Nirvana. Schleiermacher was a pantheist and mystic. No philosopher save Kant ever influenced him half so much as did Spinoza. There is something almost oriental in his mood at times. An occasional fragment of description of religion might pass as a better delineation of Buddhism than of Christianity. This universality of his mind is interesting. These elements have not been unattractive to some portions of his following. One wearied with the Philistinism of the modern popular urgency upon practicality turns to Schleiermacher, as indeed sometimes to Spinoza, and says, here is a man who at least knows what religion is. Yet nothing is further from the truth than to say that Schleiermacher had no sense for the meaning of religion in the outward life and present world.

In the *Reden* Schleiermacher had contended that religion is a condition of devout feeling, specifically the feeling of dependence upon God. This view dominates his treatment of Christianity. It gives him his point of departure. A Christian is possessed of the devout feeling of dependence upon God through Jesus Christ or, as again he phrases it, of dependence upon Christ. Christianity is a positive religion in the sense that it has direct relation to certain facts in the history of the race, most of all to the person of Jesus of Nazareth. But it does not consist in any positive propositions whatsoever. These have arisen in the process of interpretation of the faith. The substance of the faith is the experience of renewal in Christ, of redemption through Christ. This inward experience is neither produced by pure thought nor dependent upon it. Like all other experience it is simply an object to be described and reckoned with. Orthodox dogmatists had held that the content of the Christian faith is a doctrine given in revelation. Schleiermacher held that it is a consciousness inspired primarily by the personality of Jesus. It must be connected with the other data and acta of our consciousness under the general laws of the operation of the mind. Against rationalism and much so-called liberal Christianity, Schleiermacher contended that Christianity is not a new set of propositions periodically brought up to date and proclaimed as if these alone were true. New propositions can have only the same relativity of truth which belonged to the old ones in their day. They may stand between men and religion as seriously as the others had done.

The condition of the heart, which is religion, the experience through Jesus which is Christianity, is primarily an individual matter. But it is not solely such. It is a common experience also. Schleiermacher recognises the common element in the Christian consciousness, the element which shows itself in the Christian experience of all ages, of different races and of countless numbers of men. By this recognition of the Christian Church in its deep and spiritual sense, Schleiermacher hopes to escape the vagaries and eccentricities, and again the narrowness and bigotries of pure individualism. No liberal theologian until Schleiermacher had had any similar sense of the meaning of the Christian Church, and of the privilege and duty of Christian thought to contribute to the welfare of that body of men believing in God and following Christ which is meant by the Church. This is in marked contrast with the individualism of Kant. Of course, Schleiermacher would never have recognised as the Church that part of humanity which is held together by adherence to particular dogmas, since, for him, Christianity is not dogma. Still less could he recognise as the Church that part of mankind which is held together by a common tradition of worship, or by a given theory of organisation, since these also are historical and incidental. He meant by the Church that part of humanity, in all places and at all times, which has been held

F

together by the common possession of the Christian consciousness and the Christian experience. The outline of this experience, the content of this consciousness, can never be so defined as to make it legislatively operative. If it were so defined we should have dogma and not Christianity. Nevertheless, it may be practically potent. The degree in which a given man may justly identify his own consciousness and experience with that of the Christian world is problematical. In Schleiermacher's own case, the identification of some of his contentions—as, for example, the thought that God is not personal—with the great Christian consciousness of the past, is more than problematical. To this Schleiermacher would reply that if these contentions were true, they would become the possession of spiritual Christendom with the lapse of time. Advance always originates with one or a few. If, however, in the end, a given position found no place in the consciousness of generations truly evidencing their Christian life, that position would be adjudged an idiosyncrasy, a negligible quantity. This view of Schleiermacher's as to the Church is suggestive. It is the undertone of a view which widely prevails in our own time. It is somewhat difficult of practical combination with the traditional marks of the churches, as these have been inherited even in Protestantism from the Catholic age.

In a very real sense Jesus occupied the central place in Schleiermacher's system. This centralness of Jesus Christ he himself was never weary of emphasising. It became in the next generation a favourite phrase of some who followed Schleiermacher's pure and luminous spirit afar off. Too much of a mystic to assert that it is through Jesus alone that we know God, he yet accords to Jesus an absolutely unique place in revelation. It is through the character and personality of Jesus that the change in the character of man, which is redemption, is inaugurated and sustained. Redemption is a man's being brought out of the condition in which all higher self-consciousness was dimmed and enfeebled, into one in which this higher consciousness is vivid and strong and the power of self-determination toward the good has been restored. Salvation is thus moral and spiritual, present as well as future. It is possible in the future only because actual in the present. It is the reconstruction of a man's nature and life by the action of the spirit of God, conjointly with that of man's own free spirit.

It is intelligible in Schleiermacher's context that Jesus should be spoken of as the sole redeemer of men, their only hope, and that the Christian's dependence upon him should be described as absolute. As a matter of fact, however, the idea of dependence upon Christ alone has been often, indeed, one may say generally, associated with a conception of salvation widely different from that of Schleiermacher. It has been oftenest associated with the notion of something purely external, forensic, even magical. It is connected, even down to our own time, with reliance upon the blood of Christ, almost as if this were externally applied. It has postulated a propitiatory sacrifice, a vicarious atonement, a completed transaction, something which was laid up for all and waiting to be availed of by some. Now every external, forensic, magical notion of salvation, as something purchased for us, imputed to us, conferred upon us, would have been utterly impossible to Schleiermacher. It is within the soul of man that redemption takes place. Conferment from the side of God and Christ, or from God through Christ, can be nothing more, as also it can be nothing less, than the imparting of wisdom and grace and spiritual power from the personality of Jesus, which a man then freely takes up within himself and gives forth as from himself. The Christian consciousness contains, along with the sense of dependence upon Jesus, the sense of moral alliance and spiritual sympathy with him, of a free relation of the will of man to the will of God as revealed in Jesus. The will of man is set upon the reproduction within himself, so far as possible, of the consciousness, experience and character of Jesus.

The sin from which man is to be delivered is described by Schleiermacher thus : It is the dominance of the lower nature in us, of the sense-consciousness. It is the determination of our course of life by the senses. This preponderance of the

senses over the consciousness of God is the secret of unhappiness, of the feeling of defeat and misery in men, of the
need of salvation. One has to read Schleiermacher's phrase,
' the senses' here, as we read Paul's phrase, ' the flesh.' On the
other hand, the preponderance of the consciousness of God,
the willing obedience to it in every act of life, becomes to us
the secret of strength and of blessedness in life. This is the
special experience of the Christian. It is the effect of the
impulse and influence of Christ. We receive this impulse in
a manner wholly consistent with the laws of our psychological
and moral being. We carry forward this impulse with varying fortunes and by free will. It comes to us, however, from
without and from above, through one who was indeed true
man, but who is also, in a manner not further explicable, to
be identified with the moral ideal of humanity. This identification of Jesus with the moral ideal is complete and un-
questioning with Schleiermacher. It is visible in the interchangeable use of the titles Jesus and Christ. Our saving
consciousness of God could proceed from the person of Jesus
only if that consciousness were actually present in Jesus
in an absolute measure. Ideal and person in him perfectly
coincide.

As typical and ideal man, according to Schleiermacher,
Jesus was distinguished from all other founders of religions.
These come before us as men chosen from the number of
their fellows, receiving, quite as much for themselves as for
others, that which they received from God. It is nowhere
implied that Jesus himself was in need of redemption, but
rather that he alone possessed from earliest years the fulness
of redemptive power. He was distinguished from other men
by his absolute moral perfection. This excluded not merely
actual sin, but all possibility of sin and, accordingly, all real
moral struggle. This perfection was characterised also by
his freedom from error. He never originated an erroneous
notion nor adopted one from others as a conviction of his
own. In this respect his person was a moral miracle in the
midst of the common life of our humanity, of an order to
be explained only by a new spiritually creative act of God.

On the other hand, Schleiermacher says squarely that the absence of the natural paternal participation in the origin of the physical life of Jesus, according to the account in the first and third Gospels, would add nothing to the moral miracle if it could be proved and detract nothing if it should be taken away. Singular is this ability on the part of Schleiermacher to believe in the moral miracle, not upon its own terms, of which we shall speak later, but upon terms upon which the outward and physical miracle, commonly so-called, had become, we need not say incredible, but un-necessary to Schleiermacher himself. Singular is this whole part of Schleiermacher's construction, with its lapse into abstraction of the familiar sort, of which, in general, the work-ing of his mind had been so free. For surely what we here have is abstraction. It is an undissolved fragment of meta-physical theology. It is impossible of combination with the historical. It is wholly unnecessary for the religious view of salvation which Schleiermacher had distinctly taken. It is surprising how slow men have been to learn that the absolute cannot be historic nor the historic absolute.

Surely the claim that Jesus was free from error in intellectual conception is unnecessary, from the point of view of the saving influence upon character which Schleiermacher had asserted. It is in contradiction with the view of revelation to which Schleiermacher had already advanced. It is to be accounted for only from the point of view of the mistaken assumption that the divine, even in manifestation, must be perfect, in the sense of that which is static and not of that which is dynamic. The assertion is not sustained from the Gospel itself. It reduces many aspects of the life of Jesus to mere semblance. That also which is claimed in regard to the abstract impossi-bility of sin upon the part of Jesus is in hopeless contradiction with that which Schleiermacher had said as to the normal and actual development of Jesus, in moral as also in all other ways. Such development is impossible without struggle. Struggle is not real when failure is impossible. So far as we know, it is in struggle only that character is made. Even as to the actual commission of sin on Jesus' part, the assertion of the abstract necessity of his sinlessness, for the work of moral redemption, goes beyond anything which we know. The question of the sinlessness of Jesus is not an *a priori* question. To say that he was by conception free from sin is to beg the question. We thus form a conception and then read the Gospels to find evidence to sustain it. To say that he did, though tempted in all points like as we are, yet so conduct himself in the mystery of life as to remain unstained, is indeed to allege that he achieved that which, so far as we know, is without parallel in the history of the race. But it is to leave him true man, and so the moral redeemer of men who would be true. To say that, if he were true man, he must have sinned, is again to beg the question. Let us repeat that the question is one of evidence. To say that he was, though true man, so far as we have any evidence in fact, free from sin, is only to say that his humanity was uniquely penetrated by the spirit of God for the purposes of the life which he had to live. That heart-broken recollection of his own sin which one hears in *The Scarlet Letter*, giving power to the preacher who would reach men in their sins, has not the remotest parallel in any reminiscence of Jesus which we possess. There is every evidence of the purity of Jesus' consciousness. There is no evidence of the consciousness of sin. There is a passage in the *Discourses*, in which Schleiermacher himself declared that the identification of the fundamental idea of religion with the historical fact in which that religion had its rise, was a mistake. Surely it is exactly this mistake which Schleiermacher has here made.

It will be evident from all that has been said that to Schleiermacher the Scripture was not the foundation of faith. As such it was almost universally regarded in his time. The New Testament, he declared, is itself but a product of the Christian consciousness. It is a record of the Christian experience of the men of the earlier time. To us it is a means of grace because it is the vivid and original register of that experience. The Scriptures can be regarded as the work of the Holy Spirit only in so far as this was this common spirit of the early Church. This spirit has borne witness to Christ in these writings not essentially otherwise than in later writings, only more at first hand, more under the impression of intercourse with Jesus. Least of all may we base the authority of Scripture upon a theory of inspiration such as that generally current in Schleiermacher's time. It is the personality of Jesus which is the inspiration of the New Testament. Christian faith, including the faith in the Scriptures, can rest only upon the total impression of the character of Jesus.

In the same manner Schleiermacher speaks of miracles. These cannot be regarded in the conventional manner as supports of religion, for the simplest of all reasons. They presuppose religion and faith and must be understood by means of these. The accounts of external miracles contained in the Gospels are matters for unhesitating criticism. The Christian finds, for moral reasons and because of the response of his own heart, the highest revelation of God in Jesus Christ. Extraordinary events may be expected in Jesus' career. Yet these can be called miracles only relatively, as containing something extraordinary for contemporary knowledge. They may remain to us events wholly inexplicable, illustrating a law higher than any which we yet know. Therewith they are not taken out of the realm of the orderly phenomena of nature. In other words, the notion of the miraculous is purely subjective. What is a miracle for one age may be no miracle in the view of the next. Whatever the deeds of Jesus may have been, however inexplicable all ages may find them, we can but regard them as merely natural consequences of the personality of Jesus, unique because he was unique. 'In the interests of religion the necessity can never arise of regarding an event as taken out of its connection with nature, in consequence of its dependence upon God.'

It is not possible within the compass of this book to do more than deal with typical and representative persons. Schleiermacher was epoch-making. He gathered in himself the creative impulses of the preceding period.   The characteristic theological tendencies of the two succeeding generations may be traced back to him.   Many men worked in seriousness upon the theological problem.   No one of them marks an era again until we come to Ritschl.   The theologians of the interval between Schleiermacher and Ritschl have been divided into three groups.   The first group is of distinctly philosophical tendency.   The influence of Hegel was felt upon them all. To this group belong Schweitzer, Biedermann, Lipsius, and Pfleiderer.   The influence of Hegel was greatest upon Biedermann, least upon Lipsius.   An estimate of the influence of Schleiermacher would reverse that order.   Especially did Lipsius seek to lay at the foundation of his work that exact psychological study of the phenomena of religion which Schleiermacher had declared requisite.   It is possible that Lipsius will more nearly come to his own when the enthusiasm for Ritschl has waned.   The second group of Schleiermacher's followers took the direction opposite to that which we have named.   They were the confessional theologians.   Hoffmann shows himself learned, acute and full of power.   One does not see, however, why his method should not prove anything which any confession ever claimed.   He sets out from Schleiermacher's declaration concerning the content of the Christian consciousness.   In Hoffmann's own devout consciousness there had been response, since his childhood, to every item which the creed alleged.   Therefore these items must have objective truth.   One is reminded of an English parallel in Newman's *Grammar of Assent.*   Yet another group, that of the so-called mediating theologians, contains some well-known names.   Here belong Nitzsch, Rothe, Müller, Dorner. The name had originally described the effort to find, in the Union, common ground between Lutherans and Reformed. In the fact that it made the creeds of little importance and fell back on Schleiermacher's emphasis upon feeling, the movement came to have the character also of an attempt to find a middle way between confessionalists and rationalists. Its representatives had often the kind of breadth of sympathy which goes with lack of insight, rather than that breadth of

sympathy which is due to the possession of insight. Yet
Rothe rises to real distinction, especially in his forecast of the
social interpretation of religion. With the men of this group
arose a speculation concerning the person of Christ which
for a time had some currency. It was called the theory of
the kenosis. Jesus is spoken of in a famous passage of the
letter to the Philippians, as having emptied himself of divine
qualities that he might be found in fashion as a man. In
this speculation the divine attributes were divided into two
classes. Of the one class it was held Christ had emptied
himself in becoming flesh, or at least he had them in abeyance.
He had them, but did not use them. What we have here is
but a despairing effort to be just to Jesus' humanity and
yet to assert his deity in the ancient metaphysical terms. It
is but saying yes and no in the same breath. Biedermann
said sadly of the speculation that it represented the kenosis,
not of the divine nature, but of the human understanding.

RITSCHL AND THE RITSCHLIANS

If any man in the department of theology in the latter half
of the nineteenth century attained a position such as to entitle
him to be compared with Schleiermacher, it was Ritschl. He
was long the most conspicuous figure in any chair of dogmatic
theology in Germany. He established a school of theological
thinkers in a sense in which Schleiermacher never desired to
gain a following. He exerted ecclesiastical influence of a kind
which Schleiermacher never sought. He was involved in
controversy in a degree to which the life of Schleiermacher
presents no parallel. He was not a preacher, he was no philosopher. He was not a man of Schleiermacher's breadth of
interest. His intellectual history presents more than one
breach within itself, as that of Schleiermacher presented
none, despite the wide arc which he traversed. Of Ritschl,
as of Schleiermacher, it may be said that he exerted a
great influence over many who have only in part agreed
with him.

Albrecht Ritschl was born in 1822 in Berlin, the son of a

bishop in the Lutheran Church. He was educated at Bonn and at Tübingen. He established himself at Bonn, where, in 1853, he became professor extraordinarius and in 1860 ordinarius. In 1864 he was called to Göttingen. In 1874 he became consistorialrath in the new Prussian establishment for the Hanoverian Church. He died in 1888. These are the simple outward facts of a somewhat stormy professional career. There was pietistic influence in Ritschl's ancestry, as also in Schleiermacher's. Ritschl had, however, reacted violently against it. His attitude was that of repudiation of everything mystical. He had strong aversion to the type of piety which rested its assurance solely upon inward experience. This aversion is one root of the historic positivism which makes him, at the last, assert the worthlessness of all supposed revelations outside of the Bible and of all supposed Christian experience apart from the influence of the historical Christ. He began his career under the influence of Hegel. He came to the position in which he felt that the sole hope for theology was in the elimination from it of all metaphysical elements. He felt that none of his predecessors had carried out Schleiermacher's dictum, that religion is not thought, but religious thought only one of the functions of religion. Yet, of course, he was not able to discuss fundamental theological questions without philosophical basis, particularly an explicit theory of knowledge. His theory of knowledge he had derived eclectically and somewhat eccentrically, from Lotze and Kant. To this day not all, either of his friends or foes, are quite certain what it was. It is open to doubt whether Ritschl really arrived at his theory of cognition and then made it one of the bases of his theology. It is conceivable that he made his theology and then propounded his theory of cognition in its defence. In a word, the basis of distinction between religious and scientific knowledge is not to be sought in its object. It is to be found in the sphere of the subject, in the difference of attitude of the subject toward the object. Religion is concerned with what he calls *Werthurtheile*, judgments of value, considerations of our relation to the world, which are of moment solely in accordance with their value in awakening feelings of pleasure or of pain. The thought of God, for example, must be treated solely as a judgment of value. It is a conception which is of worth for the attainment of good, for our spiritual peace and victory over the world. What God is in himself we cannot know, an existential judgment we cannot form without going over to the metaphysicians. What God is to us we can know simply as religious men and solely upon the basis of religious experience. God is holy love. That is a religious value-judgment. But what sort of a being God must be in order that we may assign to him these attributes, we cannot say without leaving the basis of experience. This is pragmatism indeed. It opens up boundless possibilities of subjectivism in a man who was apparently only too matter-of-fact.

There was a time in his career when Ritschl was popular with both conservatives and liberals. There were long years in which he was bitterly denounced by both. Yet there was something in the man and in his teaching which went beyond all the antagonisms of the schools. There can be no doubt that it was the intention of Ritschl to build his theology solely upon the gospel of Jesus Christ. The joy and confidence with which this theology could be preached, Ritschl awakened in his pupils in a degree which had not been equalled by any theologian since Schleiermacher himself. Numbers who, in the time of philosophical and scientific uncertainty, had lost their courage, regained it in contact with his confident and deeply religious spirit. A wholesome nature, eminently objective in temper, concentrated with all his force upon his task, of rare dialectical gifts, he had a great sense of humour and occasionally also the faculty of bitterly sarcastic speech. His very figure radiated the delight of conflict as he walked the Göttingen wall.

A devoted pupil, writing immediately after Ritschl's death, used concerning Schleiermacher a phrase which we may transfer to Ritschl himself. 'One wonders whether such a theology ever existed as a connected whole, except in the mind of its originator. Neither by those about him, nor by those

after him, has it been reproduced in its entirety or free from
glaring contradictions.' It was not free from contradictions
in Ritschl's own mind. His pupils divided his inheritance
among them. Each appropriated that which accorded with
his own way of looking at things and viewed the remainder
as something which might be left out of the account. It is
long since one could properly speak of a Ritschlian school.
It will be long until we shall cease to reckon with a Ritschlian
influence. He did yeoman service in breaking down the high
Lutheran confessionalism which had been the order of the
day. In his recognition of the excesses of the Tübingen
school all would now agree. In his feeling against mere
sentimentalities of piety many sympathise. In his emphasis
upon the ethical and practical, in his urgency upon the actual
problem of a man's vocation in the world, he meets in striking
manner the temper of our age. In his emphasis upon the
social factor in religion, he represents a popular phase of
thought. With all of this, it is strange to find a man of so
much learning who had so little sympathy with the com-
parative study of religions, who was such a dogmatist on
behalf of his own inadequate notion of revelation, the logical
effect of whose teaching concerning the Church would be the
revival of an institutionalism and externalism such as Protestantism has hardly known.

Since Schleiermacher the German theologians had made
the problem of the person of Christ the centre of discussion.
In the same period the problem of the person of Christ had
been the central point of debate in America. Here, as there,
all the other points arranged themselves about this one.
The new movement which went out from Ritschl took as its
centre the work of Christ in redemption. This is obvious
from the very title of Ritschl's great book, *Die Christliche
Lehre von der Rechtfertigung und Versöhnung.* Of this work the
first edition of the third and significant volume was published
in 1874. Before that time the formal treatises on theology had
followed a traditional order of topics. It had been assumed
as self-evident that one should speak of a person before
one talked of his work. It did not occur to the theologians

that in the case of the divine person, at all events, we can
securely say that we know something as to his work. Much
concerning his person must remain a mystery to us, exactly
because he is divine. Our safest course, therefore, would be
to infer the unknown qualities of his person from the known
traits of his work. Certainly this would be true as to the
work of God in nature. This was not the way, however, in
which the minds of theologians worked. The habit of dealing with conceptions as if they were facts had too deep
hold upon them. So long as men believed in revelation as
giving them, not primarily God and the transcendental
world itself, but information about God and the transcendental, they naturally held that they knew as much of the
persons of God and Christ as of their works.

Schleiermacher had opened men's eyes to the fact that the
great work of Christ in redemption is an inward one, an
ethical and spiritual work, the transformation of character.
He had said, not merely that the transformation of man's
character follows upon the work of redemption. It is the
work of redemption. The primary witness to the work of
Christ is, therefore, in the facts of consciousness and history.
These are capable of empirical scrutiny. They demand
psychological investigation. When thus investigated they
yield our primary material for any assertion we may make
concerning God. Above all, it is the nature of Jesus, as
learned on the evidence of his work in the hearts of men,
which is our great revelation and source of inference concerning the nature of God. Instead of saying in the famous
phrase, that the Christians think of Christ as God, we say that
we are able to think of God, as a religious magnitude, in no
other terms than in those of his manifestation and redemptive
activity in Jesus.

None since Kant, except extreme confessionalists, and
these in diminishing degree, have held that the great effect
of the work of Christ was upon the mind and attitude of God.
Less and less have men thought of justification as forensic
and judicial, a declaring sinners righteous in the eye of the
divine law, the attribution of Christ's righteousness to men,

so far at least as to relieve these last of penalty. This was the Anselmic scheme. Indeed, it had been Tertullian's. Less and less have men thought of reconciliation as that of an angry God to men, more and more as of alienated men with God. The phrases of the orthodoxy of the seventeenth century, Lutheran as well as Calvinistic, survive. More and more new meaning, not always consistent, is injected into them. No one would deny that the loftiest moral enthusiasm, the noblest sense of duty, animated the hearts of many who thought in the terms of Calvinism. The delineation of God as unreconciled, of the work and sufferings of Christ as a substitution, of salvation as a conferment, caused gratitude, tender devotion, heroic allegiance in some. It worked revulsion in others. It was protested against most radically by Kant, as indeed it had been condemned by many before him. For Kant the renovation of character was the essential salvation. Yet the development of his doctrine was deficient through the individualistic form which it took. Salvation was essentially a change in the individual mind, brought about through the practical reason, and having its ideal in Jesus. Yet for Kant our salvation had no closer relation to the historic revelation in Jesus. Furthermore, so much was this change an individual issue that we may say that the actualisation of redemption would be the same for a given man, were he the only man in the universe. To hold fast to the ethical idealism of Kant, and to overcome its subjectivity and individualism, was the problem.

The reference to experience which underlies all that was said above was particularly congruous with the mood of an age grown weary of Hegelianism and much impressed with the value of the empirical method in all the sciences. Another great contention of our age is for the recognition of the value of what is social. Its emphasis is upon that which binds men together. Salvation is not normally achieved except in the life of a man among and for his fellows. It is by doing one's duty that one becomes good. One is saved, not in order to become a citizen of heaven by and by, but in order to be an active citizen of a kingdom of real human goodness here and now. In reality no man is being saved, except as he does actively and devotedly belong to that kingdom. The individual would hardly be in God's eyes worth the saving, except in order that he might be the instrumentality of the realisation of the kingdom. These are ideas which it is possible to exaggerate in statement or, at least, to set forth in all the isolation of their quality as half-truths. But it is hardly possible to exaggerate their significance as a reversal of the immemorial one-sidedness, inadequacy, and artificiality both of the official statement and of the popular apprehension of Christianity. These ideas appeal to men in our time. They are popular because men think them already. Men are pleased, even when somewhat incredulous, to learn that Christianity will bear this social interpretation. Most Christians are in our time overwhelmingly convinced that in this direction lies the interpretation which Christianity must bear, if it is to do the work and meet the needs of the age. Its consonance with some of the truths underlying socialism may account, in a measure, for the influence which the Ritschlian theology has had.

As was indicated, Ritschl's epoch-making book bears the title, *The Christian Doctrine of Justification and Reconciliation.* The book might be described in the language of the schools as a monograph upon one great dogma of the Christian faith, around which, as the author treats it, all the other doctrines are arranged. The familiar topic of justification, of which Luther made so much, was thus given again the central place. What the book really offered was something quite different from this. It was a complete system of theology, but it differed from the traditional systems of theology. These had followed helplessly a logical scheme which begins with God as he is in himself and apart from any knowledge which we have of him. They then slowly proceeded to man and sin and redemption, one empirical object and two concrete experiences which we may know something about. Ritschl reversed the process. He aimed to begin with certain facts of life. Such facts are sin and the consciousness of forgiveness, awareness of restoration to the will and power of goodness, the gift of love and of a spirit which can feel itself victorious even in the midst of ills in life, confidence that this life is not all. These phrases, taken together, would describe the consciousness of salvation. This consciousness of sin and salvation is a fact in individual men. It has evidently been a fact in the life of masses of men for many generations. The facts have thus a psychology and a history from which reflection on the phenomenon of faith must take its departure. There is no reason why, upon this basis, and until it departs from the scientific methods which are given with the nature of its object, theology should not be as truly a science as is any other known among men.

This science starts with man, who is the object of many other sciences. It confines itself to man in this one aspect of his relation to moral life and to the transcendent meaning of the universe. It notes the fact that men, when awakened, usually have the sense of not being in harmony with the life of the universe or on the way to realisation of its meaning. It notes the fact that many men have had the consciousness of progressive restoration to that harmony. It inquires as to the process of that restoration. It asks as to the power of it. It discovers that that power is a personal one. Men have believed that this power has been exerted over them, either in personal contact, or across the ages and through generations of believers, by one Jesus, whom they call Saviour. They have believed that it was God who through Jesus saved them. Jesus' consciousness thus became to them a revelation of God. The thought leads on to the consideration of that which a saved man does, or ought to do, in the life of the world and among his fellows, of the institution in which this attitude of mind is cherished and of the sum total of human institutions and relations of which the saved life should be the inward force. There is room even for a clause in which to compress the little that we know of anything beyond this life. We have written in unconventional words. There is no one place, either in Ritschl's work or elsewhere, where this grand and simple scheme stands together in one context. This is unfortunate. Were this

the case, even wayfaring men might have understood somewhat better than they have what Ritschl was aiming at.

It is a still greater pity that the execution of the scheme
should have left so much to be desired. That this execution
would prove difficult needs hardly to be said. That it could
never be the work of one man is certainly true. To have had
so great an insight is title enough to fame. Ritschl falls off
from his endeavour as often as did Schleiermacher—more often
and with less excuse. The might of the past is great. The
lumber which he meekly carries along with him is surprising,
as one feels his lack of meekness in the handling of the lumber
which he recognised as such. The putting of new wine into
old bottles is so often reprobated by Ritschl that the reader
is justly surprised when he nevertheless recognises the bottles.
The system is not ' all of one piece '—distinctly not. There
are places where the rent is certainly made worse by the old
cloth on the new garment. The work taken as a whole is
so bewildering that one finds himself asking, ' What is Ritschl's
method ? ' If what is meant is not a question of detail, but
of the total apprehension of the problem to be solved, the
apprehension which we strove to outline above, then Ritschl's
courageous and complete inversion of the ancient method,
his demand that we proceed from the known to the unknown,
is a contribution so great that all shortcomings in the execution of it are insignificant. His first volume deals with the
history of the doctrine of justification, beginning with Anselm
and Abelard. In it Ritschl's eminent qualities as historian
come out. In it also his prejudices have their play. The
second volume deals with the Biblical foundations for the
doctrine. Ritschl was bred in the Tübingen school. Yet
here is much forced exegesis. Ritschl's positivistic view of
the Scripture and of the whole question of revelation, was
not congruous with his well-learned biblical criticism. The
third volume is the constructive one. It is of immeasurably greater value than the other two. It is this third
volume which has frequently been translated.

In respect of his contention against metaphysics it is hardly
necessary that we should go into detail. With his empirical

G

and psychological point of departure, given above, most men will find themselves in entire sympathy. The confusion of religion, which is an experience, with dogma which is reasoning about it, and the acceptance of statements in Scripture which are metaphysical in nature, as if they were religious truths— these two things have, in time past, prevented many earnest thinkers from following the true road. When it comes to the constructive portion of his work, it is, of course, impossible for Ritschl to build without the theoretical supports which philosophy gives, or to follow up certain of the characteristic magnitudes of religion without following them into the realm of metaphysics, to which, quite as truly as to that of religion, they belong. It would be unjust to Ritschl to suppose that these facts were hidden from him.

As to his attitude toward mysticism, there is a word to say. In the long history of religious thought those who have revolted against metaphysical interpretation, orthodox or unorthodox, have usually taken refuge in mysticism. Hither the prophet Augustine takes refuge when he would flee the ecclesiastic Augustine, himself. The Brethren of the Free Spirit, Tauler, à Kempis, Suso, the author of the *Theologia Germanica*, Molinos, Madame Guyon, illustrate the thing we mean. Ritschl had seen much of mysticism in pietist circles. He knew the history of the movement well. What impressed his sane mind was the fact that unhealthy minds have often claimed, as their revelation from God, an experience which might, with more truth, be assigned to almost any other source. He desired to cut off the possibility of what seemed to him often a tragic delusion. The margin of any mystical movement stretches out toward monstrosities and absurdities. For that matter, what prevents a Buddhist from declaring his thoughts and feelings to be Christianity? Indeed, Ritschl asks, why is not Buddhism as good as such Christianity? He is, therefore, suspicious of revelations which have nothing by which they can be measured and checked. The claim of mystics that they come, in communion with God, to the point where they have no need of Christ, seemed to him impious. There is no way of knowing that we are in fellowship with God, except by comparing what we feel that this fellowship has given us, with that which we historically learn that the fellowship with God gave to Christ. This is the sense and this the connexion in which Ritschl says that we cannot come to God save in and through the historic Christ as he is given us in the Gospels. The inner life, at least, which is there depicted for us is, in this outward and authoritative sense, our norm and guide.

Large difficulties loom upon the horizon of this positivistic insistence upon history. Can we know the inner life of Christ well enough to use it thus as test in every, or even in any case ? Does not the use of such a test, or of any test in this external way, take us out of the realm of the religion of the spirit ? Men once said that the Church was their guide. Others said the Scripture was their guide. Now, in the sense of the outwardness of its authority, we repudiate even this. It rings devoutly if we say Christ is our guide. Yet, as Ritschl describes this guidance, in the exigency of his contention against mysticism, have we anything different ? What becomes of Confucianists and Shintoists, who have never heard of the historic Christ ? And all the while we have the sense of a query in our minds. Is it open to any man to repudiate mysticism absolutely and with contumely, and then leave us to discover that he does not mean mysticism as historians of every faith have understood it, but only the margin of evil which is apparently inseparable from it ? That margin of evil others see and deplore. Against it other remedies have been suggested, as, for example, intelligence. Some would feel that in Ritschl's remedy the loss is greater than the gain.

This historical character of revelation is so truly one of the fountain heads of the theology which takes its rise in Ritschl, that it deserves to be considered somewhat more at length. The Ritschlian movement has engaged a generation of more or less notable thinkers in the period since Ritschl's death. These have dissented at many points from Ritschl's views, diverged from his path and marked out courses of their own. We shall do well in the remainder of this chapter to attempt the delineation in terms, not exclusively of Ritschl, but of that which may with some laxity be styled Ritschlianism. The value judgments of religion indicate only the subjective form of religious knowledge, as the Ritschlians understand it. Faith, however, does not invent its own contents. Historical facts, composing the revelation, actually exist, quite independent of the use which the believer makes of them. No group of thinkers have more truly sought to draw near to the person of the historic Jesus. The historical person, Jesus of Nazareth, is the divine revelation. That sums up this aspect of the Ritschlian position. Some negative consequences of this position we have already noted. Let us turn to its positive significance.

Herrmann is the one of the Ritschlians who has dealt with this matter not only with great clearness, but also with deep Christian feeling in his *Verkehr des Christen mit Gott*, 1886, and notably in his address, *Der Begriff der Offenbarung*, 1887. If the motive of religion were an intellectual curiosity, a verbal communication would suffice. As it is a practical necessity, this must be met by actual impulse in life. That passing out of the unhappiness of sin, into the peace and larger life which is salvation, does indeed imply the movement of God's spirit on our hearts, in conversion and thereafter. This is essentially mediated to us through the Scriptures, especially through those of the New Testament, because the New Testament contains the record of the personality of Jesus. In that our personality is filled with the spirit which breathes in him, our salvation is achieved. The image of Jesus which we receive acts upon us as something indubitably real. It vindicates itself as real, in that it takes hold upon our manhood. Of course, this assumes that the Church has been right in accepting the Gospels as historical. Herrmann candidly faces this question. Not every word or deed, he says, which is recorded concerning Jesus, belongs to this central and dynamic revelation of which we speak. We do not help men to see Jesus in a saving way if, on the strength of accounts in the New Testament, we insist concerning Jesus that he was born of a virgin, that he raised the dead, that he himself rose from the dead. We should not put these things before men with the declaration that they must assent to them. We must not try to persuade ourselves that that which acted upon the disciples as indubitably real must of necessity act similarly upon us. We are to allow ourselves to be seized and uplifted by that which, in our position, touches us as indubitably real. This is, in the first place, the moral character of Jesus. It is his inner life which, on the testimony of the disciples, meets us as something real and active in the world, as truly now as then. What are some facts of this inner life ? The Jesus of the New Testament shows a firmness of religious conviction, a clearness of moral judgment, a purity and force of will, such as are not found united in any other figure in history. We have the image of a man who is conscious that he does not fall short of the ideal for which he offers himself. It is this consciousness which is yet united in him with the most perfect humility. He lives out his life and faces death in a confidence and independence which have never been approached. He has confidence that he can lift men to such a height that they also will partake with him in the highest good, through their full surrender to God and their life of love for their fellows.

It is clear that Herrmann aims to bring to the front only those elements in the life of Jesus which are likely to prove most effectual in meeting the need and winning the faith of the men of our age. He would cast into the background those elements which are likely to awaken doubt and to hinder the approach of men's souls to God. For Herrmann himself the virgin birth has the significance that the spiritual life of Jesus did not proceed from the sinful race. But Herrmann admits that a man could hold even that without needing to allege that the physical life of Jesus did not come into being in the ordinary way. The distinction between the inner and outward life of Jesus, and the declaration that belief in the former alone is necessary, has the result of thus ridding us of questions which can scarcely fail to be present to the mind of every modern man. Yet

it would be unjust to imply that this is the purpose. Quite
the contrary, the distinction is logical for this theology.
Redemption is an affair of the inner life of a man. It is the
force of the inner life of the Redeemer which avails for it.
It is from the belief that such an inner and spiritual life was
once realised here on earth, that our own faith gathers strength
and gets guidance in the conflict for the salvation of our
souls. The belief in the historicity of such an inner life is
necessary. So Harnack also declares in his *Wesen des Christenthums*, 1900. It is noteworthy that in this connexion neither
of these writers advances to a form of speculation concerning
the exalted Christ, which in recent years has had some currency.
According to this doctrine, there is ascribed to the risen and
ascended Jesus an existence with God which is thought of
in terms different from those which we associate with the
idea of immortality. In other words, this continued existence
of Christ as God is a counterpart of that existence before
the incarnation, which the doctrine of the pre-existence
alleged. But surely this speculation can have no better standing than that of the pre-existence.

Sin in the language of religion is defection from the law
of God. It is the transgression of the divine command.
In what measure, therefore, the life of man can be thought
of as sinful, depends upon his knowledge of the will of God.
In Scripture, as in the legends of the early history of the
race, this knowledge stands in intimate connexion with the
witness to a primitive revelation. This thought has had a
curious history. The ideas of mankind concerning God and
his will have grown and changed as much as have any other
ideas. The rudimentary idea of the good is probably of social
origin. It first emerges in the contact of men one with
another. As the personalised ideal of conduct, the god then
reacts upon conduct, as the conduct reacts upon the notion of
the god. Only slowly has the ideal of the good been clarified.
Only slowly have the gods been ethicised. ' An honest God
is the noblest work of man.' The moralising and spiritualising
of the idea of Jahve lies right upon the face of the Old Testament. The ascent of man on his ethical and spiritual side

is as certain as is that on his physical side. Long struggle upward through ignorance, weakness, sin, gradual elevating of the standard of what ought to be, growingly successful effort to conform to that standard—this is what the history of the race has seen.

Athwart this lies the traditional dogma. The dogma took up into itself a legend of the childhood of the world. It elaborated that which in Genesis is vague and poetic into a vast scheme which has passed as a sacred philosophy of history. It postulated an original revelation. It affirmed the created state of man as one of holiness before a fall. To the framers of the dogma, if sin is the transgression of God's will, then it must be in light of a revelation of that will. In the Scriptures we have vague intimations concerning God's will, growingly clearer knowledge of that will, evolving through history to Jesus. In the dogma we have this grand assumption of a paradisaic state of perfectness in which the will of God was from the beginning perfectly known.

In the Platonic, as in the rabbinic, speculation the idea must precede the fact. Every step of progress is a defection from that idea. The dogma suffers from an insoluble contradiction within itself. It aims to give us the point of departure by which we are to recognise the nature of sin. At the same moment it would describe the perfection of man at which God has willed that by age-long struggle he should arrive. Now, if we place this perfection at the beginning of human history, before all human self-determination, we divest it of ethical quality. Whatever else it may be, it is not character. On the other hand, if we would make this perfection really that of moral character, then we cannot place it at the beginning of human history, but far down the course of the evolution of the higher human traits, of the consciousness of sin and of the struggle for redemption. It is not revelation from God, but naïve imagination, later giving place to adventurous speculation concerning the origin of the universe, which we have in the doctrine of the primæval perfection of man. We do not really make earnest with our Christian claim that in Jesus we have our paramount reve·

lation, until we admit this. It is through Jesus, and not from Adam that we know sin.

So we might go on to say that the dogma of inherited guilt is a contradiction in terms. Disadvantage may be inherited, weakness, proclivity to sin, but not guilt, not sin in the sense of that which entails guilt. What entails guilt is action counter to the will of God which we know. That is always the act of the individual man myself. It cannot by any possibility be the act of another. It may be the consequence of the sins of my ancestors that I do moral evil without knowing it to be such. Even my fellows view this as a mitigation, if not as an exculpation. The very same act, however, which up to this point has been only an occasion for pity, becomes sin and entails guilt, when it passes through my own mind and will as a defection from a will of God in which I believe, and as a righteousness which I refuse. The confusion of guilt and sin in order to the inclusion of all under the need of salvation, as in the Augustinian scheme, ended in bewilderment and stultification of the moral sense. It caused men to despair of themselves and gravely to misrepresent God. It is no wonder if in the age of rationalism this dogma was largely done away with. The religious sense of sin was declared to be an hallucination. Nothing is more evident in the rationalist theology than its lack of the sense of sin. This alone is sufficient explanation of the impotency and inadequacy of that theology. Kant's doctrine of radical evil testifies to his deep sense that the rationalists were wrong. He could see also the impossibility of the ancient view. But he had no substitute. Hegel, much as he prided himself upon the restoration of dogma, viewed evil as only relative, good in the making. Schleiermacher made a beginning of construing the thought of sin from the point of view of the Christian consciousness. Ritschl was the first consistently to carry out Schleiermacher's idea, placing the Christian consciousness in the centre and claiming that the revelation of the righteousness of God and of the perfection of man is in Jesus. All men being sinners, there is a vast solidarity, which he describes as the Kingdom of Evil and sets over against the Kingdom of God, yet not so that the freedom or responsibility of man is impaired. God forgives all sin save that of wilful resistance to the spirit of the good. That is, Ritschl regards all sin, short of this last, as mainly ignorance and weakness. It is from Ritschl, and more particularly from Kaftan, that the phrases have been mainly taken which served as introduction to this paragraph.

For the work of God through Christ, in the salvation of men from the guilt and power of sin, various terms have been used. Different aspects of the work have been described by different names. Redemption, regeneration, justification, reconciliation and election or predestination—these are the familiar words. This is the order in which the conceptions stand, if we take them as they occur in consciousness. Election then means nothing more than the ultimate reference to God of the mystery of an experience in which the believer already rejoices. On the other hand, in the dogma the order is reversed. Election must come first, since it is the decree of God upon which all depends. Redemption and reconciliation have, in Christian doctrine, been traditionally regarded as completed transactions, waiting indeed to be applied to the individual or appropriated by him through faith, but of themselves without relation to faith. Reconciliation was long thought of as that of an angry God to man. Especially was this last the characteristic view of the West, where juristic notions prevailed. Origen talked of a right of the devil over the soul of man until bought off by the sacrifice of Christ. This is pure paganism, of course. The doctrine of Anselm marks a great advance. It runs somewhat thus : The divine honour is offended in the sin of man. Satisfaction corresponding to the greatness of the guilt must be rendered. Man is under obligation to render this satisfaction ; yet he is unable so to do. A sin against God is an infinite offence. It demands an infinite satisfaction. Man can render no satisfaction which is not finite. The way out of this dilemma is the incarnation of the divine Logos. For the god-man, as man, is entitled to bring this satisfaction for men. On the other hand, as God he is able so to do. In his death this satisfaction is embodied. He gave his life freely. God having received satisfaction through him demands nothing more from us.

Abelard had, almost at the same time with Anselm, interpreted the death of Christ in far different fashion. It was a revelation of the love of God which wins men to love in turn. This notion of Abelard was far too subtle. The crass objective dogma of Anselm prevailed. The death of Christ was a sacrifice. The purpose was the propitiation of an angry God. The effect was that, on the side of God, a hindrance to man's salvation was removed. The doctrine accurately reflects the feudal ideas of the time which produced it. In Grotius was done away the notion of private right, which lies at the basis of the theory of Anselm. That of public duty took its place. A sovereign need not stand upon his offended honour, as in Anselm's thought. Still, he cannot, like a private citizen, freely forgive. He must maintain the dignity of his office, in order not to demoralise the world. The sufferings of Christ did not effect a necessary private satisfaction. They were an example which satisfied the moral order of the world. Apart from this change, the conception remains the same.

As Kaftan argues, we can escape the dreadful externality and artificiality of this scheme, only as redemption and regeneration are brought back to their primary place in consciousness. These are the initial experiences in which we become aware of God's work through Christ in us and for us. The reconciliation is of us. The redemption is from our sins. The regeneration is to a new moral life. Through the influence of Jesus, reconciled on our part to God and believing in His unchanging love to us, we are translated into God's kingdom and live for the eternal in our present existence. Redemption is indeed the work of God through Christ, but it has intelligible parallel in the awakening of the life of the mind, or again of the spirit of self-sacrifice, through the personal influence of the wise and good. Salvation begins in such an awakening through the personal influence of the wisest and best. It is transformation of our personality through the personality of Jesus, by the personal God of truth, of goodness and of love. All that which God through Jesus has done for us is futile, save as we make the actualisation of our deliverance from sin our continuous and unceasing task. When this connexion of thought is broken through, we transfer the whole matter of salvation from the inner to the outer world and make of it a transaction independent of the moral life of man.

Justification and reconciliation also are primarily acts and gifts of God. Justification is a forensic act. The sense is not that in justification we are made just. We are, so to say, temporarily thus regarded, not that leniency may become the occasion of a new offence, but that in grateful love we may make it the starting point of a new life. We must justify our justification. It is easy to see the objections to such a course on the part of a civil judge. He must consider the rights of others. It was this which brought Grotius and the rest, with the New England theologians down to Park, to feel that forgiveness could not be quite free. If we acknowledge that this symbolism of God as judge or sovereign is all symbolism, mere figure of speech, not fact at all, then that objection—and much else—falls away. If we assert that another figure of speech, that of God as Father, more perfectly suggests the relation of God and man, then forgiveness may be free. Then justification and forgiveness are only two words for one and the same idea. Then the nightmare of a God who would forgive and cannot, of a God who will forgive but may not justify until something further happens, is all done away. Then the relation of the death of Jesus to the forgiveness of our sins cannot be other than the relation of his life to that forgiveness. Both the one and the other are a revelation of the forgiving love of God. We may say that in his death the whole meaning of his life was gathered. We may say that his death was the consummation of his life, that without it his life would not have been what it is. This is, however, very far from being the ordinary statement of the relation of Jesus' death, either to his own life or to the forgiveness of our sins.

The doctrinal tradition made much also of the deliverance from punishment which follows after the forgiveness of sin. In fact, in many forms of the dogma, it has been the escape from punishment which was chiefly had in mind. Along with the forensic notion of salvation we largely or wholly discard the notion of punishment. We retain only the sense that the consequence of continuing in sin is to become more sinful. God himself is powerless to prevent that. Punishment is immanent, vital, necessary. The penalty is gradually taken away if the sin itself is taken away—not otherwise. It returns with the sin, it continues in the sin, it is inseparable from the sin. Punishment is no longer the right word. Reward is not the true description of that growing better which is the consequence of being good. Reward or punishment as *quid pro quo*, as arbitrary assignments, as external equivalents, do not so much as belong to the world of ideas in which we move. For this view the idea that God laid upon Jesus penalties due to us, fades into thin air. Jesus could by no possibility have met the punishment of sin, except he himself had been a sinner. Then he must have met the punishment of his own sin and not that of others. That portion which one may gladly bear of the consequences of another's sin may rightfully be called by almost any other name. It cannot be called punishment since punishment is immanent. Even eternal death is not a judicial assignment for our obstinate sinfulness. Eternal death is the obstinate sinfulness, and the sinfulness the death.

It must be evident that reconciliation can have, in this scheme, no meaning save that of man's being reconciled to God. Jesus reveals a God who has no need to be reconciled to us. The alienation is not on the side of God. That, being alienated from God, man may imagine that God is hostile to him, is only the working of a familiar law of the human mind. The fiction of an angry God is the most awful survival among us of primitive paganism. That which Jesus by his revelation of God brought to pass was a true ' at-one-ment,' a causing of God and man to be at one again. To the word atonement, as currently pronounced, and as, until a half century ago, almost universally apprehended, the notion of that which is sacrificial attached. To the life and death of Jesus, as revelation of God and Saviour of men, we can no longer attach any sacrificial meaning whatsoever. There is indeed the perfectly general sense in which so beautiful a life and so heroic a death were, of course, a grand exemplification of self-sacrifice. Yet this is a sense so different from the other and in itself so obvious, that one hesitates to use the same word in the immediate context with that other, lest it should appear that the intention was to obscure rather than to make clear the meaning. For atonement in a sense different from that of reconciliation, we have no significance whatever. Reconciliation and atonement describe one and the same fact. In the dogma the words were as far as possible from being synonyms. They referred to two facts, the one of which was the means and essential prerequisite of the other. The vicarious sacrifice was the antecedent condition of the reconciling of God. In our thought it is not a reconciliation of God which is aimed at. No sacrifice is necessary. No sacrifice such as that postulated is possible. Of the reconciliation of man to God the only condition is the revelation of the love of God in the life and death of Jesus and the obedient acceptance of that revelation on the part of men.

CHAPTER IV

THE CRITICAL AND HISTORICAL MOVEMENT

IT has been said that in Christian times the relation of philosophy and religion may be determined by the attitude of reason toward a single matter, namely, the churchly doctrine of revelation.[1] There are three possible relations of reason to this doctrine. First, it may be affirmed that the content of religion and theology is matter communicated to man in extraordinary fashion, truth otherwise unattainable, on which it is beyond the competence of reason to sit in judgment. We have then the two spheres arbitrarily separated. As regards their relation, theology is at first supreme. Reason is the handmaiden of faith. It is occupied in applying the principles which it receives at the hands of theology. These are the so-called Ages of Faith. Notably was this the attitude of the Middle Age. But in the long run either authoritative revelation, thus conceived, must extinguish reason altogether, or else reason must claim the whole man. After all, it is in virtue of his having some reason that man is the subject of revelation. He is continually asked to exercise his reason upon certain parts of the revelation, even by those who maintain that he must do so only within limits. It is only because there is a certain reasonableness in the conceptions of revealed religion that man has ever been able to make them his own or to find in them meaning and edification. This external relation of reason to revelation cannot continue. Nor can the encroachments of reason be met by temporary distinctions such as that between the natural and the supernatural. The antithesis to the natural is not the supernatural, but the unnatural. The antithesis to reason is not faith, but irra-

[1] Seth Pringle-Pattison, *The Philosophical Radicals*, p. 216.

tionality. The antithesis to human truth is not the divine truth. It is falsehood.

When men have made this discovery, a revulsion carries their minds to the second position of which we spoke. This is, namely, the position of extreme denial. It is an attitude of negation toward revelation, such as prevailed in the barren and trivial rationalism of the end of the eighteenth century. The reason having been long repressed revenges itself, usurping everything. The explanation of the rise of positive religion and of the claim of revelation is sought in the hypothesis of deceit, of ambitious priestcraft and incurable credulity. The religion of those who thus argue, in so far as they claim any religion, is merely the current morality. Their explanation of the religion of others is that it is merely the current morality plus certain unprovable assumptions. Indeed, they may think it to be but the obstinate adherence to these assumptions minus the current morality. It is impossible that this shallow view should prevail. To overcome it, however, there is need of a philosophy which shall give not less, but greater scope to reason and at the same time an inward meaning to revelation.

This brings us to the third possible position, to which the best thinkers of the nineteenth century have advanced. So long as deistic views of the relation of God to man and the world held the field, revelation meant something interjected *ab extra* into the established order of things. The popular theology which so abhorred deism was yet essentially deistic in its notion of God and of his separation from the world. Men did not perceive that by thus separating God from the world they set up alongside of him a sphere and an activity to which his relations were transient and accidental. No wonder that other men, finding their satisfying activity within the sphere which was thus separated from God, came to think of this absentee God as an appendage to the scheme of things. But if man himself be inexplicable, save as sharing in the wider life of universal reason, if the process of history be realised as but the working out of an inherent divine purpose, the manifestation of an indwelling divine force, then revelation denotes no longer an interference with that evolution. It is a factor in that evolution. It is but the normal relation of the immanent spirit of God to the children of men at the crises of their fate. Then revelation is an experience of men precisely in the line and according to the method of all their nobler experiences. It is itself reasonable and moral. Inspiration is the normal and continuous effect of the contact of the God who is spirit with man who is spirit too. The relation is never broken. But there are times in which it has been more particularly felt. There have been personalities to whom in eminent degree this depth of communion with God has been vouchsafed. To such persons and eras the religious sense of mankind, by a true instinct, has tended to restrict the words 'revelation' and 'inspiration.' This restriction, however, signifies the separation of the grand experience from the ordinary, only in degree and not in kind. Such an experience was that of prophets and lawgivers under the ancient covenant. Such an experience, in immeasurably greater degree, was that of Jesus himself. Such a turning-point in the life of the race was the advent of Christianity. The world has not been wrong in calling the documents of these revelations sacred books and in attributing to them divine authority. It has been largely wrong in the manner in which it construed their authority. It has been wholly wrong in imagining that the documents themselves were the revelation. They are merely the record of a personal communion with the transcendent. It was Lessing who first cast these fertile ideas into the soil of modern thought. They were never heartily taken up by Kant. One can think, however, with what enthusiasm men recurred to them after their postulates had been verified and the idea of God, of man and of the world which they implied, had been confirmed by Fichte and Schelling.

In the philosophical movement, the outline of which we have suggested, what one may call the *nidus* of a new faith in Scripture had been prepared. The quality had been forecast which the Scripture must be found to possess, if it were to retain its character as document of revelation. In those

very same years the great movement of biblical criticism was
gathering force which, in the course of the nineteenth century,
was to prove by stringent literary and historical methods,
what qualities the documents which we know as Scripture
do possess. It was to prove in the most objective fashion
that the Scripture does not possess those qualities which
men had long assigned to it. It was to prove that, as a
matter of fact, the literature does possess the qualities which
the philosophic forecast, above hinted, required. It was
thus actually to restore the Bible to an age in which many
reasonable men had lost their faith in it. It was to give a
genetic reconstruction of the literature and show the progress
of the history which the Scripture enshrines. After a contest
in which the very foundations of faith seemed to be removed,
it was to afford a basis for a belief in Scripture and revelation
as positive and secure as any which men ever enjoyed, with
the advantage that it is a foundation upon which the modern
man can and does securely build. The synchronism of the
two endeavours is remarkable. The convergence upon one
point, of studies starting, so to say, from opposite poles and
having no apparent interest in common, is instructive. It
is an illustration of that which Comte said, that all the great
intellectual movements of a given time are but the manifestation of a common impulse, which pervades and possesses
the minds of the men of that time.

The attempt to rationalise the narrative of Scripture was
no new one. It grew in intensity in the early years of the
nineteenth century. The conflict which was presently
precipitated concerned primarily the Gospels. It was
natural that it should do so. These contain the most important Scripture narrative, that of the life of Jesus. Strauss
had in good faith turned his attention to the Gospels, precisely
because he felt their central importance. His generation
was to learn that they presented also the greatest difficulties.

The old rationalistic interpretation had started from the assumption that what we have in the gospel narrative is fact. Yet, of course, for the rationalists, the facts must be natural They had the appearance of being supernatural only througk the erroneous judgment of the narrators. It was for the interpreter to reduce everything which is related to its simple, natural cause. The water at Cana was certainly not turned into wine. It must have been brought by Jesus as a present and opened thus in jest. Jesus was, of course, begotten in the natural manner. A simple maiden must have been deceived. The execution of this task of the rationalising of the narratives by one Dr. Paulus, was the *reductio ad absurdum* of the claim. The most spiritual of the narratives, the finest flower of religious poetry, was thus turned into the meanest and most trivial incident without any religious significance whatsoever. The obtuseness of the procedure was exceeded only by its vulgarity.

STRAUSS

On the other hand, as Pfleiderer has said, we must remember the difficulty which beset the men of that age. Their general culture made it difficult for them to accept the miraculous element in the gospel narrative as it stood. Yet their theory of Scripture gave them no notion as to any other way in which the narratives might be understood. The men had never asked themselves how the narratives arose. In the preface to his *Leben Jesu*, Strauss said : ' Orthodox and rationalists alike proceed from the false assumption that we have always in the Gospels testimony, sometimes even that of eye-witnesses, to fact. They are, therefore, reduced to asking themselves what can have been the real and natural fact which is here witnessed to in such extraordinary way. We have to realise,' Strauss proceeds, ' that the narrators testify sometimes, not to outward facts, but to ideas, often most poetical and beautiful ideas, constructions which even eye-witnesses had unconsciously put upon facts, imagination concerning them, reflexions upon them, reflexions and imaginings such as were natural to the time and at the author's level of culture. What we have here is not falsehood, not misrepresentation of the truth. It is a plastic, naïve, and, at the same time, often most profound apprehension of truth, within the area of religious feeling and poetic insight. It results in narrative, legendary, mythical in nature, illustrative often of spiritual truth in a manner more perfect than any hard, prosaic statement could achieve.' Before Strauss men had appreciated that particular episodes, like the virgin birth and the bodily resurrection, might have some such explanation as this. No one had ever undertaken to apply this method consistently, from one end to the other of the gospel narrative. What was of more significance, no one had clearly defined the conception of legend. Strauss was sure that in the application of this notion to certain portions of the Scripture no irreverence was shown. No moral taint was involved. Nothing which could detract from the reverence in which we hold the Scripture was implied. Rather, in his view, the history of Jesus is more wonderful than ever, when some, at least, of its elements are viewed in this way, when they are seen as the product of the poetic spirit, working all unconsciously at a certain level of culture and under the impulse of a great enthusiasm.

There is no doubt that Strauss, who was at that time an earnest Christian, felt the relief from certain difficulties in the biography of Jesus which this theory affords. He put it forth in all sincerity as affording to others like relief. He said that while rationalists and supernaturalists alike, by their methods, sacrificed the divine content of the story and clung only to its form, his hypothesis sacrificed the historicity of the narrative form, but kept the eternal and spiritual truth. In his opinion, the lapse of a single generation was enough to give room for this process of the growth of the legendary elements which have found place in the written Gospels which we have. Ideas entertained by primitive Christians relative to their lost Master, have been, all unwittingly, transformed into facts and woven into the tale of his career. The legends of a people are in their basal elements never the work of a single individual. They are never intentionally produced. The imperceptible growth of a joint creative work of this kind was possible, however, only on the supposition that oral tradition was, for a time, the means of transmission of the reminiscences of Jesus. Strauss' explanation of his theory has been given above, to some extent in his own words. We may see how he understood himself. We may appreciate also the genuineness of the religious spirit of his work. At the same time the thorough-going way in which he applied his principle, the relentless march of his argument, the character of his results, must sometimes have been startling even to himself. They certainly startled others. The effect of his work was instantaneous and immense. It was not at all the effect which he anticipated. The issue of the furious controversy which broke out was disastrous both to Strauss' professional career and to his whole temperament and character.

David Friedrich Strauss was born in 1808 in Ludwigsburg in Württemberg. He studied in Tübingen and in Berlin. He became an instructor in the theological faculty in Tübingen in 1832. He published his *Leben Jesu* in 1835. He was almost at once removed from his position. In 1836 he withdrew altogether from the professorial career. His answer to his critics, written in 1837, was in bitter tone. More conciliatory was his book, *Über Vergängliches und Bleibendes im Christenthum*, published in 1839. Indeed there were some concessions in the third edition of his *Leben Jesu* in 1838, but these were all repudiated in 1840. His *Leben Jesu für das deutsche Volk*, published in 1860, was the effort to popularise that which he had done. It is, however, in point of method, superior to his earlier work. Comments were met with even greater bitterness. Finally, not long before his death in 1874, he published *Der Alte und der Neue Glaube*, in which he definitely broke with Christianity altogether and went over to materialism and pessimism.

Pfleiderer, who had had personal acquaintance with Strauss and held him in regard, once wrote : ' Strauss' error did not lie in his regarding some of the gospel stories as legends, and some of the narratives of the miraculous as symbols of ideal truths. So far Strauss was right. The contribution which he made is one which we have all appropriated and built upon. His error lay in his looking for those religious truths which are thus symbolised, outside of religion itself, in adventurous metaphysical speculations. He did not seek them in the facts of the devout heart and moral will, as these are illustrated in the actual life of Jesus.' If Strauss, after the disintegration in criticism of certain elements in the biography of Jesus, had given us a positive picture of Jesus as the ideal of religious character and ethical force, his work would indeed have been attacked. But it would have outlived the attack and conferred a very great benefit. It conferred a great benefit as it was, although not the benefit which Strauss supposed. The benefit which it really conferred was in its critical method, and not at all in its results.

Of the mass of polemic and apologetic literature which Strauss' *Leben Jesu* called forth, little is at this distance worth the mentioning. Ullmann, who was far more appreciative than most of his adversaries, points out the real weakness of Strauss' work. That weakness lay in the failure to draw any distinction between the historical and the mythical. He threatened to dissolve the whole history into myth. He had no sense for the ethical element in the personality and teaching of Jesus nor of the creative force which this must have exerted. Ullmann says with cogency that, according to Strauss, the Church created its Christ virtually out of pure imagination. But we are then left with the query : What created the Church ? To this query Strauss has absolutely no answer to give. The answer is, says Ullmann, that the ethical personality of Jesus created the Church. This ethical personality is thus a supreme historic fact and a sublime historic cause, to which we must endeavour to penetrate, if need be through the veil of legend. The old rationalists had made themselves ridiculous by their effort to explain everything in some natural way. Strauss and his followers often appeared frivolous, since, according to them, there was little left to be explained. If a portion of the

narrative presented a difficulty, it was declared mythical.
What was needed was such a discrimination between the
legendary and historical elements in the Gospels as could
be reached only by patient, painstaking study of the
actual historical quality and standing of the documents.
No adequate study of this kind had ever been undertaken. Strauss did not undertake it, nor even perceive
that it was to be undertaken. There had been many men
of vast learning in textual and philological criticism. Here,
however, a new sort of critique was applied to a problem
which had but just now been revealed in all its length and
breadth. The establishing of the principles of this historical
criticism—the so-called Higher Criticism—was the herculean
task of the generation following Strauss. To the development of that science another Tübingen professor, Baur,
made permanent contribution. With Strauss himself,
sadder than the ruin of his career, was the tragedy of
the uprooting of his faith. This tragedy followed in many
places in the wake of the recognition of Strauss' fatal
half-truth.

BAUR

Baur, Strauss' own teacher in Tübingen, afterward famous
as biblical critic and church-historian, said of Strauss' book,
that through it was revealed in startling fashion to that
generation of scholars, how little real knowledge they had of
the problem which the Gospels present. To Baur it was clear
that if advance was to be made beyond Strauss' negative
results, the criticism of the gospel history must wait upon
an adequate criticism of the documents which are our
sources for that history. Strauss' failure had brought
home to the minds of men the fact that there were certain
preliminary studies which must needs be taken up. Meantime the other work must wait. As one surveys the literature of the next thirty years this fact stands out. Many
apologetic lives of Jesus had to be written in reply to Strauss.
But they are almost completely negligible. No constructive

work was done in this field until nearly a generation had passed.

Since all history, said Baur, before it reaches us must pass through the medium of a narrator, our first question as to the gospel history is not, what objective reality can be accorded to the narrative itself.   There is a previous question. This concerns the relation of the narrative to the narrator. It might be very difficult for us to make up our minds as to what it was that, in a given case, the witness saw.   We have not material for such a judgment.   We have probably much evidence, up and down his writings, as to what sort of man the witness was, in what manner he would be likely to see anything and with what personal equation he would relate that which he saw.   Baur would seem to have been the first vigorously and consistently to apply this principle to the gospel narratives.   Before we can penetrate deeply into the meaning of an author we must know, if we may, his purpose in writing.   Every author belongs to the time in which he lives.   The greater the importance of his subject for the parties and struggles of his day, the safer is the assumption that both he and his work will bear the impress of these struggles.   He will represent the interests of one or another of the parties.   His work will have a tendency of some kind. This was one of Baur's oft-used words—the tendency of a writer and of his work.   We must ascertain that tendency. The explanation of many things both in the form and substance of a writing would be given could we but know that. The letters of Paul, for example, are written in palpable advocacy of opinions which were bitterly opposed by other apostles.   The biographies of Jesus suggest that they also represent, the one this tendency, the other that.   We have no cause to assert that this trait of which we speak implies conscious distortion of the facts which the author would relate. The simple-minded are generally those least aware of the bias in the working of their own minds.   It is obvious that until we have reckoned with such elements as these, we cannot truly judge of that which the Gospels say.   To the elaboration of the principles of this historical criticism Baur gave the labour of his life. His biblical work alone would have been epoch-making.

Ferdinand Christian Baur was born in 1793 in Schmieden, near Stuttgart. He became a professor in Tübingen in 1826 and died there in 1860. He was an ardent disciple of Hegel. His greatest work was surely in the field of the history of dogma. His works, *Die Christliche Lehre von der Versöhnung*, 1838, *Die Christliche Lehre von der Dreieinigkeit und Mensch-werdung Gottes*, 1841-1843, his *Lehrbuch der Christlichen Dogmen-geschichte*, 1847, together constitute a contribution to which Harnack's work in our own time alone furnishes a parallel. Baur had begun his thorough biblical studies before the publication of Strauss' book. The direction of those studies was more than ever confirmed by his insight of the short-comings of Strauss' work. Very characteristically also he had begun his investigations, not at the most difficult point, that of the Gospels, as Strauss had done, but at the easiest point, the Epistles of Paul. As early as 1831 he had pub-lished a tractate, *Die Christus-Partei in der Corinthischen Gemeinde*. In that book he had delineated the bitter contest between Paul and the Judaising element in the Apostolic Church which opposed Paul whithersoever he went. In 1835 his disquisition, *Die sogenannten Pastoral-Briefe*, appeared. In the teachings of these letters he discovered the antithesis to the gnostic heresies of the second century. He thought also that the stage of organisation of the Church which they imply, accorded better with this supposition than with that of their apostolic authorship. The same general theme is treated in a much larger way in Baur's *Paulus, der Apostel Jesu Christi*, in 1845. Here the results of his study of the book of the Acts are combined with those of his inquiries as to the Pauline Epistles. In the history of the apostolic age men had been accustomed to see the evidence only of peace and harmony. Baur sought to show that the period had been one of fierce struggle, between the narrow Judaic and legalistic form of faith in the Messiah and that conception, introduced by Paul, of a world-religion free from the law. Out of this conflict, which lasted a hundred and fifty years, went forth the Catholic Church. The monuments of this struggle and witnesses of this process of growth are the New Testament writings, most of which were produced in the second century. The only documents which we have which were written before A.D. 70, were the four great Epistles of Paul, those to the Galatians, to the Romans, and to the Corinthians, together with the Apocalypse.

Many details in Baur's view are now seen to have been overstated and others false. Yet this was the first time that a true historical method had been applied to the New Testament literature as a whole. Baur's contribution lay in the originality of his conception of Christianity, in his emphasis upon Paul, in his realisation of the magnitude of the struggle which Paul inaugurated against Jewish prejudices in the primitive Church. In his idea, the issue of that struggle was, on the one hand, the freeing of Christianity from Judaism and on the other, the developing of Christian thought into a system of dogma and of the scattered Christian communities into an organised Church. The Fourth Gospel contains, according to Baur, a Christian gnosis parallel to the gnosis which was more and more repudiated by the Church as heresy. The Logos, the divine principle of life and light, appears bodily in the phenomenal world in the person of Jesus. It enters into conflict with the darkness and evil of the world. This speculation is but thinly clothed in the form of a biography of Jesus. That an account completely dominated by speculative motives gives but slight guarantee of historical truth, was for Baur self-evident. The author remains unknown, the age uncertain. The book, however, can hardly have appeared before the time of the Montanist movement, that is, toward the end of the second century. Scholars now rate far more highly than did Baur the element of genuine Johannine tradition which may lie behind the Fourth Gospel and account for its name. They do not find traces of Montanism or of paschal controversies. But the main contention stands. The Fourth Gospel represents the beginning of elaborate reflexion upon the life and work of Jesus. It is what it is because of the fusion of the ethical and spiritual content of the revelation in the personality of Jesus, with metaphysical abstractions and philosophical interpretation.

Baur was by no means so fortunate in the solution which he offered of the problem which the synoptic Gospels present. His opinions are of no interest except as showing that he too worked diligently upon a question which for a long time seemed only to grow in complexity and which has busied scholars practically from Baur's day to our own. His zeal here also to discover dogmatic purposes led him astray. The *Tendenzkritik* had its own tendencies. The chief was to exaggeration and one-sidedness. Baur had the kind of ear which hears grass grow. There is much overstrained acumen. Many radically false conclusions are reached by prejudiced operation with an historical formula, which in the last analysis is that of Hegel. Everything is to be explained on the principle of antithesis. Again, the assumption of conscious purpose in everything which men do or write is a grave exaggeration. It is often in contradiction of that wonderful unconsciousness with which men and institutions move to the fulfilment of a purpose for the good, the purpose of God, into which their own life is grandly taken up. To make each phase of such a movement the contribution of some one man's scheme or endeavour is, as was once said, to make God act like a professor.

The method of this book is that it seeks to deal only with men who have inaugurated movements, or marked some turning-point in their course which has proved of more than usual significance. The compass of the book demands such a limitation. But by this method whole chapters in the life of learning are passed over, in which the substance of achievement has been the carrying out of a plan of which we have been able to note only the inception. There is a sense in which the carrying out of a plan is both more difficult and more worthy than the mere setting it in motion. When one thinks of the labour and patience which have been expended, for example, upon the problem of the Gospels in the past seventy years, these truths come home to us. When one reminds himself of the hypotheses which have been made but to be abandoned, which have yet had the value that they at least indicated the area within which solutions do not lie,— when one thinks of the wellnigh immeasurable toil by which we have been led to large results which now seem secure, one is made to realise that the conditions of the advance of science are, for theologians, not different from those which obtain for scholars who, in any other field, would establish truth and lead men. In a general way, however, it may be said that the course of opinion in these two generations, in reference to such questions as those of the dates and authorship of the New Testament writings, has been one of rather note-worthy retrogression from many of the Tübingen positions. Harnack's *Geschichte der altchristlichen Literatur*, 1893, and his *Chronologie der altchristlichen Literatur*, 1897, present a marked contrast to Baur's scheme.

The Canon

The minds of New Testament scholars in the last generation have been engaged with a question which, in its full significance, was hardly present to the attention of Baur's school. It is the question of the New Testament as a whole. It is the question as to the time and manner and motives of the gathering together of the separate writings into a canon of Scripture which, despite the diversity of its elements, exerted its influence as a unit and to which an authority was ascribed, which the particular writings cannot originally have had. When and how did the Christians come to have a sacred book which they placed on an equality with the Old Testament, which last they had taken over from the synagogue ? How did they choose the writings which were to belong to this new collection ?   Why did they reject books which we know were read for edification in the early churches?   Deeper even than the question of the growth of the collection is that of the growth of the apprehension concerning it.   This apprehension

of these twenty-seven different writings as constituting the
sole document of Christian revelation, given by the Holy
Spirit, the identical holy book of the Christian Church, gave
to the book a significance altogether different from that which
its constituent elements must have had for men to whom
they had appeared as but the natural literary deposit of the
religious movement of the apostolic age. This apprehension
took possession of the mind of the Christian community.
It was made the subject of deliverances by councils of the
Church. How did this great transformation take place ?
Was it an isolated achievement, or was it part of a general
movement ?   Did not this development of life in the Christian
communities which gave them a New Testament belong to
an evolution which gave them also the so-called Apostles'
Creed and a monarchical organisation of the Church and
the beginnings of a ritual of worship ?

It is clear that we have here a question of greatest moment.
With the rise of this idea of the canon, with the assigning to
this body of literature the character of Scripture, we have the
beginning of the larger mastery which the New Testament has
exerted over the minds and life of men.   Compared with this
question, investigations as to the authorship and as to the
time, place and circumstance of the production of particular
books, came, for the time, to occupy a secondary rank.
As they have emerged again, they wear a new aspect and are
approached in a different spirit.   The writings are revealed as
belonging to a far larger context, that of the whole body of
the Christian literature of the age.   It in no way follows
from that which we have said that the body of documents,
which ultimately found themselves together in the New
Testament, have not a unity other than the outward one
which was by consensus of opinion or conciliar decree imposed
upon them.   They do represent, in the large and in varying
degrees, an inward and spiritual unity.   There was an inspiration of the main body of these writings, the outward
condition of which, at all events, was the nearness of their
writers to Jesus or to his eye-witnesses, and the consequence
of which was the unique relation which the more important

of these documents historically bore to the formation of the
Christian Church.   There was a heaven which lay about
the infancy of Christianity which only slowly faded into the
common light of day.   That heaven was the spirit of the
Master himself.   The chief of these writings do centrally
enshrine the first pure illumination of that spirit.   But the
churchmen who made the canon and the Fathers who argued
about it very often gave mistaken reasons for facts in respect
of which they nevertheless were right.   They gave what they
considered sound external reasons.   They alleged apostolic
authorship.   They should have been content with internal
evidence and spiritual effectiveness.   The apostles had come,
in the mind of the early Church, to occupy a place of unique
distinction.   Writings long enshrined in affection for their
potent influence, but whose origin had not been much considered, were now assigned to apostles, that they might have
authority and distinction.   The theory of the canon came
after the fact.   The theory was often wrong.   The canon had
been, in the main and in its inward principle, soundly con-
stituted.   Modern critics reversed the process.   They began
where the Church Fathers left off.   They tore down first
that which had been last built up.   Modern criticism, too,
passed through a period in which points like those of authorship and date of Gospels and Epistles seemed the only ones
to be considered.   The results being here often negative,
complete disintegration of the canon seemed threatened,
through discovery of errors in the processes by which the
canon had been outwardly built up.   Men realise now that
that was a mistake.

Two things have been gained in this discussion.   There is
first the recognition that the canon is a growth.   The holy
book and the conception of its holiness, as well, were evolved.
Christianity was not primarily a book-religion save in the
sense that almost all Christians revered the Old Testament.
Other writings than those which we esteem canonical were
long used in churches.   Some of those afterward canonical
were not used in all the churches.   In similar fashion we have
learned that identical statements of faith were not current

in the earliest churches. Nor was there one uniform system
of organisation and government. There was a time concerning which we cannot accurately use the word Church.
There were churches, very simple, worshipping communities.
But the Church, as outward magnitude, as triumphant organisation, grew. So there were many creeds or, at least, in-
formally accredited and current beginnings of doctrine. By and
by there was a formally accepted creed. So there were first
dearly loved memorials of Jesus and letters of apostolic men.
Only by and by was there a New Testament. The first gain
is the recognition of this state of things. The second follows.
It is the recognition that, despite a sense in which this literature is unique, there is also a sense in which it is but a part of
the whole body of early Christian literature. From the exact
and exhaustive study of the early Christian literature as a
whole, we are to expect a clearer understanding and a juster
estimate of the canonical part of it. It is not easy to say to
whom we have to ascribe the discovery and elaboration of
these truths. The historians of dogma have done much for
this body of opinion. The historians of Christian literature
have perhaps done more. Students of institutions and of the
canon law have had their share. Baur had more than an
inkling of the true state of things. But by far the most conspicuous teacher of our generation, in two at least of these
particular fields, has been Harnack. In his lifelong labour
upon the sources of Christian history, he had come upon this
question of the canon again and again. In his *Lehrbuch der
Dogmengeschichte*, 1887-1890, 4te. Aufl., 1910, the view
of the canon, which was given above, is absolutely fundamental. In his *Geschichte der altchristlichen Literatur bis
Eusebius*, 1893, and *Chronologie der altchristlichen Literatur*,
1897-1904, the evidence is offered in rich detail. It was
in his tractate, *Das Neue Testament um das Jahr 200*,
1889, that he contended for the later date against Zahn,
who had urged that the outline of the New Testament was
established and the conception of it as Scripture present, by
the end of the first century. Harnack argues that the decision
practically shaped itself between the time of Justin Martyr,

c. A.D. 150, and that of Irenæus, c. **A.D.** 180. The studies of
the last twenty years have more and more confirmed this
view.

LIFE OF JESUS

We said that the work of Strauss revealed nothing so clearly
as the ignorance of his time concerning the documents of the
early Christian movement. The labours of Baur and of his
followers were directed toward overcoming this difficulty.
Suddenly the public interest was stirred and the earlier excitement recalled by the publication of a new life of Jesus.
The author was a Frenchman, Ernest Renan, at one time a
candidate for the priesthood in the Roman Church. He was
a man of learning and literary skill, who made his *Vie de
Jésus,* which appeared in 1863 the starting-point for a series
of historical works under the general title, *Les Origines du
Christianisme.* In the next year appeared Strauss' popular
work, *Leben Jesu für das deutsche Volk.* In 1864 was published also Weizsäcker's contribution to the life of Christ,
his *Untersuchungen über die evangelische Geschichte.* To the
same year belonged Schenkel's *Charakterbild Jesu.* In the
years from 1867-1872 appeared Keim's *Geschichte Jesu von
Nazara.* There is something very striking in this recurrence
to the topic. After all, this was the point for the sake of
which those laborious investigations had been undertaken.
This was and is the theme of undying religious interest, the
character and career of the Nazarene. Renan's philosophical
studies had been mainly in English, studies of Locke and
Hume. But Herder also had been his beloved guide. For his
biblical and oriental studies he had turned almost exclusively
to the Germans. There is a deep religious spirit in the work
of the period of his conflict with the Church. The enthusiasm
for Christ sustained him in his struggle. Of the days before
he withdrew from the Church he wrote : ' For two months
I was a Protestant like a professor in Halle or Tübingen.'
French was at that time a language much better known in the
world at large, particularly the English-speaking world, than
was German. Renan's book had great art and charm. It

took a place almost at once as a bit of world-literature. The
number of editions in French and of translations into other
languages is amazing. Beyond question, the critical position
was made known through Renan to multitudes who would
never have been reached by the German works which were
really Renan's authorities. It is idle to say with Pfleiderer
that it is a pity that, having possessed so much learning,
Renan had not possessed more. That is not quite the point.
The book has much breadth and solidity of learning. Yet
Renan has scarcely the historian's quality. His work is a
work of art. It has the halo of romance. Imagination and
poetical feeling make it in a measure what it is.

Renan was born in 1823 in Treguier in Brittany. He set
out for the priesthood, but turned aside to the study of
oriental languages and history. He made long sojourn in
the East. He spoke of Palestine as having been to him a
fifth Gospel. He became Professor of Hebrew in the *Collège
de France*. He was suspended from his office in 1863, and
permitted to read again only in 1871. He had formally
separated himself from the Roman Church in 1845. He was
a member of the Academy. His diction is unsurpassed.
He died in 1894. In his own phrase, he sought to bring
Jesus forth from the darkness of dogma into the midst of the
life of his people. He paints him first as an idyllic national
leader, then as a struggling and erring hero, always aiming
at the highest, but doomed to tragic failure through the resistance offered by reality to his ideal. He calls the traditional
Christ an abstract being who never was alive. He would
bring the marvellous human figure before our eyes. He
heightens the brilliancy of his delineation by the deep shadows
of mistakes and indiscretion upon Jesus' part. In some
respects an epic or an historical romance, without teaching
us history in detail, may yet enable us by means of the artist's
intuition to realise an event or period, or make presentation
to ourselves of a personality, better than the scant records
acknowledged by the strict historian could ever do.

Our materials for a real biography of Jesus are inadequate. This was the fact which, by all these biographies

of Jesus, was brought home to men's minds. Keim's book, the most learned of those mentioned, is hardly more than a vast collection of material for the history of Jesus' age, which has now been largely superseded by Schürer's *Geschichte des Jüdischen Volkes im Zeitalter Jesu Christi*, 2 Bde., 1886-1890. There have been again, since the decade of the sixties, periods of approach to the great problem. Weiss and Beyschlag published at the end of the eighties lives of Jesus which, especially the former, are noteworthy in their treatment of the critical material. They do not for a moment face the question of the person of Christ. The same remark might be made, almost without exception, as to those lives of Jesus which have appeared in numbers in England and America. The best books of recent years are Albert Réville's *Jésus de Nazareth*, 1897, and Oscar Holtzmann's *Leben Jesu*, 1901. So great are the difficulties and in such disheartening fashion are they urged from all sides, that one cannot withhold enthusiastic recognition of the service which Holtzmann particularly has here rendered, in a calm, objective, and withal deeply devout handling of his theme. Meantime new questions have arisen, questions of the relation of Jesus to Messianism, like those touched upon by Wrede in his *Das Messias Geheimniss in den Evangelien*, 1901, and questions as to the eschatological trait in Jesus' own teaching. Schweitzer's book, *Von Reimarus zu Wrede: eine Geschichte der Leben Jesu-Forschung*, 1906, not merely sets forth this deeply interesting chapter in the history of the thought of modern men, but has also serious interpretative value in itself. For English readers Sanday's *Life of Christ in Recent Research*, 1907, follows the descriptive aspect, at least, of the same purpose with Schweitzer's book, covering, however, only the last twenty years.

It is characteristic that Ritschl, notwithstanding his emphasis upon the historical Jesus, asserted the impossibility of a biography of Jesus. The understanding of Jesus is through faith. For Wrede, on the other hand, such a biography is impossible because of the nature of our sources. Not alone are they scant, but they are not biographical.

They are apologetic, propagandist, interested in everything except those problems which a biographer must raise. The last
few years have even conjured up the question whether Jesus
ever lived. One may say with all simplicity, that the question
has, of course, as much rightfulness as has any other question
any man could raise. The somewhat extended discussion has,
however, done nothing to make evident how it could arise,
save in minds unfamiliar with the materials and unskilled
in historical research. The conditions which beset us when
we ask for a biography of Jesus that shall answer scientific
requirement are not essentially different from those which
meet us in the case of any other personage equally remote in
point of time, and equally woven about—if any such have
been—by the love and devotion of men. Bousset's little
book, *Was Wissen wir von Jesus?* 1904, convinces a quiet
mind that we know a good deal. Qualities in the personality
of Jesus obviously worked in transcendent measure to call
out devotion. No understanding of history is adequate
which has no place for the unfathomed in personality. Exactly
because we ourselves share this devotion, we could earnestly
wish that the situation as to the biography of Jesus were
other than it is.

The Old Testament

We have spoken thus far as if the whole biblical-critical
problem had been that of the New Testament. In reality
the same impulses which had opened up that question to the
minds of men had set them working upon the problem of
the Old Testament as well. We have seen how the Christians
made for themselves a canon of the New Testament. By
the force of that conception of the canon, and through the
belief that, almost in a literal sense, God was the author of the
whole book, the obvious differences among the writings had
been obscured. Men forgot the evolution through which the
writings had passed. The same thing had happened for the
Old Testament in the Jewish synagogues and for the rabbis
before the Christian movement. When the Christians took

over the Old Testament they took it over in this sense.   It was a closed book wherein all appreciation of the long road which the religion of Israel had traversed in its evolution had been lost.   The relation of the old covenant to the new was obscured.   The Old Testament became a Christian book. Not merely were the Christian facts prophesied in the Old Testament, but its doctrines also were implied.   Almost down to modern times texts have been drawn indifferently from either Testament to prove doctrine and sustain theology. Moses and Jesus, prophets and Paul, are cited to support an argument, without any sense of difference.   What we have said is hardly more true of Augustine or Anselm than of the classic Puritan divines.   This was the state of things which the critics faced.

The Old Testament critical movement is a parallel at all points of the one which we have described in reference to the New.   Of course, elder scholars, even Spinoza, had raised the question as to the Mosaic authorship of certain portions of the Pentateuch.   Roman Catholic scholars in the seventeenth century, for whom the stringent theory of inspiration had less significance than for Protestants, had set forth views which showed an awakening to the real condition.   Yet, at the beginning of the nineteenth century, no one would have forecast a revolution in opinion which would recognise the legendary quality of considerable portions of the Pentateuch and historical books, which would leave but little that is of undisputed Mosaic authorship, which would place the prophets before the law, which would concede the growth of the Jewish canon, which would perceive the relation of Judaism to the religions of the other Semite peoples and would seek to establish the true relation of Judaism to Christianity.

In the year 1835, the same year in which Strauss' *Leben Jesu* saw the light, Wilhelm Vatke published his *Religion des Alten Testaments*.   Vatke was born in 1806, began to teach in Berlin in 1830, was professor extraordinarius there in 1837 and died in 1882, not yet holding a full professorship.   His book was obscurely written and scholastic.   Public attention was largely occupied by the conflict which Strauss' work had caused. Reuss in Strassburg was working on the same lines, but published the main body of his results much later. The truth for which these scholars and others like their argued, worked its way slowly by force of its own merit. Perhaps it was due to this fact that the development of Old Testament critical views was subject to a fluctuation less marked than that which characterised the case of the New Testament. It is not necessary to describe the earlier stages of the discussion in Vatke's own terms. To his honour be it said that the views which he thus early enunciated were in no small degree identical with those which were in masterful fashion substantiated in Holland by Kuenen about 1870, in Germany by Wellhausen after 1878, and made known to English readers by Robertson Smith in 1881.

Budde has shown in his *Kanon des Alten Testaments*, 1900, that the Old Testament which lies before us finished and complete, assumed its present form only as the result of the growth of several centuries. At the beginning of this process of the canonisation stands that strange event, the sudden appearance of a holy book of the law under King Josiah, in 621 B.C. The end of the process, through the decisions of the scribes, falls after the destruction of Jerusalem, possibly even in the second century. Lagarde seems to have proved that the rabbis of the second century succeeded in destroying all copies of the Scripture which differed from the standard then set up. This state of things has enormously increased a difficulty which was already great enough, that of the detection and separation of the various elements of which many of the books in this ancient literature are made up. Certain books of the New Testament also present the problem of the discrimination of elements of different ages, which have been wrought together into the documents as we now have them, in a way that almost defies our skill to disengage. The synoptic Gospels are, of course, the great example. The book of the Acts presents a problem of the same kind. But the Pentateuch, or rather Hexateuch, the historical books in less degree, the writings even of some of the prophets, the codes which formulate the law and ritual, are composites which have been whole centuries in the making and re-making. There was no such thing as right of authorship in ancient Israel, little of it in the ancient world at all. What was once written was popular or priestly property. Histories were newly narrated, laws enlarged and rearranged, prophecies attributed to conspicuous persons. All this took place not in deliberate intention to pervert historic truth, but because there was no interest in historic truth and no conception of it. The rewriting of a nation's history from the point of view of its priesthood bore, to the ancient Israelite, beyond question, an aspect altogether different from that which the same transaction would bear to us. The difficulty of the separation of these materials, great in any case, is enhanced by the fact alluded to, that we have none but internal evidence. The success of the achievement, and the unanimity attained with reference to the most significant questions, is one of the marvels of the life of learning of our age.

In the Jewish tradition it had been assumed that the Mosaic law was written down in the wilderness. Then, in the times of the Judges and of the Kings, the historical books took shape, with David's Psalms and the wise words of Solomon. At the end of the period of the Kings we have the prophetic literature and finally Ezra and Nehemiah. De Wette had disputed this order, but Wellhausen in his *Prolegomena zur Geschichte Israels*, 1883, may be said to have proved that this view was no longer tenable. Men ask, could the law, or even any greater part of it, have been given to nomads in the wilderness ? Do not all parts of it assume a settled state of society and an agricultural life ? Do the historical books from Judges to the II. Kings know anything about the law ? Are the practices of worship which they imply consonant with the supposition that the law was in force ? How is it that the law appears both under Josiah, and again under Ezra, as something new, thus far unknown, and yet as ruling the religious life of the people from that day forth ? It seems impossible to escape the conclusion that only after Josiah's reformation, more completely after the restoration under Ezra, did the religion of the law exist. The centralisation of worship at one point, such as the book of Deuteronomy demands, seems to have been the thing achieved by the reform under Josiah. The establishment of the priestly hierarchy such as the code ordains was the issue of the religious revolution wrought in Ezra's time. To put it differently, the so-called Book of the Covenant, the nucleus of the law-giving, itself implies the multiplicity of the places of worship. Deuteronomy demands the centralisation of the worship as something which is yet to take place. The priestly Code declares that the limitation of worship to one place was a fact already in the time of the journeys of Israel in the wilderness. It is assumed that the Hebrews in the time of Moses shared the almost universal worship of the stars. Moses may indeed have concluded a covenant between his people and Jahve, their God, hallowing the judicial and moral life of the people, bringing these into relation to the divine will. Jahve was a holy God whose will was to guide the people coming up out of the degradation of nature-worship. That part of the people held to the old nature-worship is evident in the time of Elijah. The history of Israel is not that of defection from a pure revelation. It is the history of a gradual attainment of purer revelation, of enlargement in the application of it, of discovery of new principles contained in it. It is the history also of the decline of spiritual religion. The zeal of the prophets against the ceremonial worship shows that. Their protest reveals at that early date the beginning of that antithesis which had become so sharp in Jesus' time.

This determination of the relative positions of law and prophets was the first step in the reconstruction of the history, both of the nation of Israel and of its literature. At the beginning, as in every literature, are songs of war and victory, of praise and grief, hymns, even riddles and phrases of magic. Everywhere poetry precedes prose. Then come myths relating to the worship and tales of the fathers and heroes. Elements of both these sorts are embedded in the simple chronicles which began now to be written, primitive historical works, such as those of the Jahvist and

Elohist, of the narrators of the deeds of the judges and of David and of Saul. Perhaps at this point belong the earliest attempts at fixing the tradition of family and clan rights, and of the regulation of personal conduct, as in the Book of the Covenant. Then comes the great outburst of the prophetic spirit, the preaching of an age of great religious revival. Then follows the law, with its minute regulation of all details of life upon which would depend the favour of the God who had brought punishment upon the people in the exile. The prophecy runs on into apocalyptic like that of the book of Daniel. The contact with the outside world makes possible a phase of literature such as that to which the books of Job and Ecclesiastes belong. The deepening of the inner life gave the world the lyric of the Psalms, some of which are credibly assigned to a period so late as that of the Maccabees.

In this which has been said of the literature we have the clue also for the reconstruction of the nation's history. The naïve assumption in the writing of all history had once been that one must begin with the beginning. But to Wellhausen, Stade, Eduard Meyer and Kittel and Cornill, it has been clear that the history of the earliest times is the most uncertain. It is the least adapted to furnish a secure point of departure for historical inquiry. There exist for it usually no contemporary authorities, or only such as are of problematical worth. This earliest period constitutes a problem, the solution of which, so far as any solution is possible, can be hoped for only through approach from the side of ascertained facts. We must start from a period which is historically known. For the history of the Hebrews, this is the time of the first prophets of whom we have written records, or from whom we have written prophecies. We get from these, as also from the earliest direct attempts at history writing, only that conception of Israel's pre-historic life which was entertained in prophetic circles in the eighth century. We learn the heroic legends in the interpretation which the prophets put upon them. We have still to seek to interpret them for ourselves. We must begin in the middle and work both backward and

forward. Such a view of the history of Israel affords every
opportunity for the connecting of the history and religion
of Israel with those of the other Semite stocks. Some of these
have in recent years been discovered to offer extraordinary
parallels to that which the Old Testament relates.

THE HISTORY OF DOCTRINE

When speaking of Baur's contribution to New Testament
criticism, we alluded to his historical works. He was in a distinct sense a reformer of the method of the writing of church
history. To us the notions of the historical and of that which
is genetic are identical. Of course, naïve religious chronicles
do not meet that test. A glance at the histories produced
by the age of rationalism will show that these also fall short
of it. The perception of the relativity of institutions like the
papacy is here wholly wanting. Men and things are brought
summarily to the bar of the wisdom of the author's year of
grace. They are approved or condemned by this criterion.
For Baur, all things had come to pass in the process of the
great life of the world. There must have been a rationale
of their becoming. It is for the historian with sympathy and
imagination to find out what their inherent reason was. One
other thing distinguishes Baur as church historian from his
predecessors. He realised that before one can delineate one
must investigate. One must go to the sources. One must
estimate the value of these sources. One must have ground
in the sources for every judgment. Baur was himself a great
investigator. Yet the movement for the investigation of the
sources of biblical and ecclesiastical history which his generation initiated has gone on to such achievements that, in some
respects, we can but view the foundations of Baur's own work
as precarious, the results at which he arrived as unwarranted.
New documents have come to light since his day. Forgeries
have been proved to be such. The whole state of learning
as to the literature of the Christian origins has been vastly
changed. There is still one other thing to say concerning
Baur. He was a Hegelian. He has the disposition always

to interpret the movements of the religious spirit in the sense of philosophical ideas. He frankly says that without speculation every historical investigation remains but a play upon the surface of things. Baur's fault was that in his search for, or rather in his confident discovery of, the great connecting forces of history, the biographical element, the significance of personality, threatened altogether to disappear. The force in the history was the absolute, the immanent divine will. The method everywhere was that of advance by contrasts and antagonisms. One gets an impression, for example, that the Nicene dogma became what it did by the might of the idea, that it could not by any possibility have had any other issue.

The foil to much of this in Baur's own age was represented in the work of Neander, a converted Jew, professor of church history in Berlin, who exerted great influence upon a generation of English and American scholars. He was not an investigator of sources. He had no talent for the task. He was a delineator, one of the last of the great painters of history, if one may so describe the type. He had imagination, sympathy, a devout spirit. His great trait was his insight into personality. He wrote history with the biographical interest. He almost resolves history into a series of biographical types. He has too little sense for the connexion of things, for the laws of the evolution of the religious spirit. The great dramatic elements tend to disappear behind the emotions of individuals. The old delineators were before the age of investigation. Since that impulse became masterful, some historians have been completely absorbed in the effort to make contribution to this investigation. Others, with a sense of the impossibility of mastering the results of investigation in all fields, have lost the zeal for the writing of church history on a great scale. They have contented themselves with producing monographs upon some particular subject, in which, at the most, they may hope to embody all that is known as to some specific question.

We spoke above of the new conception of the relation of the canonical literature of the New Testament to the extra-canonical. We alluded to the new sense of the continuity of the history of the apostolic churches with that of the Church of the succeeding age. The influence of these ideas has been to set all problems here involved in a new light. Until 1886 it might have been said with truth that we had no good history of the apostolic age. In that year Weizsäcker's book, *Das Apostolische Zeitalter der Christlichen Kirche*, admirably filled the place. A part of the problem of the historian of the apostolic age is difficult for the same reason which was given when we were speaking of the biography of Jesus. Our materials are inadequate. First with the beginning of the activities of Paul have we sources of the first rank. The relation of statements in the Pauline letters to data in the book of the Acts was one of the earliest problems which the Tübingen school set itself. An attempt to write the biography of Paul reminds us sharply of our limitations. We know almost nothing of Paul prior to his conversion, or subsequent to the enigmatical breaking off of the account of the beginnings of his work at Rome. Harnack's *Mission und Ausbreitung des Christenthums*, 1902 (translated, Moffatt, 1908), takes up the work of Paul's successors in that cardinal activity. It offers, strange as it may seem, the first discussion of the dissemination of Christianity which has dealt adequately with the sources. It gives also a picture of the world into which the Christian movement went. It emphasises anew the truth which has for a generation past grown in men's apprehension that there is no possibility of understanding Christianity, except against the background of the religious life and thought of the world into which it came. Christianity had vital relation, at every step of its progress, to the religious movements and impulses of the ancient world, especially in those centres of civilisation which Paul singled out for his endeavour and which remained the centres of the Christian growth. It was an age which has often been summarily described as corrupt. Despite its corruption, or possibly because it was corrupt, it gives evidence, however, of religious stirring, of strong ethical reaction, of spiritual endeavour rarely paralleled. In the Roman Empire everything travelled. Religions travelled. In the centres of civilisation there was scarcely a faith of mankind which had not its votaries.

It was an age of religious syncretism, of hospitality to diverse religious ideas, of the commingling of those ideas. These things facilitated the progress of Christianity. They made certain that if the Christian movement had in it the divine vitality which men claimed, it would one day conquer the world. Equally, they made certain that, as the very condition of this conquest, Christianity would be itself transformed. This it is which has happened in the evolution of Christianity from its very earliest stages and in all phases of its life. Of any given rite, opinion or institution, of the many which have passed for almost two millenniums unchallenged under the Christian name, men about us are now asking : But how much of it is Christian ?   In what measure have we to think of it as derived from some other source, and representing the accommodation and assimilation of Christianity to its environment in process of its work ?   What is Christianity ? Not unnaturally the ancient Church looked with satisfaction upon the great change which passed over Christianity when Constantine suddenly made that which had been the faith of a despised and persecuted sect, the religion of the world.   The Fathers can have thought thus only because their minds rested upon that which was outward and spectacular.   Not unnaturally the metamorphosis in the inward nature of Christianity which had taken place a century and a quarter earlier was hidden from their eyes.   In truth, by that earlier and subtler transformation Christianity had passed permanently beyond the stage in which it had been preponderantly a moral and spiritual enthusiasm, with its centre and authority in the person of Jesus.   It became a system and an institution, with a canon of New Testament Scripture, a monarchical organisation and a rule of faith which was formulated in the Apostles' Creed.

To Baur the truth as to the conflict of Paul with the Judaisers had meant much. He thought, therefore, with reference to the rise of priesthood and ritual among the Christians, to the emphasis on Scripture in the fashion of the scribes, to the insistence upon rules and dogmas after the manner of the Pharisees, that they were but the evidence of the decline and defeat of Paul's free spirit and of the resurgence of Judaism in Christianity. He sought to explain the rise of the episcopal organisation by the example of the synagogue. Ritschl in his *Entstehung der alt-catholischen Kirche*, 1857, had seen that Baur's theory could not be true. Christianity did not fall back into Judaism. It went forward to embrace the Hellenic and Roman world. The institutions, dogmas, practices of that which, after A.D. 200, may with propriety be called the Catholic Church, are the fruit of that embrace. There was here a falling off from primitive and spiritual Christianity. But it was not a falling back into Judaism. There were priests and scribes and Pharisees with other names elsewhere. The phenomenon of the waning of the original enthusiasm of a period of religious revelation has been a frequent one. Christianity on a grand scale illustrated this phenomenon anew. Harnack has elaborated this thesis with unexampled brilliancy and power. He has supported it with a learning in which he has no rival and with a religious interest which not even hostile critics would deny. The phrase, ' the Hellenisation of Christianity,' might almost be taken as the motto of the work to which he owes his fame.

HARNACK

Adolf Harnack was born in 1851 in Dorpat, in one of the Baltic provinces of Russia. His father, Theodosius Harnack, was professor of pastoral theology in the University of Dorpat. Harnack studied in Leipzig and began to teach there in 1874. He was called to the chair of church history in Giessen in 1879. In 1886 he removed to Marburg and in 1889 to Berlin. Harnack's earlier published work was almost entirely in the field of the study of the sources and materials of early church history. His first book, published in 1873, was an inquiry as to the sources for the history of Gnosticism. His *Patrum Apostolicorum Opera*, 1876, prepared by him jointly with von Gebhardt and Zahn, was in a way only a forecast of the great collection, *Texte und Untersuchungen zur Geschichte der alt-christlichen Literatur*, begun in 1882, upon which numbers of scholars have worked together with him. The collection has already more than thirty-five volumes. In his own two works, *Die Geschichte der alt-christlichen Literatur bis Eusebius*, 1893, and *Die Chronologie der alt-christlichen Literatur bis Eusebius*, 1897, are deposited the results of his reflexion on the mass of this material. His *Beiträge zur Einleitung in das Neue Testament*, 1906, etc., should not be overlooked. He has had the good fortune to be among those who have discovered manuscripts of importance. He has had to do with the Prussian Academy's edition of the Greek Fathers. A list of his published works, which was prepared in connexion with the celebration of his sixtieth birthday in 1911, bears witness to his amazing diligence and fertility. He was for thirty-five years associated with Schürer in the publication of the *Theologische Literaturzeitung*. He has filled important posts in the Church and under the government. To this must be added an activity as a teacher which has placed a whole generation of students from every portion of the world under undying obligation. One speaks with reserve of the living, but surely no man of our generation has done more to make the history of which we write.

Harnack's epoch-making work was his *Lehrbuch der Dogmengeschichte*, 1886-88, fourth edition, 1910. The book met, almost from the moment of its appearance, with the realisation of the magnitude of that which had been achieved. It rested upon a fresh and independent study of the sources. It departed from the mechanism which had made the old treatises upon the history of doctrine formal and lifeless. Harnack realised to the full how many influences other than theological had had part in the development of doctrine. He recognised the reaction of modes of life and practice, and of external circumstances on the history of thought. His history of doctrine has thus a breadth and human quality never before attained. Philosophy, worship, morals, the development of Church government and of the canon, the common interests and passions of the age and those of the individual participants, are all made tributary to his delineation.

Harnack cannot share Baur's view that the triumph of the Logos-Christology at Nicaea and Chalcedon was inevitable. A certain historic naturalness of the movement he would concede, the world on which Christianity entered being what it was. He is aware, however, that many elements other than Christian have entered into the development. He has phrased his apprehension thus. That Hellenisation of Christianity which Gnosticism represented, and against which, in this, its acute form, the Church contended was, after all, the same thing which, by slower process and more unconsciously, befell the Church itself. That pure moral enthusiasm and inspiration which had been the gist of the Christian movement, in its endeavour to appropriate the world, had been appropriated by the world in far greater measure than its adherents knew. It had taken up its mission to change the world. It had dreamed that while changing the world it had itself remained unchanged. The world was changed, the world of life, of feeling and of thought. But Christianity was also changed. It had conquered the world. It had no perception of the fact that it illustrated the old law that the conquered give laws to the conquerors. It had fused the ancient culture with the flame of its inspiration. It did not appreciate the degree in which the elements of that ancient culture now coloured its far-shining flame. It had been a maker of history. Meantime it had been unmade and remade by its own history. It confidently carried back its canon, dogma, organisation, ritual to Christ and the apostles. It did not realise that the very fact that it could find these things natural and declare them ancient, proved with conclusiveness that it had itself departed from the standard of Christ and the apostles. It esteemed that these were its defences against the world. It little dreamed that they were, by their very existence, the evidence of the fact that the Church had not defended itself against the world. Its dogma was the Hellenisation of its thought. Its organisation was the Romanising of its life. Its canon and ritual were the externalising, and

conventionalising of its spirit and enthusiasm. These are
positive and constructive statements of Harnack's main
position.

When, however, they are turned about and stated negatively,
these statements all convey, more or less, the impression
that the advance of Christianity had been its destruction, and
the evolution of dogma had been a defection from Christ. This
is the aspect of the contention which gave hostile critics
opportunity to say that we have before us the history of the
loss of Christianity. Harnack himself has many sentences
which superficially will bear that construction. Hatch had
said in his brilliant book, *The Influence of Greek Ideas and
Usages upon the Christian Church*, 1891, that the domestication
of Greek philosophy in the Church signified a defection from
the Sermon on the Mount. The centre of gravity of the
Gospel was changed from life to doctrine, from morals to
metaphysics, from goodness to orthodoxy. The change was
portentous. The aspect of pessimism is, however, removed
when one recognises the inevitableness of some such process,
if Christianity was ever to wield an influence in the world
at all. Again, one must consider that the process of the
recovery of pure Christianity must begin at exactly this point,
namely, with the recognition of how much in current Christianity is extraneous. It must begin with the sloughing off
of these extraneous elements, with the recovery of the sense
for that which original Christianity was. Such a recovery
would be the setting free again of the power of the religion
itself.

The constant touchstone and point of reference for every
stage of the history of the Church must be the gospel of Jesus.
But what was the gospel of Jesus ? In what way did the
very earliest Christians apprehend that gospel ? This question is far more difficult for us to answer than it was for those
to whom the New Testament was a closed body of literature,
externally differentiated from all other, and with a miraculous
inspiration extending uniformly to every phrase in any book.
These men would have said that they had but to find the
proper combination of the sacred phrases. But we acknow-

ledge that the central inspiration was the personality of Jesus. The books possess this inspiration in varying degree. Certain of the books have distinctly begun the fusion of Christian with other elements. They themselves represent the first stages of the history of doctrine. We acknowledge that those utterances of Jesus which have been preserved for us, shaped themselves by the antitheses in which Jesus stood. There is much about them that is palpably incidental, practically relevant and unquestionably only relative. In a large sense, much of the meaning of the gospel has to be gathered out of the evidence of the operation of its spirit in subsequent ages of the Christian Church, and from remoter aspects of the influence of Jesus on the world. Thus the very conception of the gospel of Jesus becomes inevitably more or less subjective. It becomes an ideal construction. The identification of this ideal with the original gospel proclamation becomes precarious. We seem to move in a circle. We derive the ideal from the history, and then judge the history by the ideal.

Is there any escape from this situation, short of the return to the authority of Church or Scripture in the ancient sense ? Furthermore, even the men to whom the gospel was in the strictest sense a letter, identified the gospel with their own private interpretation of this letter. Certainly the followers of Ritschl who will acknowledge no traits of the gospel save those of which they find direct witness in the Gospels, thus ignore that the Gospels are themselves interpretations. This undue stress upon the documents which we are fortunate enough to possess, makes us forget the limitations of these documents. We tend thus to exaggerate that which must be only incidental, as, for example, the Jewish element, in the teaching of Jesus. We thus underrate phases of Jesus' teaching which, no doubt, a man like Paul would have apprehended better than did the evangelists themselves. In truth, in Harnack's own delineation of the teaching of Jesus those elements of it which found their way to expression in Paul, or again in the fourth Gospel, are rather underrated than overstated, in the author's anxiety to exclude elements which are acknowledged to be interpretative in their nature. We are driven, in some measure, to seek to find out what the gospel was from the way in which the earliest Christians took it up. We return ever afresh to questions nearly unanswerable from the materials at hand. What was the central principle in the shaping of the earliest stages of the new community, both as to its thought and life ? Was it the longing for the coming of the Kingdom of God, the striving after the righteousness of the Sermon on the Mount ? Or was it the faith of the Messiah, the reverence for the Messiah, directed to the person of Jesus ? What word dominated the preaching ? Was it that the Kingdom of God was near, that the Son of Man would come ? Or was it that in Jesus Messiah has come ? What was the demand upon the hearer ? Was it, Repent, or was it, Believe on the Lord Jesus, or was it both, and which had the greater emphasis ? Was the name of Jesus used in the formulas of worship before the time of Paul ? What do we know about prayer in the name of Jesus, or baptism in that name, or miracles in the name of Jesus, or of the Lord's Supper and the conception of the Lord as present with his disciples in the rite ? Was this revering of Jesus, which was fast moving toward a worship of him, the inner motive force of the whole construction of the dogma of his person and of the trinity ?

In the second volume Harnack treats of the development primarily of the Christological and trinitarian dogma, from the fourth to the seventh centuries. The dramatic interest of the narrative exceeds anything which has been written on this theme. A debate which to most modern men is remote and abstruse almost to the point of unintelligibility, and of which many of the external aspects are disheartening in the extreme, is here brought before us in something of the reasonableness which it must have had for those who took part in it. Tertullian shaped the problem and established the nomenclature for the Christological solution which the Orient two hundred years later made its own. It was he who, from the point of view of the jurist, rather than of the philosopher, gave the words ' person ' and ' substance,' which continually occur in this discussion, the meaning which in the

Nicene Creed they bear. Most brilliant is Harnack's characterisation of Arius and Athanasius. In Arius the notion of the Son of God is altogether done away. Only the name remains. The victory of Arianism would have resolved Christianity into cosmology and formal ethics. It would have destroyed it as religion. Yet the perverse situation into which the long and fierce controversy had drifted cannot be better illustrated than by one undisputed fact. Athanasius, who assured for Christianity its character as a religion of the living communion of God with man, is yet the theologian in whose Christology almost every possible trace of the recollection of the historic Jesus has disappeared. The purpose of the redemption is to bring men into community of life with God. But Athanasius apprehended this redemption as a conferment, from without and from above, of a divine nature. He subordinated everything to this idea. The whole narrative concerning Jesus falls under the interpretation that the only quality requisite for the Redeemer in his work was the possession in all fulness of the divine nature. His incarnation, his manifestation in real human life, held fast to in word, is reduced to a mere semblance. Salvation is not an ethical process, but a miraculous bestowment. The Christ, who was God, lifts men up to godhood. They become God. These phrases are of course capable of ethical and intelligible meaning. The development of the doctrine, however, threw the emphasis upon the metaphysical and miraculous aspects of the work. It gloried in the fact that the presence of divine and human, two natures in one person forever, was unintelligible. In the end it came to the pass that the enthusiastic assent to that which defied explanation became the very mark of a humble and submissive faith. One reads the so-called Athanasian Creed, and hears the ring of its determination to exact assent. It had long since been clear to these Catholics and churchmen that, with the mere authority of Scripture, it was not possible to defend Christianity against the heretics. The heretics read their heresies out of the Bible. The orthodox read orthodoxy from the same page. Marcion had proved that, in the very days when the canon took its shape. There must be an authority to define the interpretation of the Scripture. Those who would share the benefits which the Church dispensed must assent unconditionally to the terms of membership.

All these questions were veiled for the early Christians behind the question of the kind of Christ in whom their hearts believed. With all that we have said about the reprehensible admixture of the metaphysical element in the dogma, with all the accusation which we bring concerning acute or gradual Hellenisation, secularisation and defection from the Christ, we ought not to hide from ourselves that in this gigantic struggle there were real religious interests at stake, and that for the men of both parties. Dimly, or perhaps vividly, the man of either party felt that the conception of the Christ which he was fighting for was congruous with the conception of religion which he had, or felt that he must have. It is this religious issue, everywhere present, which gives dignity to a struggle which otherwise does often sadly lack it. There are two religious views of the person of Christ which have stood, from the beginning, the one over against the other.[1] The one saw in Jesus of Nazareth a man, distinguished by his special calling as the Messianic King, endued with special powers, lifted above all men ever known, yet a man, completely subject to God in faith, obedience and prayer. This view is surely sustained by many of Jesus' own words and deeds. It shines through the testimony of the men who followed him. Even the belief in his resurrection and his second coming did not altogether do away with it. The other view saw in him a new God who, descending from God, brought mysterious powers for the redemption of mankind into the world, and after short obscuring of his glory, returned to the abode of God, where he had been before. From this belief come all the hymns and prayers to Jesus as to God all miracles and exorcisms in his name.

In the long run, the simpler view did not maintain itself. If false gods and demons were expelled, it was the God

[1] Wernle, *Einführung in das Theologische Studium*, 1908, s. 204.

Jesus who expelled them. The more modest faith believed that in the man Jesus, being such an one as he was, men had received the greatest gift which the love of God had to bestow. In turn the believer felt the assurance that he also was a child of God, and in the spirit of Jesus was to realise that sonship. Syncretist religions suggested other thoughts. We see that already even in the synoptic tradition the calling upon the name of Jesus had found place. One wonders whether that first apprehension ever stood alone in its purity. The Gentile Churches founded by Paul, at all events, had no such simple trust. Equally, the second form of faith seems never to have been able to stand alone in its peculiar quality. Some of the gnostic sects had it. Marcion again is our example. The new God Jesus had nothing to do with the cruel God of the Old Testament. He supplanted the old God and became the only God. In the Church the new God, come down from heaven, must be set in relation with the long-known God of Israel. No less, must he stand in relation to the simple hero of the Gospels with his human traits. The problem of theological reflexion was to find the right middle course, to keep the divine Christ in harmony, on the one side, with monotheism, and on the other, with the picture which the Gospels gave. Belief knew nothing of these contradictions. The same simple soul thanked God for Jesus with his sorrows and his sympathy, as man's guide and helper, and again prayed to Jesus because he seemed too wonderful to be a man. The same kind of faith achieves the same wondering and touching combination to-day, after two thousand years. With thought comes trouble. Reflexion wears itself out upon the insoluble difficulty, the impossible combination, the flat contradiction, which the two views present, so soon as they are clearly seen.

In the earliest Christian writings the fruit of this reflexion lies before us in this form:—The Creator of worlds, the mediator, the lord of angels and demons, the Logos which was God and is our Saviour, was yet a humble son of man, undergoing suffering and death, having laid aside his divine glory. This picture is made with materials which the

canonical writings themselves afford. Theological study had
henceforth nothing to do but to avoid extremes and seek
to make this image, which reflexion upon two polar opposites had yielded, as nearly thinkable as possible. It has
been said that the trinitarian doctrine is not in the New
Testament, that it was later elaborated by a different kind
of mind. This is not true. But the inference is precisely
the contrary of that which defenders of the dogma would
formerly have drawn from this concession. The same kind
of mind, or rather the same two kinds of mind, are at work
in the New Testament. Both of the religious elements
above suggested are in the Gospels and Epistles. The
New Testament presents attempts at their combination.
Either form may be found in the literature of the later
age. If we ask ourselves, What is that in Jesus which
gives us the sense of redemption, surely we should answer,
It is his glad and confident resting in the love of God
the Father. It is his courage, his faith in men, which
becomes our faith in ourselves. It is his wonderful mingling
of purity and love of righteousness with love of those who
have sinned. You may find this in the ancient literature,
as the Fathers describe that to which their souls cling. But
this is not the point of view from which the dogma is organised.
The Nicene Christology is not to be understood from this
approach. The cry of a dying civilisation after power and
light and life, the feeling that these might come to it,
streaming down as it were, from above, as a physical, a
mechanical, a magical deliverance, this is the frame within
which is set what is here said of the help and redemption
wrought by Christ. The resurrection and the incarnation
are the points at which this streaming in of the divine light
and power upon a darkened world is felt.

That religion seemed the highest, that interpretation of
Christianity the truest, the absolute one, which could boast
that it possessed the power of the Almighty through his
physical union with men. He who contended that Jesus was
God, contended therewith for a power which could come
upon men and make them in some sense one with God. This

is the view which has been almost exclusively held in the Greek Church. It is the view which has run under and through and around the other conception in the Roman and Protestant Churches. The sense that salvation is inward, moral, spiritual, has rarely indeed been absent from Christendom. It would be preposterous to allege that it had. Yet this sense has been overlaid and underrun and shot through with that other and disparate idea of salvation, as of a pure bestowment, something achieved apart from us, or, if one may so say, some alteration of ourselves upon other than moral and spiritual terms. The conception of the person Christ shows the same uncertainty. Or rather, with a given view of the nature of religion and salvation, the corresponding view of Christ is certain. In the age-long and world-wide contest over the trinitarian formula, with all that is saddening in the struggle and all that was misleading in the issue, it is because we see men struggling to come into the clear as to these two meanings of religion, that the contest has such absorbing interest. Men have been right in declining to call that religion in which a man saves himself. They have been wrong in esteeming that they were then only saved of God or Christ when they were saved by an obviously external process. Even this antinomy is softened when one no longer holds that God and men are mutually exclusive conceptions. It is God working within us who saves, the God who in Jesus worked such a wonder of righteousness and love as else the world has never seen.

CHAPTER V

THE CONTRIBUTION OF THE NATURAL AND SOCIAL SCIENCES

By the middle of the nineteenth century the empirical sciences had undergone vast expansion in the study of detail and in the discovery of principles. Men felt the necessity of some adequate discussion of the relation of these sciences one to another and of their unity. There was need of the organisation of the mass of knowledge, largely new and ever increasing, which the sciences furnished. It lay in the logic of the case that some of these attempts should advance the bold claim to deal with all knowledge whatsoever and to offer a theory of the universe as a whole. Religion, both in its mythological and in its theological stages, had offered a theory of the universe as a whole. The great metaphysical systems had offered theories of the universe as a whole. Both had professed to include all facts. Notoriously both theology and metaphysics had dealt in most inadequate fashion with the material world, in the study of which the sciences were now achieving great results. Indeed, the methods current and authoritative with theologians and metaphysicians had actually prevented study of the physical universe. Both of these had invaded areas of fact to which their methods had no application and uttered dicta which had no relation to truth. The very life of the sciences depended upon deliverance from this bondage. The record of that deliverance is one of the most dramatic chapters in the history of thought. Could one be surprised if, in the resentment which long oppression had engendered and in the joy which overwhelming victory had brought, scientific men now invaded the fields of their opponents? They repaid their enemies in their own coin.

There was with some a disposition to deny that there exists an area of knowledge to which the methods of metaphysicians and theologians might apply. This was Comte's contention. Others conceded that there might be such an area, but claimed that we can have no knowledge of it. Even the theologians, after their first shock, were disposed to concede that, concerning the magnitudes in which they were most interested, as for example, God and soul, we have no knowledge of the sort which the method of the physical sciences would give. They fell back upon Kant's distinction of the two reasons and two worlds. They exaggerated the sharpness of that distinction. They learned that the claim of agnosticism was capable of being viewed as a line of defence, behind which the transcendental magnitudes might be secure. Indeed, if one may take Spencer as an example, it is not certain that this was not the intent of some of the scientists in their strong assertion of agnosticism. Spencer's later work reveals that he had no disposition to deny that there are foundations for belief in a world lying behind the phenomenal, and from which the latter gets its meaning.

Meantime, after positivism was buried and agnosticism dead, a thing was achieved for which Comte himself laid the foundation and in which Spencer as he grew older was ever more deeply interested. This was the great development of the social sciences. Every aspect of the life of man, including religion itself, has been drawn within the area of the social sciences. To all these subjects, including religion, there have been applied empirical methods which have the closest analogy with those which have reigned in the physical sciences. Psychology has been made a science of experiment, and the psychology of religion has been given a place within the area of its observations and generalisations. The ethical, and again the religious consciousness has been subjected to the same kind of investigation to which all other aspects of consciousness are subjected. Effort has been made to ascertain and classify the phenomena of the religious life of the race in all lands and in all ages. A science of religions is taking its place among the other sciences. It is as purely an inductive science as is any other. The history of religions and the philosophy of religion are being rewritten from this point of view.

In the first lines of this chapter we spoke of the empirical sciences, meaning the sciences of the material world. It is clear, however, that the sciences of mind, of morals and of religion have now become empirical sciences. They have their basis in experience, the experience of individuals and the experience of masses of men, of ages of observable human life. They all proceed by the method of observation and inference, of hypothesis and verification. There is a unity of method as between the natural and social and psychical sciences, the reach of which is startling to reflect upon. Indeed, the physiological aspects of psychology, the investigations of the relation of adolescence to conversion, suggest that the distinction between the physical and the psychical is a vanishing distinction. Science comes nearer to offering an interpretation of the universe as a whole than the opening paragraphs of this chapter would imply. But it does so by including religion, not by excluding it. No one would any longer think of citing Kant's distinction of two reasons and two worlds in the sense of establishing a city of refuge into which the persecuted might flee. Kant rendered incomparable service by making clear two poles of thought. Yet we must realise how the space between is filled with the gradations of an absolute continuity of activity. Man has but one reason. This may conceivably operate upon appropriate material in one or the other of these polar fashions. It does operate in infinite variations of degree, in unity with itself, after both fashions, at all times and upon all materials.

Positivism was a system. Agnosticism was at least a phase of thought. The broadening of the conception of science and the invasion of every area of life by a science thus broadly conceived, has been an influence less tangible than those others but not, therefore, less effective. Positivism was bitterly hostile to Christianity, though, in the mind of Comte himself and of a few others, it produced a curious substitute, possessing many of the marks of Roman Catholicism. The name

' agnostic ' was so loosely used that one must say that the contention was hostile to religion in the minds of some and not of others. The new movement for an inclusive science is not hostile to religion. Yet it will transform current conceptions of religion as those others never did. In proportion as it is scientific it cannot be hostile. It may at most be indifferent. Nevertheless, in the long run, few will choose the theme of religion for the scientific labour of life who have not some interest in religion. Men of these three classes have accepted the doctrine of evolution. Comte thought he had discovered it. Spencer and those for whom we have taken him as type, did service in the elaboration of it. To the men of our third group, the truth of evolution seems no longer debatable. Here too, in the word ' evolution,' we have a term which has been used with laxity. It corresponds to a notion which has only gradually been evolved. Its implications were at first by no means understood. It was associated with a mechanical view of the universe which was diametrically opposed to its truth. Still, there could not be a doubt that the doctrine contravened those ideas as to the origin of the world, and more particularly of man, of the relations of species, and especially of the human species to other forms of animal life, which had immemorially prevailed in Christian circles and which had the witness of the Scriptures on their behalf. If we were to attempt, with acknowledged latitude, to name a book whose import might be said to be cardinal for the whole movement treated of in this chapter, that book would be Darwin's *Origin of Species*, which was published in 1859.

Long before Darwin the creation legend had been recognised as such. The astronomy of the seventeenth century had removed the earth from its central position. The geology of the eighteenth had shown how long must have been the ages of the laying down of the earth's strata. The question of the descent of man, however, brought home the significance of evolution for religion more forcibly than any other aspect of the debate had done. There were scientific men of distinction who were not convinced of the truth of the evolutionary hypothesis. To most Christian men the theory seemed to leave no unique distinction or spiritual quality for man. It seemed to render impossible faith in the Scriptures as revelation. To many it seemed that the whole issue as between a spiritual and a purely materialistic view of the universe was involved. Particularly was this true of the English-speaking peoples.

One other factor in the transformation of the Christian view needs to be dwelt upon. It is less theoretical than those upon which we have dwelt. It is the influence of socialism, taking that word in its largest sense. An industrial civilisation has developed both the good and the evil of individualism in incredible degree. The unity of society which the feudal system and the Church gave to Europe in the Middle Age had been destroyed. The individualism and democracy which were essential to Protestantism notoriously aided the civil and social revolution, but the centrifugal forces were too great. Initiative has been wonderful, but cohesion is lacking. Democracy is yet far from being realised. The civil liberations which were the great crises of the western world from 1640 to 1830 appear now to many as deprived of their fruit. Governments undertake on behalf of subjects that which formerly no government would have dreamed of doing. The demand is that the Church, too, become a factor in the furtherance of the outward and present welfare of mankind. If that meant the call to love and charity it would be an old refrain. That is exactly what it does not mean. It means the attack upon evils which make charity necessary. It means the taking up into the idealisation of religion the endeavour to redress all wrongs, to do away with all evils, to confer all goods, to create a new world and not, as heretofore, mainly at least, a new soul in the midst of the old world. No one can deny either the magnitude of the evils which it is sought to remedy, or the greatness of the goal which is thus set before religion. The volume of religious and Christian literature devoted to these social questions is immense. It is revolutionary in its effect. For, after all, the very gist of religion has been held to be that it deals primarily with the inner life and the transcendent world. That it has dealt with the problem of the inner life and transcendent world in such a manner as to retard, or even only not to further, the other aspects of man's life is indeed a grave indictment. That it should, however, see ends in the outer life and present world as ends fully sufficient in themselves, that it should cease to set these in the light of the eternal, is that it should cease to be religion. The physical and social sciences have given to men an outward setting in the world, a basis of power and happiness such as men never have enjoyed. Yet the tragic failure of our civilisation to give to vast multitudes that power and happiness, is the proof that something more than the outward basis is needed. The success of our civilisation is its failure. This is by no means a recurrence to the old antithesis of religion and civilisation, as if these were contradictory elements. On the contrary, it is but to show that the present world of religion and of economics are not two worlds, but merely different aspects of the same world. Therewith it is not alleged that religion has not a specific contribution to make.

POSITIVISM

The permanent influence of that phase of thought which called itself Positivism has not been great. But a school of thought which numbered among its adherents such men and women as John Stuart Mill, George Henry Lewes, George Eliot, Frederic Harrison, and Matthew Arnold, cannot be said to have been without significance. A book upon the translation of which Harriet Martineau worked with sustained enthusiasm cannot be dismissed as if it were merely a curiosity. Comte's work, *Cours de Philosophie Positive*, appeared between the years 1830 and 1842. Littré was his chief French interpreter. But the history of the positivist movement belongs to the history of English philosophical and religious thought, rather than to that of France.

Comte was born at Montpellier in 1798, of a family of intense Roman Catholic piety. He showed at school a precocity which might bear comparison with Mill's. Expelled from school, cast off by his parents, dismissed by the elder Casimir Périer, whose secretary he had been, he eked out a living by tutoring in mathematics. Friends of his philosophy rallied to his support. He never occupied a post comparable with his genius. He was unhappy in his marriage. He passed through a period of mental aberration, due, perhaps, to the strain under which he worked. He did not regain his liberty without an experience which embittered him against the Church. During the fourteen years of the production of his book he cut himself off from any reading save that of current scientific discovery. He came under the influence of Madame Vaux, whom, after her death, he idolised even more than before. For the problem which, in the earlier portion of his work, he set himself, that namely, of the organising of the sciences into a compact body of doctrine, he possessed extraordinary gifts. Later, he took on rather the air of a high priest of humanity, legislating concerning a new religion. It is but fair to say that at this point Littré and many others parted company with Comte. He developed a habit and practice ascetic in its rigour and mystic in its devotion to the positivists' religion—the worship of humanity. He was the friend and counsellor of working-men and agitators, of little children, of the poor and miserable. He ended his rather pathetic and turbulent career in 1857, gathering a few disciples about his bed as he remembered that Socrates had done.

Comte begins with the natural sciences and postulates the doctrine of evolution. To the definition of this doctrine he makes some interesting approaches. The discussion of the order and arrangement of the various sciences and of their characteristic differences is wonderful in its insight and suggestiveness. He asserts that in the study of nature we are concerned solely with the facts before us and the relations which connect those facts. We have nothing to do with the supposed essence or hidden nature and meaning of those facts. Facts and the invariable laws which govern them are the only legitimate objects of pursuit. Comte infers that because we can know, in this sense, only phenomena and their relations, we should in consequence guard against illusions which creep in again if we so much as use the words principle, or cause, or will, or force.   By phenomena must be understood objects of perception, to the exclusion, for example, of psychological changes reputed to be known in self-consciousness. That there is no knowledge but of the physical, that there is no knowing except by perception—this is ever reiterated as self-evident.   Even psychology, resting as it does largely upon the observation of the self by the self, must be illusive. Physiology, or even phrenology, with the value of which Comte was much impressed, must take its place.   Every object of knowledge is other than the knowing subject.   Whatever else the mind knows, it can never know itself.   By invincible necessity the human mind can observe all phenomena except its own.   Commenting upon this, James Martineau observed : ' We have had in the history of thought numerous forms of idealism which construed all outward phenomena as mere appearances within the mind.   We have hitherto had no strictly corresponding materialism, which claimed certainty for the outer world precisely because it was foreign to ourselves.'   Man is the highest product of nature, the highest stage of nature's most mature and complex form. Man as individual is nothing more.   Physiology gives us not merely his external constitution and one set of relations.   It is the whole science of man.   There is no study of mind in which its actions and states can be contemplated apart from the physical basis in conjunction with which mind exists.

Thus far man has been treated only biologically, as individual.   We must advance to man in society.   Almost one half of Comte's bulky work is devoted to this side of the inquiry.   Social phenomena are a class complex beyond any which have yet been investigated.   So much is this the case and so difficult is the problem presented, that Comte felt constrained in some degree to change his method.   We proceed from experience, from data in fact, as before.   But the facts are not mere illustrations of the so-called laws of individual human nature.   Social facts are the results also of situations which represent the accumulated influence of past generations. In this, as against Bentham, for example, with his endless recurrence to human nature, as he called it, Comte was right. Comte thus first gave the study of history its place in sociology. In this study of history and sociology, the collective phenomena are more accessible to us and better known by us, than are the parts of which they are composed. We therefore proceed here from the general to the particular, not from the particular to the general, as in research of the kinds previously named. The state of every part of the social organisation is intimately connected with the contemporaneous state of all the other parts. Philosophy, science, the fine arts, commerce, navigation, government, are all in close mutual dependence. When any considerable change takes place in one, we may know that a parallel change has preceded or will follow in the others. The progress of society is not the aggregate of partial changes, but the product of a single impulse acting through all the partial agencies. It can therefore be most easily traced by studying all together. These are the main principles of sociological investigation as set forth by Comte, some of them as they have been phrased by Mill.

The most sweeping exemplification of the axiom last alluded to, as to parallel changes, is Comte's so-called law of the three states of civilisation. Under this law, he asserts, the whole historical evolution can be summed up. It is as certain as the law of gravitation. Everything in human society has passed, as has the individual man, through the theological and then through the metaphysical stage, and so arrives at the positive stage. In this last stage of thought nothing either of superstition or of speculation will survive. Theology and metaphysics Comte repeatedly characterises as the two successive stages of nescience, unavoidable as preludes to science. Equally unavoidable is it that science shall ultimately prevail in their place. The advance of science having once begun, there is no possibility but that it will ultimately possess itself of all. One hears the echo of this confidence in Haeckel also. There is a persistence about the denial of any knowledge whatsoever that goes beyond

external facts, which ill comports with the pretensions of
positivism to be a philosophy.   For its final claim is not
that it is content to rest in experimental science.   On the
contrary, it would transform this science into a homogeneous
doctrine which is able to explain everything in the universe.
This is but a *tour de force*.   The promise is fulfilled through
the denial of the reality of everything which science cannot
explain.   Comte was never willing to face the fact that the
very existence of knowledge has a noumenal as well as a
phenomenal side.   The reasonableness of the universe is
certainly a conception which we bring to the observation of
nature.   If we did not thus bring it with us, no mere observation of nature would ever give it to us.   It is impossible for
science to get rid of the conception of force, and ultimately
of cause.   There can be no phenomenon which is not a manifestation of something.   The very nomenclature falls into
hopeless confusion without these conceptions.   Yet the
moment we touch them we transcend science and pass into
the realm of philosophy.   It is mere juggling with words to
say that our science has now become a philosophy.

The adjective ' positive ' contains the same fallacy.   Apparently Comte meant by the choice of it to convey the sense that
he would limit research to phenomena in their orders of resemblance, co-existence and succession.   But to call the inquiry
into phenomena positive, in the sense that it alone deals with
reality, to imply that the inquiry into causes deals with that
which has no reality, is to beg the question.   This is not a
premise with which he may set out in the evolution of his
system.

Comte denied the accusation of materialism and atheism.
He did the first only by changing the meaning of the term
materialism.   Materialism the world has supposed to be the
view of man's condition and destiny which makes these to
begin and end in nature.   That certainly was Comte's view.
The accusation of atheism also he avoids by a mere play on
words.   He is not without a God.   Humanity is God.   Mankind is the positivist's Supreme.   Altruism takes the place of
devotion.   The devotion so long wasted upon a mere creature

of the imagination, to whom it could do no good, he would now give to men who sorely need it and can obviously profit by it. Surely the antithesis between nature and the supernatural, in the form in which Comte argues against it, is now abandoned by thoughtful people. Equally the antithesis of altruism to the service of God is perverse. It arouses one's pity that Comte should not have seen how, in true religion these two things coalesce.

Moreover, this deification of mankind, in so far as it is not a sounding phrase, is an absurdity. When Comte says, for example, that the authority of humanity must take the place of that of God, he has recognised that religion must have authority. Indeed, the whole social order must have authority. However, this is not for him, as we are accustomed to say, the authority of the truth and of the right. There is no such abstraction as the truth, coming to various manifestations. There is no such thing as right, apart from relatively right concrete measures. There is no larger being indwelling in men. Society, humanity in its collective capacity, must, if need be, override the individual. Yet Comte despises the mere rule of majorities. The majority which he would have rule is that of those who have the scientific mind. We may admit that in this he aims at the supremacy of truth. But, in fact, he prepares the way for a doctrinaire tyranny which, of all forms of government, might easily turn out to be the worst which a long-suffering humanity has yet endured.

In the end, we are told, love is to take the place of force. Humanity is present to us first in our mothers, wives and daughters. For these it is present in their fathers, husbands, sons. From this primary circle love widens and worship extends as hearts enlarge. It is the prayer to humanity which first rises above the mere selfishness of the effort to get something out of God. Remembrance in the hearts of those who loved us and owe something to us is the only worthy form of immortality. Clearly it is only the caricature of prayer or of the desire of immortality which rises before Comte's mind as the thing to be escaped. For this caricature religious men, both Catholic and Protestant, without doubt, gave him cause. There were to be seven sacraments, corresponding to seven significant epochs in a man's career. There were to be priests for the performance of these sacraments and for the inculcation of the doctrines of positivism. There were to be temples of humanity, affording opportunity for and reminder of this worship. In each temple there was to be set up the symbol of the positivist religion, a woman of thirty years with her little son in her arms. Littré spoke bitterly of the positivist religion as a lapse of the author into his old aberration. This religion was certainly regarded as negligible by many to whom his system as a whole meant a great deal. At least, it is an interesting example, as is also his transformation of science into a philosophy, of the resurgence of valid elements in life, even in the case of a man who has made it his boast to do away with them.

NATURALISM AND AGNOSTICISM

We may take Spencer as representative of a group of men who, after the middle of the nineteenth century, laboured enthusiastically to set forth evolutionary and naturalistic theories of the universe. These theories had also, for the most part, the common trait that they professed agnosticism as to all that lay beyond the reach of the natural-scientific methods, in which the authors were adept. Both Ward and Boutroux accept Spencer as such a type. Agnosticism for obvious reasons could be no system. Naturalism is a tendency in interpretation of the universe which has many ramifications. There is no intention of making the reference to one man's work do more than serve as introduction to the field.

Spencer was eager in denial that he had been influenced by Comte. Yet there is a certain reminder of Comte in Spencer's monumental endeavour to systematise the whole mass of modern scientific knowledge, under the general title of ' A Synthetic Philosophy.' He would show the unity of the sciences and their common principles or, rather, the one great common principle which they all illustrate, the doctrine of

evolution, as this had taken shape since the time of Darwin.
Since 1904 we have an autobiography of Herbert Spencer,
which, to be sure, seems largely to have been written prior to
1889. The book is interesting, as well in the light which it
throws upon the expansion of the sciences and the development of the doctrine of evolution in those years, as in the
revelation of the personal traits of the man himself. Concerning these Tolstoi wrote to a friend, apropos of a gift of
the book : ' In autobiographies the most important psychological phenomena are often revealed quite independently
of the author's will.'

Spencer was born in 1820 in Derby, the son of a school-
master. He came of Nonconformist ancestry of most marked
individuality. His early education was irregular and inadequate. Before he reached the age of seventeen his reading had been immense. He worked with an engineer in the
period of the building of the railways in the Midlands. He
always retained his interest in inventions. He wrote for the
newspapers and magazines and definitely launched upon a
literary career. At the age of thirty he published his first
book, on *Social Statics*. He made friends among the most
notable men and women of his age. So early as 1855 he
was the victim of a disease of the heart which never left him.
It was on his recovery from his first grave attack that he
shaped the plan which henceforth held him, of organising the
modern sciences and incorporating them into what he called a
synthetic philosophy. There was immense increase in actual
knowledge and in the power of his reflection on that knowledge, as the years went by. A generation elapsed between
the publication of his *First Principles* and the conclusion of
his more formal literary labours. There is something cap-
tivating about a man's life, the energy of which remains so
little impaired that he esteems it better to write a new
book, covering some untouched portion of his scheme, than
to give to an earlier volume the revision which in the light
of his matured convictions it may need. His philosophical
limitations he never transcended. He does not so naïvely
offer a substitute for philosophy as does Comte. But he was

no master in philosophy. There is a reflexion of the consciousness of this fact in his agnosticism.

That the effect of the agnostic contention has been great, and on the whole salutary, few would deny. Spencer's own later work shows that his declaration, that the absolute which lies behind the universe is unknowable, is to be taken with considerable qualification. It is only a relative unknowableness which he predicates. Moreover, before Spencer's death the doctrine of evolution had made itself profoundly felt in the discussion of all aspects of life, including that of religion. There seemed no longer any reason for the barrier between science and religion which Spencer had once thought requisite.

The epithet agnostic, as applied to a certain attitude of scientific mind, is just, as over against excessive claims to valid knowledge made, now by theology and now by speculative philosophy. It is hardly descriptive in any absolute sense. Spencer had coined the rather fortunate illustration which describes science as a gradually increasing sphere, such that every addition to its surface does but bring us into more extensive contact with surrounding nescience. Even upon this illustration Ward has commented that the metaphor is misleading. The continent of our knowledge is not merely bounded by an ocean of ignorance. It is intersected and cut up by straits and seas of ignorance. The author of *Ecce Cœlum* has declared : ' Things die out under the microscope into the same unfathomed and, so far as we can see, unfathomable mystery, into which they die off beyond the range of our most powerful telescope.' This sense of the circumambient unknown has become cardinal with the best spirits of the age. Men have a more rigorous sense of what constitutes knowledge. They have reckoned more strictly with the methods by which alone secure and solid knowledge may be attained. They have undisguised scepticism as to alleged knowledge not arrived at in these ways. It was the working of these motives which gave to the labours of the middle of the nineteenth century so prevailingly the aspect of denial, the character which Carlyle described as an everlasting No. This was but a preparatory stage, a retrogression for a new and firmer advance.

In the sense of the recognition of our ignorance and of a becoming modesty of affirmation, over against the mystery into which all our thought runs out, we cannot reject the correction which agnosticism has administered. It is a fact which has had disastrous consequences, that precisely the department of thought, namely the religious, which one might suppose would most have reminded men of the outlying mystery, that phase of life whose very atmosphere is mystery, has most often been guilty of arrant dogmatism. It has been thus guilty upon the basis of the claim that it possessed a revelation. It has allowed itself unlimited licence of affirmation concerning the most remote and difficult matters. It has alleged miraculously communicated information concerning those matters. It has clothed with a divine authoritativeness, overriding the mature reflexion and laborious investigation of learned men, that which was, after all, nothing but the innocent imaginings of the childhood of the race. In this good sense of a parallel to that agnosticism which scientists profess for themselves within their own appointed realm, there is a religious agnosticism which is one of the best fruits of the labour of the age. It is not that religious men have abandoned the thought of revelation. They apprehended more justly the nature of revelation. They confess that there is much ignorance which revelation does not mitigate. *Exeunt omnia in mysterium.* They are prepared to say concerning many of the dicta of religiosity, that they cannot affirm their truth. They are prepared to say concerning the experience of God and the soul, that they know these with an indefeasible certitude. This just and wholesome attitude toward religious truth is only a corollary of the attitude which science has taught us toward all truth whatsoever.

The strictly philosophic term phenomenon, to which science has taken so kindly, is in itself an explicit avowal of something beyond the phenomenal. Spencer is careful to insist upon this relation of the phenomenal to the noumenal. His *Synthetic Philosophy* opens with an exposition of this non-relative or

absolute, without which the relative itself becomes contradictory. It is an essential part of Spencer's doctrine to
maintain that our consciousness of the absolute, indefinite as
it is, is positive and not negative. 'Though the absolute
cannot in any manner or degree be known, in the strict sense
of knowing, yet we find that its positive existence is a necessary datum of consciousness. The belief which this datum
of consciousness constitutes has a higher warrant than any
other belief whatsoever.' In short, the absolute or noumenal,
according to Spencer, though not known as the phenomenal
or relative is known, is so far from being for knowledge a
pure blank, that the phenomenal, which is said to be known,
is in the strict sense inconceivable without it. This actuality
behind appearances, without which appearances are unthink-
able, is by Spencer identified with that ultimate verity upon
which religion ever insists. Religion itself is a phenomenon,
and the source and secret of most complex and interesting
phenomena. It has always been of the greatest importance
in the history of mankind. It has been able to hold its own
in face of the attacks of science. It must contain an element
of truth. All religions, however, assert that their God is for
us not altogether cognisable, that God is a great mystery.
The higher their rank, the more do they acknowledge this.
It is by the flippant invasion of this mystery that the
popular religiosity offends. It talks of God as if he were a
man in the next street. It does not distinguish between
merely imaginative fetches into the truth, and presumably
accurate definition of that truth. Equally, the attempts
which are logically possible at metaphysical solutions of the
problem, namely, theism, pantheism, and atheism, if they are
consistently carried out, assert, each of them, more than we
know and are involved in contradiction with themselves.
But the results of modern physics and chemistry reveal, as
the constant element in all phenomena, force. This manifests itself in various forms which are interchangeable, while
amid all these changes the force remains the same. This
latter must be regarded as the reality, and basis of all that
is relative and phenomenal. The entire universe is to be

explained from the movements of this absolute force. The phenomena of nature and of mental life come under the same general laws of matter, motion, and force.

Spencer's doctrine, as here stated, is not adequate to account for the world of mental life or adapted to serve as the basis of a reconciliation of science and religion. It does not carry us beyond materialism. Spencer's real intention was directed to something higher than that. If the absolute is to be conceived at all, it is as a necessary correlative of our self-consciousness. If we get the idea of force from the experience of our own power of volition, is it not natural to think of mind-force as the prius of physical force, and not the reverse ? Accordingly, the absolute force, basis of all specific forces, would be mind and will. The doctrine of evolution would harmonise perfectly with these inferences. But it would have to become idealistic evolution, as in Schelling, instead of materialistic, as in Comte. We are obliged, Spencer owns, to refer the phenomenal world of law and order to a first cause. He says that this first cause is incomprehensible. Yet he further says, when the question of attributing personality to this first cause is raised, that the choice is not between personality and something lower. It is between personality and something higher. To this may belong a mode of being as much transcending intelligence and will as these transcend mechanical motion. It is strange, he says, that men should suppose the highest worship to lie in assimilating the object of worship to themselves. And yet, again, in one of the latest of his works he writes : ' Unexpected as it will be to most of my readers, I must assert that the power which manifests itself in consciousness is but a differently conditioned form of the power which manifests itself beyond consciousness. The conception to which the exploration of nature everywhere tends is much less that of a universe of dead matter than that of a universe everywhere alive.'

Similar is the issue in the reflexion of Huxley. Agnosticism had at first been asserted in relation to the spiritual and the teleological. It ended in fastening upon the material and mechanical. After all, says Huxley, in one of his essays :—

'What do we know of this terrible matter, except as a name for an unknown and hypothetical cause of states of our own consciousness ?   Again, what do we know of that spirit over whose threatened extinction by matter so great lamentation has now arisen, except that it is also a name for an unknown and hypothetical cause of states of our consciousness ? '   He concedes that matter is inconceivable apart from mind, but that mind is not inconceivable apart from matter.   He concedes that the conception of universal and necessary law is an ideal.   It is an invention of the mind's own devising.   It is not a physical fact.   In brief, taking agnostic naturalism just as it seemed disposed a generation ago to present itself, it now appears as if it had been turned exactly inside out. Instead of the physical world being primary and fundamental and the mental world secondary, if not altogether problematical, the precise converse is true.

Nature, as science regards it, may be described as a system whose parts, be they simple or complex, are wholly governed by universal laws.   Knowledge of these laws is an indispensable condition of that control of nature upon which human welfare in so large degree depends.   But this reign of law is an hypothesis.   It is not an axiom which it would be absurd to deny.   It is not an obvious fact, thrust upon us whether we will or no.   Experiences are possible without the conception of law and order.   The fruit of experience in knowledge is not possible without it.   That is only to say that the reason why we assume that nature is a connected system of uniform laws, lies in the fact that we ourselves are self-conscious personalities.   When the naturalists say that the notion of cause is a fetish, an anthropomorphic superstition which we must eliminate, we have to answer : ' from the realm of empirical science perhaps, but not from experience as a whole.'   Indeed, a glance at the history, and particularly at the popular literature, of science affords the interesting spectacle of the rise of an hallucination, the growth of a habit of mythological speech, which is truly surprising.   We begin to hear of self-existent laws which reign supreme and bind nature fast in fact.   By this learned substitution for God, it was once confidently assumed that the race was to emerge from mythical dawn and metaphysical shadows into the noonday of positive knowledge. Rather, it would appear that at this point a part of the human race plunged into a new era of myth-making and fetish worship—the homage to the fetish of law. Even the great minds do not altogether escape. ' Fact I know and law I know,' says Huxley, with a faint suggestion of sacred rhetoric. But surely we do not know law in the same sense in which we know fact. If there are no causes among our facts, then we do not know anything about the laws. If we do know laws it is because we assume causes. If, in the language of rational beings, laws of nature are to be spoken of as self-existent and independent of the phenomena which they are said to govern, such language must be merely analogous to the manner in which we often speak of the civil law. We say the law does that which we know the executive does. But the thorough-going naturalist cast off these implications as the last rags of a creed outworn. Physicists were fond of talking of the movement of molecules, just as the ancient astrologers imagined that the planets had souls and guided their own courses. We had supposed that this was anthropomorphism. In truth, this would-be scientific mode of speech is as anthropomorphic as is the cosmogony of Hesiod, only on a smaller scale. Primitive religion ascribed life to everything of which it talked. Polytheism in religion and independent forces and self-existent laws in science are thus upon a par. The gods many and lords many, so amenable to concrete presentation in poetry and art, have given place to one Supreme Being. So also light, heat, and other natural agencies, palpable and ready to hand for the explanation of everything, in the myth-making period of science which living men can still remember, have by this time paled. They have become simply various manifestations of one underlying spiritual energy, which is indeed beyond our perception.[1] When Comte said that the universe could not rest upon will, because then it would be arbitrary, incalculable, subject to caprice, one feels the humour and pathos

[1] Ward, *Naturalism and Agnosticism*, vol. ii. p. 248.

of it. Comte's experience with will, his own and that of others, had evidently been too largely of that sad sort. Real freedom consists in conformity to what ought to be. In God, whom we conceive as perfect, this conformity is complete. With us it remains an ideal. Were we the creatures of a blind mechanical necessity there could be no talk of ideal standards and no meaning in reason at all.

EVOLUTION

In the progress of the thought of the generation, say, from 1870 to the present day, the conception of evolution has been much changed. The doctrine of evolution has itself been largely evolved within that period. The application of it has become familiar in fields of which there was at first no thought. The bearing of the acceptance of it upon religion has been seen to be quite different from that which was at first supposed. The advocacy of the doctrine was at first associated with the claims of naturalism or positivism. Wider applications of the doctrine and deeper insight into its meaning have done away with this misunderstanding. Evolution, as originally understood, was as far as possible from suggesting anything mechanical. By the term was meant primarily the gradual unfolding of a living germ from its embryonic beginning to its mature and final stage. This adult form was regarded not merely as the goal actually reached through successive stages of growth. It was conceived as the end aimed at, and achieved through the force of some vital or ideal principle shaping the plastic material and directing the process of growth. In short, evolution implied ideal ends controlling physical means. Yet we find with Spencer, as prevailingly also with others in the study of the natural sciences, the ideas of end and of cause looked at askance. They are regarded as outside the pale of the natural sciences. In a very definite sense that is true. The logical consequence of this admission should be merely the recognition that the idea of evolution as developed in the natural sciences can-not be the whole idea.

The entire history of anything, Spencer tells us, must include its appearance out of the imperceptible, and its disappearance again into the imperceptible. Be it a single object, or the whole universe, an account which begins with it in a concrete form, or leaves off with its concrete form, is incomplete. He uses a familiar instance, that of a cloud appearing when vapour drifts over a cold mountain top, and again disappearing when it emerges into warmer air. The cloud emerges from the imperceptible as heat is dissipated. It is dissolved again as heat is absorbed and the watery particles evaporate. Spencer esteems this an analogue of the appearance of the universe itself, according to the nebular hypothesis. Yet assuredly, as the cl)ud presupposes vapours which had previously condensed, and the vapour clouds that had previously evaporated, and as clouds dissolve in one place even at the moment that they are forming in another, so we are told of nebulæ which are in every phase of advance or of decline. To ask which was first, solid masses or nebulous haze, is much like recurring to the riddle of the hen and the egg. Still, we are told, we have but to extend our thought beyond this emergence and subsidence of sidereal systems, of continents, nations, men, to find a permanent totality made up of transient individuals in every stage of change. The physical assumption with which Spencer sets out is that the mass of the universe and its energy are fixed in quantity. All the phenomena of evolution are included in the conservation of this matter and force.

Besides the criticism which was offered above, that the mere law of the persistence of force does not initiate our series, there is a further objection. Even within the series, once it has been started, this law of the persistence of force is solely a quantitative law. When energy is transformed there is an equivalence between the new form and the old. Of the reasons for the direction evolution takes, for the permanence of that direction once it has been taken, so that the sequence of forms is a progression, the explication of a latent nature —of all this, the mere law of the persistence of force gives us no explanation whatever. The change at random from one

form of manifestation to another might be a striking illustration of the law of the persistence of force, but it would be
the contradiction of evolution. The very notion of evolution
is that of the sequence of forms, so that something is expressed
or achieved. That achievement implies more than the mere
force. Or rather, it involves a quality of the force with which
the language of mechanism does not reckon. It assumes the
idea which gives direction to the force, an ideal quality of
the force.

Unquestionably that which men sought to be rid of was
the idea of purpose in nature, in the old sense of design in the
mind of God, external to the material universe, of force
exerted upon nature from without, so as to cause nature to
conform to the design of its ' Great Original,' in Addison's
high phrase. In this effort, however, the reducing of all to mere
force and permutation of force, not merely explains nothing,
but contradicts facts which stare us in the face. It deprives
evolution of the quality which makes it evolution. To put in
this incongruous quality at the beginning, because we find
it necessary at the end, is, to say the least, naïve. To deny
that we have put it in, to insist that in the marvellous
sequence we have only an illustration of mechanism and of
conservation of force, is perverse. We passed through an
era in which some said that they did not believe in God ;
everything was accounted for by evolution. In so far as they
meant that they did not believe in the God of deism and of
much traditional theology, they did not stand alone in this
claim. In so far as they meant by evolution mere mechanism,
they explained nothing and destroyed the notion of evolution
besides. In so far as they meant more than mere mechanism,
they lapsed into the company of the scientific myth-makers
to whom we alluded above. They attributed to their abstraction, evolution, qualities which other people found in
the forms of the universe viewed as the manifestation of an
immanent God. Only by so doing were they able to ascribe
to evolution that which other people describe as the work
of God. At this level the controversy becomes one simply
about words.

Of course, the great illumination as to the meaning of evolution has come with its application to many fields besides the physical. Darwin was certainly the great inaugurator of the evolutionary movement in England. Still, Darwin's problem was strictly limited. The impression is widespread that the biological evolutionary theories were first developed, and furnished the basis for the others. Yet both Hegel and Comte, not to speak of Schelling, were far more interested in the intellectual and historical, the ethical and social aspects of the question. Both Hegel and Comte were, whether rightly or wrongly, rather contemptuous of the appeal to biology and organic life. Both had the sense that they used a great figure of speech when they spoke of society as an organism, and compared the working of institutions to biological functions. This is indeed the question. It is a question over which Spencer sets himself lightly. He passes back and forth between organic evolution and the ethical, economic, and social movements which are described by the same term, as if we were in possession of a perfectly safe analogy, or rather as if we were assured of an identical principle. Much that is already archaic in Spencer's economic and social, his historical and ethical, not to say his religious, chapters is due to the influence of this fact. Of his own mind it was true that he had come to the doctrine of evolution from the physical side. He brought to his other subjects a more or less developed method of operating with the conception. He never fully realised how new subjects would alter the method and transform the conception. Spencerian evolution is an assertion of the all-sufficiency of natural law. The authority of conscience is but the experience of law-abiding and dutiful generations flowing in our veins. The public weal has hold over us, because the happiness and misery of past ages are inherited by us.

It marked a great departure when Huxley began vigorously to dissent from these views. According to him evolutionary science has done nothing for ethics. Men become ethical only as they set themselves against the principles embodied in the evolutionary process of the world. Evolution is the struggle for existence. It is preposterous to say that man became good by succeeding in the struggle for existence. Instead of the old single movement, as in Spencer, straight from the nebula to the saint, Huxley has place for suffering. Suffering is most intense in man precisely under conditions most essential to the evolution of his nobler powers. The loss of ease or money may be gain in character. The cosmical process is not only full of pain. It is full of mercilessness and of wickedness. Good has been evolved, but so has evil. The fittest may have survived. There is no guarantee that they are the best. The continual struggle against our fellows poisons our higher life. It will hardly do to say with Huxley that the ethical struggle is the reverse of the cosmical process. Nevertheless, we have here a most interesting transformation in thought.

These ideas and principles, as is well known, were elaborated and advanced upon in a very popular book, Drummond's *Ascent of Man*, 1894. Even the title was a happy and suggestive one. Struggle for life is a fact, but it is not the whole fact. It is balanced by the struggle for the life of others. This latter reaches far down into the levels of what we call brute life. Its divinest reach is only the fulfilment of the real nature of humanity. It is the living with men which develops the moral in man. The prolongation of infancy in the higher species has had to do with the development of moral nature. So only that we hold a sufficiently deep view of reason, provided we see clearly that reason transforms, perfects, makes new what we inherit from the beast, we need not fear for morality, though it should universally be taught that morality came into being by the slow and gradual fashioning of brute impulse.

Benjamin Kidd in his *Social Evolution*, 1895, has reverted again to extreme Darwinism in morals and sociology. The law is that of unceasing struggle. Reason does not teach us to moderate the struggle. It but sharpens the conflict. All religions are præter-rational, Christianity most of all, in being the most altruistic. Kidd, not without reason, comments bitterly upon Spencer's Utopia, the passage of militarism into industrialism. The struggle in industrialism is fiercer than ever. Reason affects the animal nature of man for the worse. Clearly conscious of what he is doing, man objects to sacrificing himself for his family or tribe. Instinct might lead an ape to do that. Intelligence warns a man against it. Reason is cruel beyond anything dreamed of in the beast. That portion of the community which loves to hear the abuse of reason, rejoiced to hear this phrase. They rejoiced when they heard that religion was the only remedy, and that religion was ultra-rational, contra-rational, supernatural, in this new sense. How one comes by it, or how one can rationally justify the yielding of allegiance to it, is not clear. One must indeed have the will to believe if one believes on these terms.

These again are but examples. They convey but a superficial impression of the effort to apply the conception of evolution to the moral and religious life of man. All this has taken place, of course, in a far larger setting—that of the endeavour to elaborate the evolutionary view of politics and of the state, of economics and of trade, of social life and institutions, of culture and civilisation in every aspect. This elaboration and reiteration of the doctrine of evolution sometimes wearies us. It is but the unwearied following of the main clue to the riddle of the universe which the age has given us. It is nothing more and nothing less than the endeavour to apprehend the ideal life, no longer as something held out to us, set up before us, but also as something working within us, realising itself through us and among us. To deny the affinity of this with religion would be fatuous and also futile. Temporarily, at least, and to many interests of religion, it would be fatal.

MIRACLES

It must be evident that the total view of the universe which the acceptance of the doctrine of evolution implies, has had effect in the diminution of the acuteness of the question concerning miracles. It certainly gives to that question a new form. A philosophy which asserts the constant presence of God in nature and the whole life of the world, a criticism which has given us a truer notion of the documents which record the biblical miracles, the reverent sense of ignorance which our increasing knowledge affords, have tended to diminish the dogmatism of men on either side of the debate. The contention on behalf of the miracle, in the traditional sense of the word, once seemed the bulwark of positive religion, the distinction between the man who was satisfied with a naturalistic explanation of the universe and one whose devout soul asked for something more. On the other hand, the contention against the miracle appeared to be a necessary corollary of the notion of a law and order which are inviolable throughout the universe. Furthermore, many men have come of themselves to the conclusion for which Schleiermacher long ago contended. Whatever may be theoretically determined concerning miracles, yet the miracle can never again be regarded as among the foundations of faith. This is for the simplest of reasons. The belief in a miracle presupposes faith. It is the faith which sustains the miracle, and not the miracle the faith. Jesus is to men the incomparable moral and spiritual magnitude which he is, not on the evidence of some unparalleled things physical which it is alleged he did. Quite the contrary, it is the immediate impression of the moral and spiritual wonder which Jesus is, that prepares what credence we can gather for the wonders which it is declared he did. This is a transfer of emphasis, a redistribution of weight in the structure of our thought, the relief of which many appreciate who have not reasoned the matter through for themselves.

Schleiermacher had said, and Herrmann and others repeat the thought, that, as the Christian faith finds in Christ the highest revelation, miracles may reasonably be expected of him. Nevertheless, he adds, these deeds can be called miracles or esteemed extraordinary, only as containing something which was beyond contemporary knowledge of the regular and orderly connexion between physical and spiritual life. Therewith, it must be evident, that the notion of the miraculous is fundamentally changed. So it comes to pass that we have a book like Mackintosh's *Natural History of the Christian Religion*, 1894, whose avowed purpose is to do away with the miraculous altogether. Of course, the author means the traditional notion of the miraculous, according to which it is the essence of arbitrariness and the negation of law. It is not that he has less sense for the divine life of the world, or for the quality of Christianity as revelation. On the other hand, we have a book like Percy Gardner's *Exploratio Evangelica*, 1899. With the most searching criticism of the narratives of some miracles, there is reverent confession, on the author's part, that he is baffled by the reports of others. There is recognition of unknown possibilities in the case of a character like that of Jesus. It is not that Gardner has a less stringent sense of fact and of the inexorableness of law than has Mackintosh or an ardent physicist. The problem is reduced to that of the choice of expression. We are not able to withhold a justification of the scholar who declares : We must not say that we believe in the miraculous. This language is sure to be appropriated by those who still take their departure from the old dualism, now hopelessly obsolete, for which a breach of the law of nature was the crowning evidence of the love of God. On the other hand, the assertion that we do not believe in the miraculous will easily be taken by some to mean the denial of the whole sense of the nearness and power and love of God, and of the unimagined possibilities of such a moral nature as was that of Christ. It is to be repeated that we have here a mere difference as to terms. The debate is no longer about ideas.

The traditional notion of the miracle arose out of the confusion of two series of ideas which, in the last analysis, have nothing to do with each other. On the one hand, there is the conception of law and order, of cause and effect, of the unbroken connexion of nature. On the other hand is the thought of the divine purpose in the life of the world and of the individual. By the aid of that first sequence of thoughts we find ourselves in the universe and interpret the world of fact to ourselves. Yet in the other sequence lies the essence of religion. The two sequences may perfectly well coexist

M

in the same mind. Out of the attempt to combine them nothing clear or satisfying can issue. If one should be, to-day, brought face to face with a fact which was alleged to be a miracle, his instinctive effort would be, nevertheless, to seek to find its cause, to establish for it a connexion in the natural order. In the ancient world men did not argue thus, nor in the modern world until less than two hundred years ago. The presumption of the order of nature had not assumed for them the proportions which it has for us. For us it is overwhelming, self-evident. Therewith is not involved that we lack belief in a divine purpose for the world and for the individual life.

We do not deny that there are laws of nature of which we have no experience, facts which we do not understand, events which, if they should occur, would stand before us as unique. Still, the decisive thing is, that in face of such an event, instead of viewing it quite simply as a divine intervention, as men used to do, we, with equal simplicity and no less devoutness, conceive that same event as only an illustration of a connexion in nature which we do not understand. There is no inherent reason why we may not understand it. When we do understand it, there will be nothing more about it that is conceivably miraculous. There will be then no longer a unique quality attaching to the event. Therewith ends the possible significance of such an event as proof of divine intervention for our especial help. We have but a connexion in nature such that, whether understood or not, if it were to recur, the event would recur.

The miracles which are related in the Scripture may be divided for our consideration into three classes. To the first class belong most of those which are related in the Old Testament, but some also which are conspicuous in the New Testament. They are, in some cases, the poetical and imaginative representation of the profoundest religious ideas. So soon as one openly concedes this, when there is no longer any necessity either to attack or to defend the miracle in question, one is in a position to acknowledge how deep and wonderful the thoughts often are and how beautiful the form in which they are conveyed. It is through imagination and symbolism that we are able to convey the subtlest meanings which we have. Still more was this the case with men of an earlier age. In the second place, the narratives of miracles are, some of them, of such a sort that we may say that an event or circumstance in nature has been obviously apprehended in naïve fashion. This by no means forbids us to interpret that same event in quite a different way. The men of former time, exactly in proportion as they had less sense of the order of nature than have we, so were they also far readier to assume the immediate forthputting of the power of God. This was true not merely of the uneducated. It is difficult, or even impossible, for us to find out what the event was. Fact and apprehension are inextricably interwoven. That which really happened is concealed from us by the tale which had intended to reveal it. In the third place, there are many cases in the history of Jesus, and some in that of the apostles and prophets, in which that which is related moves in the borderland between body and soul, spirit and matter, the region of the influence of will, one's own or that of another, over physical conditions. Concerning such cases we are disposed, far more than were men even a few years ago, to concede that there is much that is by no means yet investigated, and the soundest judgment we can form is far from being sure. Even if we recognise to the full the lamentable resurgence of outworn superstitions and stupidities, which again pass current among us for an unhappy moment, if we detect the questionable or manifestly evil consequences of certain uses made or alleged of psychic influence, yet still we are not always in a position to say, with certainty, what is true in tales of healing which we hear in our own day. There are certain of the statements concerning Jesus' healing power and action which are absolutely baffling. They can be eliminated from the narrative only by a procedure which might just as well eliminate the narrative. In many of the narratives there may be much that is true. In some all may be as related. In Jesus' time, on the witness of the Scripture itself, it was assumed as something no one questioned, that miraculous deeds were performed, not alone by Jesus and the apostles, but by many others, and not always even by the good. Such deeds were performed through the power of evil spirits as well as by the power of God. To imagine that the working of miracles proved that Jesus came from God, is the most patent importation of a modern apologetic notion into the area of ancient thought. We must remember that Jesus himself laid no great weight upon the miracles which we assume that he believed he wrought, and some of which we may believe that he did work. Many he performed with hesitation and desired so far as possible to conceal.

Even if we were in a position at one point or another in the life of Jesus to defend the traditional assumptions concerning the miraculous, yet it must be evident how opposed it is to right reason, to lay stress on the abstract necessity of belief in the miraculous. The traditional conception of the miraculous is done away for us. This is not at all by the fact that we are in a position to say with Matthew Arnold : ' The trouble with miracles is that they never happen.' We do not know enough to say that. To stake all on the assertion of the impossibility of so-called miracles is as foolish as to stake much on the affirmation of their actuality. The connexion of nature is only an induction. This can never be complete. The real question is both more complex and also more simple. The question is whether, even if an event, the most unparalleled of those related in the Gospels or outside of them, should be proved before our very eyes to have taken place, the question is whether we should believe it to have been a miracle in the traditional sense, an event in which the actual—not the known, but the possible—order of nature had been broken through, and in the old sense, God had arbitrarily supervened.

Allowed that the event were, in our own experience and in the known experience of the race, unparalleled, yet it would never occur to us to suppose but that there was a law of this case, also, a connexion in nature in which, as work of God, it occurred, and in which, if the conditions were repeated, it would recur. We should unceasingly endeavour through observation, reflexion, and new knowledge, to show how we might subordinate this event in the connexion of nature which we assume. We should feel that we knew more, and not less, of God, if we should succeed. And if our effort should prove altogether futile, we should be no less sure that such natural connexion exists. This is because nature is for us the revelation of the divine. The divine, we assume, has a natural order of working. Its inviolability is the divinest thing about it. It is through this sequence of ideas that we are in a position to deny, not facts which may be inexplicable, but the traditional conception of the miracle. For surely no one needs to be told that this is not the conception of the miracle which has existed in the minds of the devout, and equally of the undevout, from the beginning of thought until the present day.

However, there is nothing in all of this which hinders us from believing with a full heart in the love and grace and care of God, in his holy and redeeming purpose for mankind and for the individual. It is true that this belief cannot any longer retain its naïve and childish form. It is true that it demands of a man far more of moral force, of ethical and spiritual mastery, of insight and firm will, to sustain the belief in the purpose of God for himself and for all men, when a man believes that he sees and feels God only in and through nature and history, through personal consciousness and the personal consciousness of Jesus. It is true that it has, apparently, been easier for men to think of God as outside and above his world, and of themselves as separated from their fellows by his special providence. It is more difficult, through glad and intelligent subjection to all laws of nature and of history, to achieve the education of one's spirit, to make good one's inner deliverance from the world, to aid others in the same struggle and to set them on their way to God. Men grow uncertain within themselves, because they say that traditional religion has apprehended the matter in a different way. This is true. It is also misleading. Whatever miracles Jesus may have performed, no one can say that he performed them to make life easier for himself, to escape the common lot, to avoid struggle, to evade suffering and disgraceful death. On the contrary, in genuine human self-distrust, but also in genuine heroism, he gave himself to his vocation, accepting all that went therewith, and finished the work of God which he had made his own. This is the more wonderful because it lay so much nearer to him than it can lie to us, to pray for special evidence of the love of God and to set his faith on the receiving of it. He had not the conception of the relation of God to nature and history which we have.

We may well view the modern tendency to belief in healings through prayer, suggestion and faith, as an intelligible, an interesting, and in part, a touching manifestation. Of course there is mingled with it much dense ignorance, some superstition and even deception. Yet behind such a phenomenon there is meaning. Men of this mind make earnest with the thought that God cares for them. Without that thought there is no religion. They have been taught to find the evidence of God's love and care in the unusual. They are quite logical. It has been a weak point of the traditional belief that men have said that in the time of Christ there were miracles, but since that time, no more. Why not, if we can only in spirit come near to Christ and God ? They are quite logical also in that they have repudiated modern science. To be sure, no inconsiderable part of them use the word science continually. But the very esoteric quality of their science is that it means something which no one else ever understood that it meant. In reality their breach with science is more radical than their breach with Christianity. They feel the contradiction in which most men are bound fast, who will let science have its way, up to a certain point, but who beyond that, would retain the miracle. Dimly the former appreciate that this position is impossible. They leave it to other men to become altogether scientific if they wish. For themselves they prefer to remain religious. What a revival of ancient superstitions they have brought to pass, is obvious. Still we shall never get beyond such adventurous and preposterous endeavours to rescue that which is inestimably precious in religion, until the false antithesis between reason and faith, the lying contradiction between the providence of God and the order of nature, is overcome. Some science mankind apparently must have. Altogether without religion the majority, it would seem, will never be. How these are related, the one to the other, not every one sees. Many attempt their admixture in unhappy ways. They might try letting them stand in peace as complement and supplement the one to the other. Still better, they may perhaps some day see how each penetrates, permeates and glorifies the other.

THE SOCIAL SCIENCES

We said that the last generation had been characterised by an unexampled concentration of intellectual interest upon problems presented by the social sciences. With this has gone an unrivalled earnestness in the interpretation of religion as a social force. The great religious enthusiasm has been that of the application of Christianity to the social aspects of life. This effort has furnished most of the watchwords of religious teaching. It has laid vigorous, not to say violent, hands on religious institutions. It has given a new perspective to effort and a new impulse to devotion. The revival of religion in our age has taken this direction, with an exclusiveness which has had both good and evil consequences. Yet, before all, it should be made clear that it constitutes a religious revival. Some are deploring the prostrate condition of spiritual interests. If one judged only by conventional standards, they have much evidence upon their side. Some are seeking to galvanise religious life by recurrence to evangelistic methods successfully operative half a century ago. The outstanding fact is that the age shows immense religious vitality, so soon as one concedes that it must be allowed to show its vitality in its own way. It is the age of the social question. One must be ignorant indeed of the activity of the churches and of the productivity of religious thinkers, if he does not own that in Christian circles also no questions are so rife as these. Whether the panaceas have been all wise or profitable may be questioned. Whether the interest has not been even excessive and one-sided, whether the accusation has not been occasionally unjust and the self-accusation morbid, these are questions which it might be possible in some quarters to ask. This is, however, only another form of proof of what we say. The religious interest in social questions has not been aroused primarily by intellectual and scientific impulses, nor fostered mainly by doctrinaire discussion. On the contrary, the initiative has been from the practical side. It has been a question of life and service. If anything, one often misses the scientific note in the flood of semi-religious literature relating to this theme, the realisation that, to do well, it is often profitable to think. Yet there is effort to mediate the best results of social-scientific thinking, through clerical education and directly to the laity. On the other hand, a deep sense of ethical and spiritual responsibility is prevalent among thinkers upon social topics.

Often indeed has the quality of Christianity been observed which is here exemplified. Each succeeding age has read into Christ's teachings, or drawn out from his example, the special meaning which that generation, or that social level, or that individual man had need to draw. To them in their enthusiasm it has often seemed as if this were the only lesson reasonable men could draw. Nothing could be more enlightening than is reflexion upon this reading of the ever-changing ideals of man's life into Christianity, or of Christianity into the ever-advancing ideals of man's life. This chameleonlike quality of Christianity is the farthest possible remove from the changelessness which men love to attribute to religion. It is the most wonderful quality which Christianity possesses. It is precisely because of the recognition of this capacity for change that one may safely argue the continuance of Christianity in the world. Yet also because of this recognition, one is put upon his guard against joining too easily in the clamour that a past apprehension of religion was altogether wrong, or that a new and urgent one, in its exclusive emphasis and its entirety, is right. Our age is haunted by the sense of terrific social and economic inequalities which prevail. It has set its heart upon the elimination of these inequalities. It is an age whose disrespect for religion is in some part due to the fact that religion has not done away with these inequalities. It is an age which is immediately interested in an interpretation of religion which will make central the contention that, before all things else, these inequalities must be done away. If religion can be made a means of every man's getting his share of the blessings of this world, well and good. If not, there are many men and women to whom religion seems utterly meaningless.

This sentence hardly overstates the case. It is the challenge of the age to religion to do something which the age profoundly needs, and which religion under its age-long dominant apprehension has not conspicuously done, nor even on a great scale attempted. It is the challenge to religion to undertake a work of surpassing grandeur—nothing less than the actualisation of the whole ideal of the life of man. Religious men respond with the quickened and conscientious conviction, not indeed that they have laid too great an emphasis upon the spiritual, but that under a dualistic conception of God and man and world, they have never sufficiently realised that the spiritual is to be realised in the material, the ideal in and not apart from the actual, the eternal in and not after the temporal. Yet with that oscillatory quality which belongs to human movements, especially where old wrongs and errors have come deeply to be felt, a part of the literature of the contention shows marked tendency to extremes. A religion in the body must become a religion of the body. A Christianity of the social state runs risk of being apprehended as merely one more means for compassing outward and material ends. Religion does stand for the inner life and the transcendent world, only not an inner life through the neglect of the outer, or a transcendent world in some far-off star or after an æon or two. There might be meaning in the argument that, exactly because so many other forces in our age do make for the realisation of the outer life and present world with an effectiveness and success which no previous age has ever dreamed,

there is the more reason, and not the less, why religion should
still be religion. Exactly this is the contention of Eucken in
one of the most significant contributions of recent years to
the philosophy of religion, his *Wahrheitsgehalt der Religion*,
1901, transl. Jones, 1911. The very source and cause of the
sure recovery of religion in our age will be the experience
of the futility, the bankruptcy, of a civilisation without
faith. No nobler argument has been heard in our time
for the spiritual meaning of religion, with the fullest recognition of all its other meanings.

The modern emphasis on the social aspects of religion may be
said to have been first clearly expressed in Seeley's *Ecce Homo*,
1867. The pith of the book is in this phrase : ' To reorganise
society and to bind the members of it together by the closest
ties was the business of Jesus' life.' Allusion has been made
to Fremantle's *The World as the Subject of Redemption*, 1885.
Worthy of note is also Fairbairn's *Religion in History and
Modern Life*, 1894 ; pre-eminently so is Bosanquet's *The
Civilisation of Christendom*, 1893. Westcott's *Incarnation
and Common Life*, 1893, contains utterances of weight.
Peabody, in his book, *Jesus Christ and the Social Question*,
1905, has given, on the whole, the best résumé of the discussion. He conveys incidentally an impression of the body
of literature produced in recent years, in which it is assumed,
sometimes with embitterment, that the centre of gravity of
Christianity is outside the Church. Sell, in the very title
of his illuminating little book, *Christenthum und Welt-
geschichte seit der Reformation : das Christenthum in seiner
Entwickelung über die Kirche hinaus*, 1910, records an impression, which is widespread and true, that the characteristic
mark of modern Christianity is that it has transcended the
organs and agencies officially created for it. It has become
non-ecclesiastical, if not actually hostile to the Church. It
has permeated the world in unexpected fashion and does
the deeds of Christianity, though rather eager to avoid the
name. The anti-clericalism of the Latin countries is not unintelligible, the anti-ecclesiasticism of the Teutonic not without
a cause. German socialism, ever since Karl Marx, has been

fundamentally antagonistic to any religion whatsoever. It is
purely secularist in tone. This is also a strained situation,
liable to become perverse. That part of the Christian Church
which understands itself, rejoices in nothing so much as in the
fact that the spirit of Christ is so widely disseminated, his
influence felt by many who do not know what influence it is
which they feel, his work done by vast numbers who would
never call themselves his workers. That part of the Church is
not therewith convinced but that there is need of the Church
as institution, and of those who are consciously disciples of
Jesus in the world.

By far the largest question, however, which is raised in this
connexion, is one different from any thus far intimated. It
is, perhaps, the last question one would have expected the
literature of the social movement to raise. It is, namely, the
question of the individual. Ever since the middle of the
eighteenth century a sort of universalistic optimism, to
which the individual is sacrificed, has obtained. Within
the period of which this book treats the world has won an
enlargement of horizon of which it never dreamed. It has
gained a forecast of the future of culture and civilisation
which is beyond imagination. The access of comfort makes
men at home in the world as they never were at home. There
has been set a value on this life which life never had before.
The succession of discoveries and applications of discovery
makes it seem as if there were to be no end in this direction.
From Rousseau to Spencer men have elaborated the view
that the historical process cannot really issue in anything
else than in ever higher stages of perfection and of happiness.
They postulate a continuous enhancement of energy and a
steady perfecting of intellectual and moral quality. As the
goal of evolution appears an ideal condition which is either
indefinitely remote, that is, which gives room for the bliss of
infinite progress in its direction, or else a definitely attainable
condition, which would have within itself the conditions of
perpetuity.

The resistlessness with which this new view of the life of
civilisation has won acknowledgment from men of all classes

is amazing. It rests upon a belief in the self-sufficiency and the all-sufficiency of the life of this world, of the bearings of which it may be assumed that few of its votaries are aware. In reality this view cannot by any possibility be described as the result of knowledge. On the contrary, it is a venture of faith. It is the peculiar, the very characteristic and suggestive form which the faith of our age takes. Men believe in this indefinite progress of the world and of mankind, because without postulating such progress they do not see how they can assume the absolute worth of an activity which is yet the only thing which has any interest to most of them. Under this view one can assign to the individual life a definite significance, only upon the supposition that the individual is the organ of realisation of a part of this progress of mankind. All happiness and suffering, all changes in knowledge and manner of conduct, are supposed to have no worth each for itself or for the sake of the individual, but only for their relation to the movement as a whole. Surely this is an illusion. Exactly that in which the characteristic quality of the world and of life is found, the individual personalities, the single generations, the concrete events—these lose, in this view, their own particular worth. What can possibly be the worth of a whole of which the parts have no worth ? We have here but a parallel on a huge scale of that deadly trait in our own private lives, according to which it makes no difference what we are doing, so only that we are doing, or whither we are going, so only that we cease-not to go, or what our noise is all about, so only that there be no end of the noise. Certainly no one can establish the value of the evolutionary process in· and of itself.

If the movement as a whole has no definite end that has absolute worth, then it has no worth except as the stages, the individual factors included in it, attain to something within themselves which is of increasing worth. If the movement achieves this, then it has worth, not otherwise. We may illustrate this question by asking ourselves concerning the existence and significance of suffering and of the evil and of the bad which are in the world, in their relation to this tendency to indefinite progress which is supposed to be inherent in civilisation. On this theory we have to say that the suffering of the individual is necessary for the development and perfecting of the whole. As over against the whole the individual has no right to make demands as to welfare or happiness. The bad also becomes only relative. In the movement taken as a whole, it is probably unavoidable. In any case it is negligible, since the movement is irresistible. All ethical values are absorbed in the dynamic ones, all personal values in the collective ones. Surely the sole intelligent question about any civilisation is, what sort of men does it produce. If it produces worthless individuals, it is so far forth a worthless civilisation. If it has sacrificed many worthy men in order to produce this ignoble result, then it is more obviously ignoble than ever.

Furthermore, this notion of an inherent necessity and an irresistible tendency to progress is a chimera. The progress of mankind is a task. It is something to which the worthy human spirit is called upon to make contribution. The unworthy never hear the call. Progress is not a natural necessity. It is an ethical obligation. It is a task which has been fulfilled by previous generations in varying degrees of perfectness. It will be participated in by succeeding generations with varying degrees of wisdom and success. But as to there being anything autonomous about it, this is sheer hallucination, myth-making again, on the part of those who boast that they despise the myth, miracle-mongering on the part of those who have abjured the miracle, nonsense on the part of those who boast that they alone are sane. There is no ultimate source of civilisation but the individual, as there is also no issue of civilisation but in individuals. Men, characters, personalities, are the makers of it. Men are the product which is made. The higher stages and achievements of the life of society have come to pass always and only upon condition that single personalities have recognised the problem, seen their individual duty and known how to inspire others with enthusiasm. Periods of decline are always those in which this personal element cannot make itself felt. Demo-

cracies and periods of the intensity of emphasis upon the
social movement, tend directly to the depression and sup-
pression of personality.[1]   Such reflexions will have served
their purpose if they give us some clear sense of what we have
to understand as the effect of the social movement on religion.
They may give also some forecast of the effect of real religion
on the social movement.   For religion is the relation of God
and personality.   It can be social only in the sense that
society, in all its normal relations, is the sphere within which
that relation of God and personality is to be wrought out.

[1] Siebeck, *Religionsphilosophie*, 1893, s. 407.

CHAPTER VI

THE ENGLISH-SPEAKING PEOPLES: ACTION AND REACTION

IN those aspects of our subject with which we have thus far dealt, leadership has been largely with the Germans. Effort was indeed made in the chapter on the sciences to illustrate the progress of thought by reference to British writers. In this department the original and creative contribution of British authors was great. There were, however, also in the earlier portion of the nineteenth century movements of religious thought in Great Britain and America related to some of those which we have previously considered. Moreover, one of the most influential movements of English religious thought, the so-called Oxford Movement, with the Anglo-Catholic revival which it introduced, was of a reactionary tendency. It has seemed, therefore, feasible to append to this chapter that which we must briefly say concerning the general movement of reaction which marked the century. This reactionary movement has indeed everywhere run parallel to the one which we have endeavoured to record. It has often with vigour run counter to our movement. It has revealed the working of earnest and sometimes anxious minds in directions opposed to those which we have been studying. No one can fail to be aware that there has been a great Catholic revival in the nineteenth century. That revival has had place in the Roman Catholic countries of the Continent as well. It was in order to include the privilege of reference to these aspects of our subject that this chapter was given a double title. Yet in no country has the nineteenth century so favourably altered the position of the Roman Catholic Church as in England. In no country has a Church

which has been esteemed to be Protestant been so much
influenced by Catholic ideas. This again is a reason for
including our reference to the reaction here.

According to Pfleiderer, a new movement in philosophy may
be said to have begun in Great Britain in the year 1825, with
the publication of Coleridge's *Aids to Reflection.* In Coleridge's
Confessions of an Enquiring Spirit, published six years after
his death in 1834, we have a suggestion of the biblical-critical
movement which was beginning to shape itself in Germany.
In the same years we have evidence in the works of Erskine
and the early writings of Campbell, that in Scotland theologians were thinking on Schleiermacher's lines. In those
same years books of more or less marked rationalistic tendency
were put forth by the Oriel School. Finally, with Pusey's
Assize Sermon, in 1833, Newman felt that the movement
later to be called Tractarian had begun. We shall not be
wrong, therefore, in saying that the decade following 1825
saw the beginnings in Britain of more formal reflexion upon
all the aspects of the theme with which we are concerned.

What went before that, however, in the way of liberal
religious thinking, though informal in its nature, should not
be ignored. It was the work of the poets of the end of the
eighteenth and of the beginning of the nineteenth centuries.
The culmination of the great revolt against the traditional
in state and society and against the conventional in religion,
had been voiced in Britain largely by the poets. So vigorous
was this utterance and so effective, that some have spoken
of the contribution of the English poets to the theological
reconstruction. It is certain that the utterances of the poets
tended greatly to the dissemination of the new ideas. There
was in Great Britain no such unity as we have observed
among the Germans, either of the movement as a whole or in
its various parts. There was a consecution nothing less than
marvellous in the work of the philosophers from Kant to
Hegel. There was a theological sequence from Schleiermacher to Ritschl. There was an unceasing critical advance
from the days of Strauss. There was nothing resembling this
in the work of the English-speaking people. The contributions

were for a long time only sporadic. The movement had no inclusiveness. There was no aspect of a solid front in the advance. In the department of the sciences only was the situation different. In a way, therefore, it will be necessary in this chapter merely to single out individuals, to note points of conflict, one and another, all along the great line of advance. Or, to put it differently, it will be possible to pursue a chronological arrangement which would have been bewildering in our study heretofore. With the one great division between the progressive spirits and the men of the reaction, it will be possible to speak of philosophers, critics and theologians together, among their own contemporaries, and so to follow the century as it advances.

In the closing years of the eighteenth century in England what claimed to be a rational supernaturalism prevailed. Men sought to combine faith in revealed religion with the empirical philosophy of Locke. They conceived God and his relation to the world under deistical forms. The educated often lacked in singular degree all deeper religious feeling. They were averse to mysticism and spurned enthusiasm. Utilitarian considerations, which formed the practical side of the empirical philosophy, played a prominent part also in orthodox belief. The theory of the universe which obtained among the religious is seen at its worst in some of the volumes of the Warburton Lectures, and at its best perhaps in Butler's *Analogy of Natural and Revealed Religion.* The character and views of the clergy and of the ruling class among the laity of the Church of England, early in the nineteenth century, are pictured with love and humour in Trollope's novels. They form the background in many of George Eliot's books, where, in more mordant manner, both their strength and weaknesses are shown. Even the remarks which introduce Dean Church's *Oxford Movement,* 1891, in which the churchly element is dealt with in deep affection, give anything but an inspiring view.

The contrast with this would-be rational and unemotional religious respectability of the upper classes was furnished, for masses of the people, in the quickening of the consciousness

of sin and grace after the manner of the Methodists. But the
Methodism of the earlier age had as good as no intellectual
relations whatsoever. The Wesleys and Whitefield had indeed influenced a considerable portion of the Anglican communion. Their pietistic trait, combined, for the most part,
with a Calvinism which Wesley abhorred and an old-fashioned
low church feeling with which also Wesley had no sympathy,
shows itself in the so-called evangelical party which was
strong before 1830. This evangelical movement in the
Church of England manifested deep religious feeling, it put
forth zealous philanthropic effort, it had among its representatives men and women of great beauty of personal character
and piety. Yet it was completely cut off from any living
relation to the thought of the age. There was among its
representatives no spirit of theological inquiry. There was,
if anything, less probability of theological reconstruction,
from this quarter, than from the circles of the older German
pietism, with which this English evangelicalism of the time of
the later Georges had not a little in common. There had been
a great enthusiasm for humanity at the opening of the period
of the French Revolution, but the excesses and atrocities of
the Revolution had profoundly shocked the English mind.
There was abroad something of the same sense for the return
to nature, and of the greatness of man, which moved Schiller
and Goethe. The exponents of it were, however, almost
exclusively the poets, Wordsworth, Shelley, Keats and
Byron. There was nothing which combined these various
elements as parts of a great whole. Britain had stood outside
the area of the Revolution, and yet had put forth stupendous
efforts, ultimately successful, to make an end of the revolutionary era and of the Napoleonic despotism. This tended
perhaps to give to Britons some natural satisfaction in the
British Constitution and the established Church which
flourished under it. Finally, while men on the Continent
were devising holy alliances and other chimeras of the sort,
England was precipitated into the earlier acute stages of the
industrial revolution in which she has led the European
nations and still leads. This fact explains a certain pre-

occupation of the British mind with questions remote from theological reconstruction or religious speculation.

THE POETS

It may now sound like a contradiction if we assert that the years from 1780 to 1830 constitute the era of the noblest English poetry since the times of great Elizabeth.   The social direction of the new theology of the present day, with its cry against every kind of injustice, with its claim of an equal opportunity for a happy life for every man—this was the forecast of Cowper, as it had been of Blake.   To Blake all outward infallible authority of books or churches was iniquitous.   He was at daggers drawn with every doctrine which set limit to the freedom of all men to love God, or which could doubt that God had loved all men.   Jesus alone had seen the true thing. God was a father, every man his child.   Long before 1789, Burns was filled with the new ideas of the freedom and brotherhood of man, with zeal for the overthrow of unjust privilege.   He had spoken in imperishable words of the holiness of the common life.   He had come into contact with the most dreadful consequences of Calvinism.   He has pilloried these mercilessly in his ' Holy Tulzie' and in his 'Holy Willie's Prayer.'   Such poems must have shaken Calvinism more than a thousand liberal sermons could have done.   What Coleridge might have done in this field, had he not so early turned to prose, it is not easy to say.   The verse of his early days rests upon the conviction, fundamental to his later philosophy, that all the new ideas concerning men and the world are a revelation of God.   Wordsworth seems never consciously to have broken with the current theology.   His view of the natural glory and goodness of humanity, especially among the poor and simple, has not much relation to that theology. His view of nature, not as created of God, in the conventional sense, but as itself filled with God, of God as conscious of himself at every point of nature's being, has still less.   Man and nature are but different manifestations of the one soul of all.   Byron's contribution to Christian thought, we need hardly say, was of a negative sort. It was destructive rather than constructive. Among the conventions and hypocrisies of society there were none which he more utterly despised than those of religion and the Church as he saw these. There is something volcanic, Voltairean in his outbreaks. But there is a difference. Both Voltaire and Byron knew that they had not the current religion. Voltaire thought, nevertheless, that he had a religion. Posterity has esteemed that he had little. Byron thought he had none. Posterity has felt that he had much. His attack was made in a reckless bitterness which lessened its effect. Yet the truth of many things which he said is now overwhelmingly obvious. Shelley began with being what he called an atheist. He ended with being what we call an agnostic, whose pure poetic spirit carried him far into the realm of the highest idealism. The existence of a conscious will within the universe is not quite thinkable. Yet immortal love pervades the whole. Immortality is improbable, but his highest flights continually imply it. He is sure that when any theology violates the primary human affections, it tramples into the dust all thoughts and feelings by which men may become good. The men who, about 1840, stood paralysed between what Strauss later called ' the old faith and the new,' or, as Arnold phrased it, were ' between two worlds, one dead, the other powerless to be born,' found their inmost thoughts written broad for them in Arthur Clough. From the time of the opening of Tennyson's work, the poets, not by destruction but by construction, not in opposition to religion but in harmony with it, have built up new doctrines of God and man and aided incalculably in preparing the way for a new and nobler theology. In the latter part of the nineteenth century there was perhaps no one man in England who did more to read all of the vast advance of knowledge in the light of higher faith, and to fill such a faith with the spirit of the glad advance of knowledge, than did Browning. Even Arnold has voiced in his poetry not a little of the noblest conviction of the age. And what shall one say of Mrs. Browning, of the Rossettis and William Morris, of Emerson and Lowell, of Lanier and Whitman, who have spoken, often with consummate power and beauty, that which one never says at all without faith and rarely says well without art ?

COLERIDGE

Samuel Taylor Coleridge was born in 1772 at his father's vicarage, Ottery St. Mary's, Devonshire. He was the tenth child of his parents, weak in frame, always suffering much. He was a student at Christ's Hospital, London, where he was properly bullied, then at Jesus College, Cambridge, where he did not take his degree. For some happy years he lived in the Lake region and was the friend of Wordsworth and Southey. He studied in Göttingen, a thing almost unheard of in his time. The years 1798 to 1813 were indeed spent in utter misery, through the opium habit which he had contracted while seeking relief from rheumatic pain. He wrote and taught and talked in Highgate from 1814 to 1834. He had planned great works which never took shape. For a brief period he severed his connexion with the English Church, coming under Unitarian influence. He then reverted to the relation in which his ecclesiastical instincts were satisfied. We read his *Aids to Reflection* and his *Confessions of an Enquiring Spirit*, and wonder how they can ever have exerted a great influence. Nevertheless, they were fresh and stimulating in their time. That Coleridge was a power, we have testimony from men differing among themselves so widely as do Hare, Sterling, Newman and John Stuart Mill. He was a master of style. He had insight and breadth. Tulloch says of the *Aids*, that it is a book which none but a thinker upon divine things will ever like. Not all even of these have liked it. Inexcusably fragmentary it sometimes seems. One is fain to ask : What right has any man to publish a scrap-book of his musings ? Coleridge had the ambition to lay anew the foundations of spiritual philosophy. The *Aids* were but of the nature of prolegomena. For substance his philosophy went back to Locke and Hume and to the Cambridge Platonists. He had learned of Kant and Schleiermacher as well. He was no metaphysician, but a

keen interpreter of spiritual facts, who himself had been
quickened by a particularly painful experience. He saw in
Christianity, rightly conceived, at once the true explanation
of our spiritual being and the remedy for its disorder. The
evangelical tradition brought religion to a man from without.
It took no account of man's spiritual constitution, beyond
the fact that he was a sinner and in danger of hell. Coleridge
set out, not from sin alone, but from the whole deep basis of
spiritual capacity and responsibility upon which sin rests.
He asserts experience. We are as sure of the capacity for the
good and of the experience of the good as we can be of the
evil. The case is similar as to the truth. There are aspects
of truth which transcend our powers. We use words without
meaning when we talk of the plans of a being who is neither
an object for our senses nor a part of our self-consciousness.
All truth must be capable of being rendered into words con-
formable to reason. Theologians had declared their doctrines
true or false without reference to the subjective standard of
judgment. Coleridge contended that faith must rest not
merely upon objective data, but upon inward experience.
The authority of Scripture is in its truthfulness, its answer to
the highest aspirations of the human reason and the most
urgent necessities of the moral life. The doctrine of an
atonement is intelligible only in so far as it too comes within
the range of spiritual experience. The apostolic language
took colour from the traditions concerning sacrifice. Much
has been taken by the Church as literal dogmatic statement
which should be taken as mere figure of speech, borrowed
from Jewish sources.

Coleridge feared that his thoughts concerning Scripture
might, if published, do more harm than good. They were
printed first in 1840. Their writing goes back into the
period long before the conflict raised by Strauss. There is
not much here that one might not have learned from Herder
and Lessing. Utterances of Whately and Arnold showed
that minds in England were waking. But Coleridge's utterances rest consistently upon the philosophy of religion and
theory of dogma which have been above implied. They are

more significant than are mere flashes of generous insight, like those of the men named. The notion of verbal inspiration or infallible dictation of the Holy Scriptures could not possibly survive after the modern spirit of historical inquiry had made itself felt. The rabbinical idea was bound to disappear. A truer sense of the conditions attending the origins and progress of civilisation and of the immaturities through which religious as well as moral and social ideas advance, brought of necessity a changed idea of the nature of Scripture and revelation. Its literature must be read as literature, its history as history. For the answer in our hearts to the spirit in the Book, Coleridge used the phrase : ' It finds me.' ' Whatever finds me bears witness to itself that it has proceeded from the Holy Ghost. In the Bible there is more that finds me than in all the other books which I have read.' Still, there is much in the Bible that does not find me. It is full of contradictions, both moral and historical. Are we to regard these as all equally inspired ? The Scripture itself does not claim that. Besides, what good would it do us to claim that the original documents were inerrant, unless we could claim also that they had been inerrantly transmitted ? Apparently Coleridge thought that no one would ever claim that. Coleridge wrote also concerning the Church. His volume on *The Constitution of Church and State* appeared in 1830. It is the least satisfactory of his works. The vacillation of Coleridge's own course showed that upon this point his mind was never clear. Arnold also, though in a somewhat different way, was zealous for the theory that Church and State are really identical, the Church being merely the State in its educational and religious aspect and organisation. If Thomas Arnold's moral earnestness and his generous spirit could not save this theory from being chimerical, no better result was to be expected from Coleridge.

The Oriel School

It has often happened in the history of the English universities that a given college has become, through its body of tutors and students, through its common-room talk and literary work, the centre, for the time, of a movement of thought which gives leadership to the college. In this manner it has been customary to speak of the group of men who, before the rise of the Oxford Movement, gathered at Oriel College, as the Oriel School. Newman and Keble were both Oriel tutors. The Oriel men were of distinctly liberal tendency. There were men of note among them. There was Whately, Archbishop of Dublin after 1831, and Copleston, from whom both Keble and Newman owned that they learned much. There was Arnold, subsequently Headmaster of Rugby. There was Hampden, Professor of Divinity after 1836. The school was called from its liberalism the Noetic school. Whether this epithet contained more of satire or of complacency it is difficult to say. These men arrested attention and filled some of the older academic and ecclesiastical heads with alarm. Without disrespect one may say that it is difficult now to understand the commotion which they made. Arnold had a truly beautiful character. What he might have done as Professor of Ecclesiastical History in Oxford was never revealed, for he died in 1842. Whately, viewed as a noetic, appears commonplace.

Perhaps the only one of the group upon whom we need dwell was Hampden. In his Bampton Lectures of 1832, under the title of *The Scholastic Philosophy considered in its Relation to Christian Theology,* he assailed what had long been the very bulwark of traditionalism. His idea was to show how the vast fabric of scholastic theology had grown up, particularly what contributions had been made to it in the Middle Age. The traditional dogma is a structure reared upon the logical terminology of the patristic and mediæval schools. It has little foundation in Scripture and no response in the religious consciousness. We have here the application, within set limits, of the thesis which Harnack in our own time has applied in a universal way. Hampden's opponents were not wrong in saying that his method would dissolve, not merely that particular system of theology, but all creeds and theologies whatsoever. Patristic, mediæval Catholic theology and scholastic Protestantism, no less, would go down before it. A pamphlet attributed to Newman, published in 1836, precipitated a discussion which, for bitterness, has rarely been surpassed in the melancholy history of theological dispute. The excitement went to almost unheard of lengths. In the controversy the Archbishop, Dr. Howley, made but a poor figure. The Duke of Wellington did not add to his fame. Wilberforce and Newman never cleared themselves of the suspicion of indirectness. This was, however, after the opening of the Oxford Movement.

Erskine and Campbell

The period from 1820 to 1850 was one of religious and intellectual activity in Scotland as well. Tulloch depicts with a Scotsman's patriotism the movement which centres about the names of Erskine and Campbell. Pfleiderer also judges that their contribution was as significant as any made to dogmatic theology in Great Britain in the nineteenth century. They achieved the same reconstruction of the doctrine of salvation which had been effected by Kant and Schleiermacher. At their hands the doctrine was rescued from that forensic externality into which Calvinism had degenerated. It was given again its quality of ethical inwardness, and based directly upon religious experience. High Lutheranism had issued in the same externality in Germany before Kant and Schleiermacher, and the New England theology before Channing and Bushnell. The merits of Christ achieved an external salvation, of which a man became participant practically upon condition of assent to certain propositions. Similarly, in the Catholic revival, salvation was conceived as an external and future good, of which a man became participant through the sacraments applied to him by priests in apostolical succession. In point of externality there was not much to choose between views which were felt to be radically opposed the one to the other.

Erskine was not a man theologically educated. He led a peculiarly secluded life. He was an advocate by profession,

but, withdrawing from that career, virtually gave himself up
to meditation. Campbell was a minister of the Established
Church of Scotland in a remote village, Row, upon the Gare
Loch. When he was convicted of heresy and driven from
the ministry, he also devoted himself to study and authorship.
Both men seem to have come to their results largely from
the application of their own sound religious sense to the
Scriptures. That the Scottish Church should have rejected
the truth for which these men contended was the heaviest
blow which it could have inflicted on itself. Thereby it
arrested its own healthy development. It perpetuated its
traditional view, somewhat as New England orthodoxy was
given a new lease of life through the partisanship which the
Unitarian schism engendered. The matter was not mended
at the time of the great rupture of the Scottish Church in 1843.
That body which broke away from the Establishment, and
achieved a purely ecclesiastical control of its own clergy, won,
indeed, by this means the name of the Free Church, though,
in point of theological opinion, it was far from representing the more free and progressive element. Tulloch pays a
beautiful tribute to the character of Erskine, whom he knew.
Quiet, brooding, introspective, he read his Bible and his own
soul, and with singular purity of intuition generalised from
his own experience. Therewith is described, however, both
the power and the limitation of his work. His first book was
entitled *Remarks on the Internal Evidence for the Truth of
Revealed Religion*, 1820. The title itself is suggestive of the
revolution through which the mind both of Erskine and of
his age was passing. His book, *The Unconditional Freeness of
the Gospel*, appeared in 1828 ; *The Brazen Serpent* in 1831.
Men have confounded forgiveness and pardon. They have
made pardon equivalent to salvation. But salvation is
character. Forgiveness is only one of the means of it. Salvation is not a future good. It is a present fellowship with
God. It is sanctification of character by means of our labour
and God's love. The fall was the rise of the spirit of freedom.
Fallen man can never be saved except through glad surrender
of his childish independence to the truth and goodness of

God. Yet that surrender is the preservation and enlargement of our independence. It is the secret of true self-realisation. The sufferings of Christ reveal God's holy love. It is not as if God's love had been purchased by the sufferings of his Son. On the contrary, it is man who needs to believe in God's love, and so be reconciled to the God whom he has feared and hated. Christ overcomes sin by obediently enduring the suffering which sin naturally entails. He endures it in pure love of his brethren. Man must overcome sin in the same way.

Campbell published, so late as 1856, his great work *The Nature of the Atonement and its Relation to the Remission of Sins and Eternal Life.* It was the matured result of the reflections of a quarter of a century, spent partly in enforced retirement after 1831. Campbell maintains unequivocally that the sacrifice of Christ cannot be understood as a punishment due to man's sin, meted out to Christ in man's stead. Viewed retrospectively, Christ's work in the atonement is but the highest example of a law otherwise universally operative. No man can work redemption for his fellows except by entering into their condition, as if everything in that condition were his own, though much of it may be in no sense his due. It is freely borne by him because of his identification of himself with them. Campbell lingers in the myth of Christ's being the federal head of the humanity. There is something pathetic in the struggle of his mind to save phrases and the paraphernalia of an ancient view which, however, his fundamental principle rendered obsolete. He struggles to save the word satisfaction, though it means nothing in his system save that God is satisfied as he contemplates the character of Christ. Prospectively considered, the sacrifice of Christ effects salvation by its moral power over men in example and inspiration. Vicarious sacrifice, the result of which was merely imputed, would leave the sinner just where he was before. It is an empty fiction. But the spectacle of suffering freely undertaken for our sakes discovers the treasures of the divine image in man. The love of God and a man's own resolve make him in the end, in fact, that which he has always been in capacity and destiny, a child of God, possessed of the secret of a growing righteousness, which is itself salvation.

MAURICE

Scottish books seem to have been but little read in England in that day. It was Maurice who first made the substance of Campbell's teaching known in England. Frederick Denison Maurice was the son of a Unitarian minister, educated at Trinity College, Cambridge, at a time when it was impossible for a Nonconformist to obtain a degree. He was ordained a priest of the Church of England in 1834, even suffering himself to be baptised again. He was chaplain of Lincoln's Inn and Professor of Theology in King's College, London. After 1866 he was Professor of Moral Philosophy in Cambridge, though his life-work was over. At the heart of Maurice's theology lies the contention to which he gave the name of universal redemption. Christ's work is for every man. Every man is indeed in Christ. Man's unhappiness lies only in the fact that he will not own this fact and live accordingly. Man as man is the child of God. He cannot undo that fact or alter that relation if he would. He does not need to become a child of God, as the phrase has been. He needs only to recognise that he already is such a child. He can never cease to bear this relationship. He can only refuse to fulfil it. With other words Erskine and Coleridge and Schleiermacher had said this same thing.

For the rest, one may speak briefly of Maurice. He was animated by the strongest desire for Church unity, but at the back of his mind lay a conception of the Church and an insistence upon uniformity which made unity impossible. In the light of his own inheritance his ecclesiastical positivism seems strange. Perhaps it was the course of his experience which made this irrational positivism natural. Few men in his generation suffered greater persecutions under the unwarranted supposition on the part of contemporaries that he had a liberal mind. In reality, few men in his generation had less of a quality which, had he possessed it, would have given him peace and joy even in the midst of his persecutions. The casual remark above made concerning Campbell is true in enhanced degree of Maurice. A large part of the industry of a very industrious life was devoted to the effort to convince others and himself that those few really wonderful glimpses of spiritual truth which he had, had no disastrous consequences for an inherited system of thought in which they certainly did not take their rise. His name was connected with the social enthusiasm that inaugurated a new movement in England which will claim attention in another paragraph.

CHANNING

Allusion has been made to a revision of traditional theology which took place in America also, upon the same general lines which we have seen in Schleiermacher and in Campbell. The typical figure here, the protagonist of the movement, is William Ellery Channing. It may be doubted whether there has ever been a civilisation more completely controlled by its Church and ministers, or a culture more entirely dominated by theology, than were those of New England until the middle of the eighteenth century. There had been indeed a marked decline in religious life. The history of the Great Awakening shows that. Remonstrances against the Great Awakening show also how men's minds were moving away from the theory of the universe which the theology of that movement implied. One cannot say that in the preaching of Hopkins there is an appreciable relaxation of the Edwardsian scheme. Interestingly enough, it was in Newport that Channing was born and with Hopkins that he associated until the time of his licensure to preach in 1802. Many thought that Channing would stand with the most stringent of the orthodox. Deism and rationalism had made themselves felt in America after the Revolution. Channing, during his years in Harvard College, can hardly have failed to come into contact with the criticism of religion from this side. There is no such clear influence of current rationalism upon Channing as, for example, upon Schleiermacher. Yet here in the West, which most Europeans thought of as a wilderness, circumstances brought about the launching of this man upon the career of a liberal religious thinker, when as yet Schleiermacher had hardly advanced beyond the position of the *Discourses*, when Erskine had not yet written a line and Campbell was still a child. Channing became minister of the Federal Street Church in Boston in 1803. The appointment of Ware as Hollis Professor of Divinity in Harvard College took place in 1805. That appointment was the first clear indication of the liberal party's strength. Channing's Baltimore Address was delivered in 1819. He died in 1847.

In the schism among the Congregational Churches in New England, which before 1819 apparently had come to be regarded by both parties as remediless, Channing took the side of the opposition to Calvinistic orthodoxy. He developed qualities as controversialist and leader which the gentler aspect of his early years had hardly led men to suspect. This American liberal movement had been referred to by Belsham as related to English Unitarianism. After 1815, in this country, by its opponents at least, the movement was consistently called Unitarian. Channing did with zeal contend against the traditional doctrines of the atonement and of the trinity. On the other hand, he saw in Christ the perfect revelation of God to humanity and at the same time the ideal of humanity. He believed in Jesus' sinlessness and in his miracles, especially in his resurrection. The keynote of Channing's character and convictions is found in his sense of the inherent greatness of man. Of this feeling his entire system is but the unfolding. It was early and deliberately adopted by him as a fundamental faith. It remained the immovable centre of his reverence and trust amid all the inroads of doubt and sorrow. Political interest was as natural to Channing's earlier manhood as it had been to Fichte in the emergency of the Fatherland. Similarly, in the later years of his life, when evils connected with slavery had made themselves felt, his participation in the abolitionist agitation showed the same enthusiasm and practical bent. He had his dream of communism, his perception of the evils of our industrial system, his contempt for charity in place of economic remedy. All was for man, all rested upon supreme faith in man. That man is endowed with knowledge of the right and with the power to realise it, was a fundamental maxim. Hence arose Channing's assertion of free-will. The denial of free-will renders the sentiment of duty but illusory. In the conscience there is both a revelation and a type of God. Its suggestions, by the very authority they carry with them, declare themselves to be God's law. God, concurring with our highest nature, present in its action, can be thought of only after the pattern which he gives us in ourselves. Whatever revelation God makes of himself, he must deal with us as with free beings living under natural laws. Revelation must be merely supplementary to those laws. Everything arbitrary and magical, everything which despairs of us or insults us as moral agents, everything which does not address itself to us through reason and conscience, must be excluded from the intercourse between God and man. What the doctrines of salvation and atonement, of the person of Christ and of the influence of the Holy Spirit, as construed from this centre would be, may without difficulty be surmised. The whole of Channing's teaching is bathed in an atmosphere of the reverent love of God which is the very source of his enthusiasm for man.

BUSHNELL

A very different man was Horace Bushnell, born in the year of Channing's licensure, 1802. He was not bred under the influence of the strict Calvinism of his day. His father was an Arminian. Edwards had made Arminians detested in New England. His mother had been reared in the Episcopal Church. She was of Huguenot origin. When about seventeen, while tending a carding-machine, he wrote a paper in which he endeavoured to bring Calvinism into logical coherence and, in the interest of sound reason, to correct St. Paul's willingness to be accursed for the sake of his brethren. He graduated from Yale College in 1827. He taught there while studying law after 1829. He describes himself at this period as sound in ethics and sceptical in religion, the soundness of his morals being due to nature and training, the scepticism, to the theology in which he was involved. His law studies were complete, yet he turned to the ministry. He had been born on the orthodox side of the great contention in which Channing was a leader of the liberals in the days of which we speak. He never saw any reason to change this relation. His clerical colleagues, for half a life-time, sought to change it for him. In 1833 he was ordained and installed as minister of the North Church in Hartford, a pastorate which he never left. The process of disintegration of the orthodox body was continuing. There was almost as much rancour between the old and the new orthodoxy as between orthodox and Unitarians themselves. Almost before his career was well begun an incurable disease fastened itself upon him. Not much later, all the severity of theological strife befell him. Between these two we have to think of him doing his work and keeping his sense of humour.

His earliest book of consequence was on *Christian Nurture*, published in 1846. Consistent Calvinism presupposes in its converts mature years. Even an adult must pass through waters deep for him. He is not a sinful child of the Father. He is a being totally depraved and damned to everlasting punishment. God becomes his Father only after he is redeemed. The revivalists' theory Bushnell bitterly opposed. It made of religion a transcendental matter which belonged on the outside of life, a kind of miraculous epidemic. He repudiated the prevailing individualism. He anticipated much that is now being said concerning heredity, environment and subconsciousness. He revived the sense of the Church in which Puritanism had been so sadly lacking. The book is a classic, one of the rich treasures which the nineteenth century offers to the twentieth.

Bushnell, so far as one can judge, had no knowledge of Kant. He is, nevertheless, dealing with Kant's own problem, of the theory of knowledge, in his rather diffuse ' Dissertation on

Language,' which is prefixed to the volume which bears the title *God in Christ*, 1849.   He was following his living principle, the reference of doctrine to conscience.   God must be a ' right God.'   Dogma must make no assertion concerning God which will not stand this test.   Not alone does the dogma make such assertions.   The Scripture makes them as well.   How can this be ?   What is the relation of language to thought and of thought to fact ?   How can the language of Scripture be explained, and yet the reality of the revelation not be explained away ?   There is a touching interest which attaches to this Hartford minister, working out, alone and clumsily, a problem the solution of which the greatest minds of the age had been gradually bringing to perfection for three-quarters of a century.

In the year 1848 Bushnell was invited to give addresses at the Commencements of three divinity schools : that at Harvard, then unqualifiedly Unitarian ; that at Andover, where the battle with Unitarianism had been fought ; and that at Yale, where Bushnell had been trained.   The address at Cambridge was on the subject of *the Atonement*; the one at New Haven on *the Divinity of Christ*, including Bushnell's doctrine of the trinity ; the one at Andover on *Dogma and Spirit*, a plea for the cessation of strife.   He says squarely of the old school theories of the atonement, which represent Christ as suffering the penalty of the law in our stead : ' They are capable, one and all of them, of no light in which they do not offend some right sentiment of our moral being.   If the great Redeemer, in the excess of his goodness, consents to receive the penal woes of the world in his person, and if that offer is accepted, what does it signify, save that God will have his modicum of suffering somehow ; and if he lets the guilty go he will yet satisfy himself out of the innocent ? '   The vicariousness of love, the identification of the sufferer with the sinner, in the sense that the Saviour is involved by his desire to help us in the woes which naturally follow sin, this Bushnell mightily affirmed.   Yet there is no pretence that he used vicariousness or satisfaction in the same sense in which his adversaries did.   He is magnificently free from all such indirection. In the New Haven address there is this same combination of fire and light. The chief theological value of the doctrine of the trinity, as maintained by the New England Calvinistic teachers, had been to furnish the *dramatis personæ* for the doctrine of the atonement. In the speculation as to the negotiation of this substitutionary transaction, the language of the theologians had degenerated into stark tritheism. Edwards, describing the councils of the trinity, spoke of the three persons as ' they.' Bushnell saw that any proper view of the unity of God made the forensic idea of the atonement incredible. He sought to replace the ontological notion of the trinity by that of a trinity of revelation, which held for him the practical truths by which his faith was nourished, and yet avoided the contradictions which the other doctrine presented both to reason and faith. Bushnell would have been far from claiming that he was the first to make this fight. The American Unitarians had been making it for more than a generation. The Unitarian protest was wholesome. It was magnificent. It was providential, but it paused in negation. It never advanced to construction. Bushnell's significance is not that he fought this battle, but that he fought it from the ranks of the orthodox Church. He fought it with a personal equipment which Channing had not had. He was decades later in his work. He took up the central religious problem when Channing's successors were following either Emerson or Parker.

The Andover address consisted in the statement of Bushnell's views of the causes which had led to the schism in the New England Church. A single quotation may give the keynote of the discourse :—' We had on our side an article of the creed which asserted a metaphysical trinity. That made the assertion of the metaphysical unity inevitable and desirable. We had theories of atonement, of depravity, of original sin, which required the appearance of antagonistic theories. On our side, theological culture was so limited that we took what was really only our own opinion for the unalterable truth of God. On the other side, it was so limited that men, perceiving the insufficiency of dogma, took the opposite contention with the same seriousness and totality of conviction. They asserted liberty, as indeed they must, to vindicate their revolt. They produced, meantime, the most intensely human and, in that sense, the most intensely opinionated religion ever invented.'

THE CATHOLIC REVIVAL

The Oxford Movement has been spoken of as a reaction against the so-called Oriel Movement, a conservative tendency over against an intellectualist and progressive one. In a measure the personal animosities within the Oxford circle may be accounted for in this way. The Tractarian Movement, however, which issued, on the one hand, in the going over of Newman to the Church of Rome and, on the other, in a great revival of Catholic principles within the Anglican Church itself, stands in a far larger setting. It was not merely an English or insular movement. It was a wave from a continental flood. On its own showing it was not merely an ecclesiastical movement. It had political and social aims as well. There was a universal European reaction against the Enlightenment and the Revolution. That reaction was not simple, but complex. It was a revolt of the conservative spirit from the new ideals which had been suddenly translated into portentous realities. It was marked everywhere by hatred of the eighteenth century with all its ways and works. On the one side we have the revolutionary thesis, the rights of man, the authority of reason, the watchwords liberty, equality, fraternity. On the other side stood forth those who were prepared to assert the meaning of community, the continuity of history, spiritual as well as civil authority as the basis of order, and order as the condition of the highest good. In literature the tendency appears as romanticism, in politics as legitimism, in religion as ultramontanism. Le Maistre with his *L'Église gallicane du Pape* ; Chateaubriand with his *Génie du Christianisme* ; Lamennais with his *Essai sur l'Indifférence en Matière de Religion*, were, from 1820 to 1860, the exponents of a view which has had prodigious consequences for France and Italy. The romantic movement arose outside of Catholicism. It was impersonated in Herder. Friedrich Schlegel, Werner and others went over to the Roman Church. The political reaction was specifically Latin and Catholic. In the lurid light of anarchy Rome seemed to have a mission again. Divine right in the State must be restored through the Church. The Catholic apologetic saw the Revolution as only the logical conclusion of the premises of the Reformation. The religious revolt of the sixteenth century, the philosophical revolt of the seventeenth, the political revolt of the eighteenth, the social revolt of the nineteenth, are all parts of one dreadful sequence. As the Church lifted up the world after the first flood of the barbarians, so must she again lift up the world after the devastations made by the more terrible barbarians of the eighteenth century. England had indeed stood a little outside of the cyclone which had devastated the world from Corunna to Moscow and from the Channel to the Pyramids, but she had been exhausted in putting down the revolution. Only God's goodness had preserved England. The logic of Puritanism would have been the same. Indeed, in England the State was weaker and worse than were the states upon the Continent. For since 1688 it had been a popular and constitutional monarchy. In Frederick William's phrase, its sovereign took his crown from the gutter. The Church was through and through Erastian, a creature of the State. Bishops were made by party representatives. Acts like the Reform Bills, the course of the Government in the matter of the Irish Church, were steps which would surely bring England to the pass which France had reached in 1789. The source of such acts was wrong. It was with the people. It was in men, not in God. It was in reason, not in authority. It would be difficult to overstate the strength of this reactionary sentiment in important circles in England at the end of the third decade of the nineteenth century.

The Oxford Movement

In so far as that complex of causes just alluded to made of the Oxford Movement or the Catholic revival a movement

of life, ecclesiastical, social and political as well, its history
falls outside the purpose of this book.   We proposed to deal
with the history of thought.   Reactionary movements have
frequently got on without much thought.   They have left
little deposit of their own in the realm of ideas.   Their avowed
principle has been that of recurrence to that which has already
been thought, of fidelity to ideas which have long prevailed.
This is the reason why the conservatives have not a
large place in such a sketch as this.   It is not that their
writings have not often been full of high learning and of the
subtlest of reasoning.   It is only that the ideas about which
they reason do not belong to the history of the nineteenth
century.   They belong, on the earnest contention of the
conservatives themselves—those of Protestants, to the history
of the Reformation—and of Catholics, both Anglican and
Roman, to the history of the early or mediæval Church.

Nevertheless, when with passionate conviction a great man,
taking the reactionary course, thinks the problem through
again from his own point of view, then we have a real pheno
menon in the history of contemporary thought.   When such
an one wrestles before God to give reason to himself and to
his fellows for the faith that is in him, then the reactionary's
reasoning is as imposing and suggestive as is any other.   He
leaves in his work an intellectual deposit which must be considered.   He makes a contribution which must be reckoned
with, even more seriously, perhaps, by those who dissent from
it than by those who may agree with it.   Such deposit Newman and the Tractarian movement certainly did make.   They
offered a rationale of the reaction.   They gave to the Catholic
revival a standing in the world of ideas, not merely in the
world of action.   Whether their reasoning has weight to-day,
is a question upon which opinion is divided.   Yet Newman
and his compeers, by their character and standing, by their
distinctively English qualities and by the road of reason
which they took in the defence of Catholic principles, made
Catholicism English again, in a sense in which it had not
been English for three hundred years.   Yet though Newman
brought to the Roman Church in England, on his conversion

to it, a prestige and qualities which in that communion were unequalled, he was never *persona grata* in that Church. Outwardly the Roman Catholic revival in England was not in large measure due to Newman and his arguments. It was due far more to men like Wiseman and Manning, who were not men of argument but of deeds.

NEWMAN

John Henry Newman was born in 1801, the son of a London banker. His mother was of Huguenot descent. He came under Calvinistic influence. Through study especially of Romaine *On Faith* he became the subject of an inward conversion, of which in 1864 he wrote : ' I am still more certain of it than that I have hands and feet.' Thomas Scott, the evangelical, moved him. Before he was sixteen he made a collection of Scripture texts in proof of the doctrine of the trinity. From Newton *On the Prophecies* he learned to identify the Pope with anti-Christ—a doctrine by which, he adds, his imagination was stained up to the year 1843. In his *Apologia*, 1865, he declares : 'From the age of fifteen, dogma has been a fundamental principle of my religion. I cannot enter into the idea of any other sort of religion.' At the age of twenty-one, two years after he had taken his degree, he came under very different influences. He passed from Trinity College to a fellowship in Oriel. To use his own phrase, he drifted in the direction of liberalism. He was touched by Whately. He was too logical, and also too dogmatic, to be satisfied with Whately's position. Of the years from 1823 to 1827 Mozley says : ' Probably no one who then knew Newman could have told which way he would go. It is not certain that he himself knew.' Francis W. Newman, Newman's brother, who later became a Unitarian, remembering his own years of stress, speaks with embitterment of his elder brother, who was profoundly uncongenial to him.

The year 1827, in which Keble's *Christian Year* was published, saw another change in Newman's views. Illness and

bereavement came to him with awakening effect. He made
the acquaintance of Hurrell Froude. Froude brought
Newman and Keble together. Henceforth Newman bore no
more traces either of evangelicalism or of liberalism. Of Froude
it is difficult to speak with confidence. His brother, James
Anthony Froude, the historian, author of the *Nemesis of Faith*,
1848, says that he was gifted, brilliant, enthusiastic. Newman
speaks of him with almost boundless praise. Two volumes
of his sermons, published after his death in 1836, make the
impression neither of learning nor judgment. Clearly he
had charm. Possibly he talked himself into a common-
room reputation. Newman says: 'Froude made me look
with admiration toward the Church of Rome.' Keble never
had felt the liberalism through which Newman had passed.
Cradled as the Church of England had been in Puritanism,
the latter was to him simply evil. Opinions differing from
his own were not simply mistaken, they were sinful. He
conceived no religious truth outside the Church of England.
In the *Christian Year* one perceives an influence which
Newman strongly felt. It was that of the idea of the sacramental significance of all natural objects or events. Pusey
became professor of Hebrew in 1830. He lent the movement
academic standing, which the others could not give. He
had been in Germany, and had published an *Inquiry into the
Rationalist Character of German Theology*, 1825. He hardly
did more than expose the ignorance of Rose. He was himself
denounced as a German rationalist who dared to speak of a
new era in theology. Pusey, mourning the defection of
Newman, whom he deeply loved, gathered in 1846 the forces
of the Anglo-Catholics and continued in some sense a leader
to the end of his long life in 1882.

The course of political events was fretting the Conservatives intolerably. The agitation for the Reform Bill was
taking shape. Sir Robert Peel, the member for Oxford, had
introduced a Bill for the emancipation of the Roman Catholics.
There was violent commotion in Oxford. Keble and Newman strenuously opposed the measure. In 1830 there was
revolution in France. In England the Whigs had come into

power. Newman's mind was excited in the last degree. ' The vital question,' he says, ' is this, how are we to keep the Church of England from being liberalised ? ' At the end of 1832 Newman and Froude went abroad together. On this journey, as he lay becalmed in the straits of Bonifacio, he wrote his immortal hymn, 'Lead, Kindly Light.' He came home assured that he had a work to do. Keble's Assize Sermon on the *National Apostasy*, preached in July 1833, on the Sunday after Newman's return to Oxford, kindled the conflagration which had been long preparing. Newman conceived the idea of the *Tracts for the Times* as a means of expressing the feelings and propagating the opinions which deeply moved him. ' From the first,' he says, ' my battle was with liberalism. By liberalism I mean the anti-dogmatic principle. Secondly, my aim was the assertion of the visible Church with sacraments and rites and definite religious teaching on the foundation of dogma ; and thirdly, the assertion of the Anglican Church as opposed to the Church of Rome.' Newman grew greatly in personal influence. His afternoon sermons at St. Mary's exerted spiritual power. They deserved so to do. Here he was at his best. All of his strength and little of his weakness shows. His insight, his subtility, his pathos, his love of souls, his marvellous play of dramatic as well as of spiritual faculty, are in evidence. Keble and Pusey were busying themselves with the historical aspects of the question. Pusey began the *Library of the Fathers*, the most elaborate literary monument of the movement. Nothing could be more amazing than the uncritical quality of the whole performance. The first check to the movement came in 1838, when the Bishop of Oxford animadverted upon the *Tracts*. Newman professed his willingness to stop them. The Bishop did not insist. Newman's own thought moved rapidly onward in the only course which was still open to it.

Newman had been bred in the deepest reverence for Scripture. In a sense that reverence never left him, though it changed its form. He saw that it was absurd to appeal to the Bible in the old way as an infallible source of doctrine. How could truth be infallibly conveyed in defective and fallible expressions ? Newman's own studies in criticism, by no means profound, led him to this correct conclusion. This was the end for him of evangelical Protestantism. The recourse was then to the infallible Church. Infallible guide and authority one must have. Without these there can be no religion. To trust to reason and conscience as conveying something of the light of God is impossible. To wait in patience and to labour in fortitude for the increase of that light is unendurable. One must have certainty. There can be no certainty by the processes of the mind from within. This can come only by miraculous certification from without.

According to Newman the authority of the Church should never have been impaired in the Reformation. Or rather, in his view of that movement, this authority, for truly Christian men, had never been impaired. The intellect is aggressive, capricious, untrustworthy. Its action in religious matters is corrosive, dissolving, sceptical. ' Man's energy of intellect must be smitten hard and thrown back by infallible authority, if religion is to be saved at all.' Newman's philosophy was utterly sceptical, although, unlike most absolute philosophical sceptics, he had a deep religious experience. The most complete secularist, in his negation of religion, does not differ from Newman in his low opinion of the value of the surmises of the mind as to the transcendental meaning of life and the world. He differs from Newman only in lacking that which to Newman was the most indefeasible thing which he had at all, namely religious experience. Newman was the child of his age, though no one ever abused more fiercely the age of which he was the child. He supposed that he believed in religion on the basis of authority. Quite the contrary, he believed in religion because he had religion or, as he says, in a magnificent passage in one of his parochial sermons, because religion had him. His scepticism forbade him to recognise that this was the basis of his belief. His diremption of human nature was absolute. The soul was of God. The mind was of the devil. He dare not trust his own intellect concerning this inestimable treasure of his

experience. He dare not trust intellect at all. He knew
not whither it might lead him. The mind cannot be broken
to the belief of a power above it. It must have its stiff neck
bent to recognise its Creator.

His whole book, *The Grammar of Assent*, 1870, is pervaded
by the intensest philosophical scepticism. Scepticism supplies
its motives, determines its problems, necessitates its distinctions, rules over the succession and gradation of its
arguments. The whole aim of the work is to withdraw
religion and the proofs of it, from the region of reason into the
realm of conscience and imagination, where the arguments
which reign may satisfy personal experience without alleging
objective validity or being able to bear the criticism which
tests it. Again, he is the perverse, unconscious child of the
age which he curses. Had not Kant and Schleiermacher,
Coleridge and Channing sought, does not Ritschl seek, to
remove religion from the realm of metaphysics and to bring
it within the realm of experience ? They had, however,
pursued the same end by different means. One is reminded
of that saying of Gretchen concerning Mephistopheles : ' He
says the same thing with the pastor, only in different words.'
Newman says the same words, but means a different thing.

Assuming the reduction of religion to experience, in which
Kant and Schleiermacher would have agreed, and asserting
the worthlessness of mentality, which they would have denied,
we are not surprised to hear Newman say that without
Catholicism doubt is invincible. ' The Church's infallibility
is the provision adopted by the mercy of the Creator to
preserve religion in the world. Outside the Catholic Church
all things tend to atheism. The Catholic Church is the one
face to face antagonist, able to withstand and baffle the fierce
energy of passion and the all-dissolving scepticism of the mind.
I am a Catholic by virtue of my belief in God. If I should be
asked why I believe in God, I should answer, because I believe
in myself. I find it impossible to believe in myself, without
believing also in the existence of him who lives as a personal,
all-seeing, all-judging being in my conscience.' These passages
are mainly taken from the *Apologia*, written long after New-

man had gone over to the Roman Church. They perfectly describe the attitude of his mind toward the Anglican Church, so long as he believed this, and not the Roman, to be the true Church. He had once thought that a man could hold a position midway between the Protestantism which he repudiated and the Romanism which he still resisted. He stayed in the *via media* so long as he could. But in 1839 he began to have doubts about the Anglican order of succession. The catholicity of Rome began to overshadow the apostolicity of Anglicanism. The Anglican formularies cannot be at variance with the teachings of the authoritative and universal Church. This is the problem which the last of the *Tracts*, *Tract Ninety*, sets itself. It is one of those which Newman wrote. One must find the sense of the Roman Church in the Thirty-Nine Articles. This tract is prefaced by an extraordinary disquisition upon reserve in the communication of religious knowledge. God's revelations of himself to mankind have always been a kind of veil. Truth is the reward of holiness. The Fathers were holy men. Therefore what the Fathers said must be true. The principle of reserve the Articles illustrate. They do not mean what they say. They were written in an uncatholic age, that is, in the age of the Reformation. They were written by Catholic men. Else how can the Church of England be now a Catholic Church ? Through their reserve they were acceptable in an uncatholic age. They cannot be uncatholic in spirit, else how should they be identical in meaning with the great Catholic creeds ? Then follows an exposition of every important article of the thirty-nine, an effort to interpret each in the sense of the Roman Catholic Church of to-day. Four tutors published a protest against the tract. Formal censure was passed upon it. It was now evident to Newman that his place in the leadership of the Oxford Movement was gone. From this time, the spring of 1841, he says he was on his deathbed as regards the Church of England. He withdrew to Littlemore and established a brotherhood there. In the autumn of 1843 he resigned the parochial charge of St. Mary's at Oxford. On the 9th of October 1845 he was formally admitted to the

Roman Church. On the 6th of October Ernest Renan had formally severed his connexion with that Church.

It is a strange thing that in his *Essay on the Development of Christian Doctrine*, written in 1845, Newman himself should have advanced substantially Hampden's contention. Here are written many things concerning the development of doctrine which commend themselves to minds conversant with the application of historical criticism to the whole dogmatic structure of the Christian ages. The purpose is with Newman entirely polemical, the issue exactly that which one would not have foreseen. Precisely because the development of doctrine is so obvious, because no historical point can be found at which the growth of doctrine ceased and the rule of faith was once for all settled, therefore an infallible authority outside of the development must have existed from the beginning, to provide a means of distinguishing true development from false. This infallible guide is, of course, the Church. It seems incredible that Newman could escape applying to the Church the same argument which he had so skilfully applied to Scripture and dogmatic history. Similar is the case with the argument of the *Grammar of Assent*. ' No man is certain of a truth who can endure the thought of its contrary.' If the reason why I cannot endure the thought of the contradictory of a belief which I have made my own, is that so to think brings me pain and darkness, this does not prove my truth. If my belief ever had its origin in reason, it must be ever refutable by reason. It is not corroborated by the fact that I do not wish to see anything that would refute it.[1] This last fact may be in the highest degree an act of arbitrariness. To make the impossibility of thinking the opposite, the test of truth, and then to shut one's eyes to those evidences which might compel one to think the opposite, is the essence of irrationality. One attains by this method indefinite assertiveness, but not certainty. Newman lived in some seclusion in the Oratory of St. Philip Neri in Birmingham for many years. A few distinguished men, and a

[1] Fairbairn, *Catholicism, Roman and Anglican*, p. 157 f.

number of his followers, in all not more than a hundred and fifty, went over to the Roman Church after him. The defection was never so great as, in the first shock, it was supposed that it would be. The outward influence of Newman upon the Anglican Church then ceased. But the ideas which he put forth have certainly been of great influence in that Church to this day. Most men know the portrait of the great cardinal, the wide forehead, ploughed deep with horizontal furrows, the pale cheek, down which 'long lines of shadow slope, which years and anxious thought and suffering give.' One looks into the wonderful face of those last days—Newman lived to his ninetieth year—and wonders if he found in the infallible Church the peace which he so earnestly sought.

Modernism

It was said that the Oxford Movement furnished the rationale of the reaction. Many causes, of course, combine to make the situation of the Roman Church and the status of religion in the Latin countries of the Continent the lamentable one that it is. That position is worst in those countries where the Roman Church has most nearly had free play. The alienation both of the intellectual and civil life from organised religion is grave. That the Roman Church occupies in England to-day a position more favourable than in almost any nation on the Continent, and better than it occupied in England at the beginning of the nineteenth century, is due in large measure to the general influence of the movement with which we have been dealing. The Anglican Church was at the beginning of the nineteenth century preponderantly evangelical, low-church and conscious of itself as Protestant. At the beginning of the twentieth it is dominantly ritualistic and disposed to minimise its relation to the Reformation. This resurgence of Catholic principles is another effect of the movement of which we speak. Other factors must have wrought for this result besides the body of arguments which Newman and his compeers offered. The argument itself, the mere intellectual factor, is not adequate. There is an inherent contradiction in the effort to ground in reason an authority which is to take the place of reason. Yet round and round this circle all the labours of John Henry Newman go. Cardinal Manning felt this. The victory of the Church was not to be won by argument. It is well known that Newman opposed the decree of infallibility. It cannot be said that upon this point his arguments had great weight. If one assumes that truth comes to us externally through representatives of God, and if the truth is that which they assert, then in the last analysis what they assert is truth. If one has given in to such authority because one distrusts his reason, then it is querulous to complain that the deliverances of authority do not comport with reason. There may be, of course, the greatest interest in the struggle as to the instance in which this authority is to be lodged. This interest attaches to the age-long struggle between Pope and Council. It attaches to the dramatic struggle of Döllinger, Dupanloup, Lord Acton and the rest, in 1870. Once the Church has spoken there is, for the advocate of authoritative religion, no logic but to submit.

Similarly as to the *Encyclical* and *Syllabus of Errors* of 1864, which forecast the present conflict concerning Modernism. The *Syllabus* had a different atmosphere from that which any Englishman in the sixties would have given it. Had not Newman, however, made passionate warfare on the liberalism of the modern world ? Was it not merely a question of degrees ? Was Gladstone's attitude intelligible ? The contrast of two principles in life and religion, the principles of authority and of the spirit, is being brought home to men's consciousness as it has never been before. One reads *Il Santo* and learns concerning the death of Fogazzaro, one looks into the literature relating to Tyrrell, one sees the fate of Loisy, comparing the really majestic achievement in his works and the spirit of his *Simple Reflections* with the *Encyclical Pascendi*, 1907. One understands why these men have done what they could to remain within the Roman Church. One recalls the attitude of Döllinger to the inauguration of the Old Catholic Movement, reflects upon the relative futility of the

Old Catholic Church, and upon the position of Hyacinthe Loyson. One appreciates the feeling of these men that it is impossible, from without, to influence as they would the Church which they have loved. The present difficulty of influencing it from within seems almost insuperable. The history of Modernism as an effective contention in the world of Christian thought seems scarcely begun. The opposition to Modernism is not yet a part of the history of thought.

ROBERTSON

In no life are reflected more perfectly the spiritual conflicts of the fifth decade of the nineteenth century than in that of Frederick W. Robertson. No mind worked itself more triumphantly out of these difficulties. Descended from a family of Scottish soldiers, evangelical in piety, a student in Oxford in 1837, repelled by the Oxford Movement, he undertook his ministry under a morbid sense of responsibility. He reacted violently against his evangelicalism. He travelled abroad, read enormously, was plunged into an agony which threatened mentally to undo him. He took his charge at Brighton in 1847, still only thirty-one years old, and at once shone forth in the splendour of his genius. A martyr to disease and petty persecution, dying at thirty-seven, he yet left the impress of one of the greatest preachers whom the Church of England has produced. He left no formal literary work such as he had designed. Of his sermons we have almost none from his own manuscripts. Yet his influence is to-day almost as intense as when the sermons were delivered. It is, before all, the wealth and depth of his thought, the reality of the content of the sermons, which commands admiration. They are a classic refutation of the remark that one cannot preach theology. Out of them, even in their fragmentary state, a well-articulated system might be made. He brought to his age the living message of a man upon whom the best light of his age had shone.

PHILLIPS BROOKS

Something of the same sort may be said concerning Phillips Brooks. He inherited on his father's side the sober rationalism and the humane and secular interest of the earlier Unitarianism, on his mother's side the intensity of evangelical pietism with the Calvinistic form of thought. The conflict of these opposing tendencies in New England was at that time so great that Brooks's parents sought refuge with the low-church element in the Episcopal Church. Brooks's education at Harvard College, where he took his degree in 1855, as also at Alexandria, and still more, his reading and experience, made him sympathetic with that which, in England in those years, was called the Broad Church party. He was deeply influenced by Campbell and Maurice. Later well known in England, he was the compeer of the best spirits of his generation there. Deepened by the experience of the great war, he held in succession two pulpits of large influence, dying as Bishop of Massachusetts in 1893. There is a theological note about his preaching, as in the case of Robertson. Often it is the same note. Brooks had passed through no such crisis as had Robertson. He had flowered into the greatness of rational belief. His sermons are a contribution to the thinking of his age. We have much finished material of this kind from his own hand, and a book or two besides. His service through many years as preacher to his university was of inestimable worth. The presentation of ever-advancing thought to a great public constituency is one of the most difficult of tasks. It is also one of the most necessary. The fusion of such thoughtfulness with spiritual impulse has rarely been more perfectly achieved than in the preaching of Phillips Brooks.

THE BROAD CHURCH

We have used the phrase, the Broad Church party. Stanley had employed the adjective to describe the real character of the English Church, over against the antithesis of the Low

Church and the High. The designation adhered to a group of which Stanley was himself a type. They were not bound together in a party. They had no ecclesiastical end in view. They were of a common spirit. It was not the spirit of evangelicalism. Still less was it that of the Tractarians. It was that which Robertson had manifested. It aimed to hold the faith with an open mind in all the intellectual movement of the age. Maurice should be enumerated here, with reservations. Kingsley beyond question belonged to this group. There was great ardour among them for the improvement of social conditions, a sense of the social mission of Christianity. There grew up what was called a Christian Socialist movement, which, however, never attained or sought a political standing. The Broad Church movement seemed, at one time, assured of ascendancy in the Church of England. Its aims appeared congruous with the spirit of the times. Yet Dean Fremantle esteems himself perhaps the last survivor of an illustrious company.

The men who in 1860 published the volume known as *Essays and Reviews* would be classed with the Broad Church. In its authorship were associated seven scholars, mostly Oxford men. Some one described *Essays and Reviews* as the *Tract Ninety* of the Broad Church. It stirred public sentiment and brought the authors into conflict with authority in a somewhat similar way. The living antagonism of the Broad Church was surely with the Tractarians rather than with the evangelicals. Yet the most significant of the essays, those on miracles and on prophecy, touched opinions common to both these groups. Jowett, later Master of Balliol, contributed an essay on the 'Interpretation of Scripture.' It hardly belongs to Jowett's best work. Yet the controversy then precipitated may have had to do with Jowett's adherence to Platonic studies instead of his devoting himself to theology. The most decisive of the papers was that of Baden Powell on the 'Study of the Evidences of Christianity.' It was mainly a discussion of the miracle. It was radical and conclusive. The essay closes with an allusion to Darwin's *Origin of Species*, which

P

had then just appeared. Baden Powell died shortly after its
publication. The fight came on Rowland Williams's paper
upon Bunsen's *Biblical Researches*. It was really upon the
prophecies and their use in 'Christian Evidences.' Baron
Bunsen was not a great archæologist, but he brought to the
attention of English readers that which was being done in
Germany in this field. Williams used the archæological
material to rectify the current theological notions concerning
ancient history. A certain type of English mind has always
shown zeal for the interpretation of prophecy. Williams's
thesis, briefly put, was this : the Bible does not always give
the history of the past with accuracy ; it does not give the
history of the future at all; prophecy means spiritual teaching, not secular prognostication. A reader of our day may
naturally feel that Wilson, with his paper on the 'National
Church,' made the greatest contribution. He built indeed
upon Coleridge, but he had a larger horizon. He knew the
arguments of the great Frenchmen of his day and of their
English imitators who, in Benn's phrase, narrowed and perverted the ideal of a world-wide humanity into that of a
Church founded on dogmas and administered by clericals.
Wilson argued that in Jesus' teaching the basis of the
religious community is ethical. The Church is but the
instrument for carrying out the will of God as manifest in
the moral law. The realisation of the will of God must
extend beyond the limits of the Church's activity, however
widely these are drawn. There arose a violent agitation.
Williams and Wilson were prosecuted. The case was tried
in the Court of Arches. Williams was defended by no
less a person than Fitzjames Stephen. The two divines
were sentenced to a year's suspension. This decision was
reversed by the Lord Chancellor. Fitzjames Stephen had
argued that if the men most interested in the Church, namely,
its clergy, are the only men who may be punished for serious
discussion of the facts and truths of religion, then respect
on the part of the world for the Church is at an end. By
this discussion the English clergy, even if Anglo-Catholic,
are in a very different position from the Roman priests,

over whom encyclicals, even if not executed, are always suspended.

Similar was the issue in the case of Colenso, Bishop of Natal. Equipped mainly with Cambridge mathematics added to purest self-devotion, he had been sent out as a missionary bishop. In the process of the translation of the Pentateuch for his Zulus, he had come to reflect upon the problem which the Old Testament presents. In a manner which is altogether marvellous he worked out critical conclusions parallel to those of Old Testament scholars on the Continent. He was never really an expert, but in his main contention he was right. He adhered to his opinion despite severe pressure and was not removed from the episcopate. With such guarantees it would be strange indeed if we could not say that biblical studies entered in Great Britain, as also in America, on a development in which scholars of these nations are not behind the best scholars of the world. The trials for heresy of Robertson Smith in Edinburgh and of Dr. Briggs in New York have now little living interest. Yet biblical studies in Scotland and America were incalculably furthered by those discussions. The publication of a book like *Supernatural Religion*, 1872, illustrates a proclivity not uncommon in self-conscious liberal circles, for taking up a contention just when those who made it and have lived with it have decided to lay it down. However, the names of Hatch and Lightfoot alone, not to mention the living, are sufficient to warrant the assertions above made.

More than once in these chapters we have spoken of the service rendered to the progress of Christian thought by the criticism and interpretation of religion at the hands of literary men. That country and age may be esteemed fortunate in which religion occupies a place such that it compels the attention of men of genius. In the history of culture this has by no means always been the case. That these men do not always speak the language of edification is of minor consequence. What is of infinite worth is that the largest minds of the generation shall engage themselves with the topic of religion. A history of thought concerning Christianity cannot but reckon with the opinions, for example, of Carlyle, of Emerson, of Matthew Arnold—to mention only types.

CARLYLE

Carlyle has pictured for us his early home at Ecclefechan on the Border; his father, a stone mason of the highest character ; his mother with her frugal, pious ways ; the minister, from whom he learned Latin, 'the priestliest man I ever beheld in any ecclesiastical guise.' The picture of his mother never faded from his memory. Carlyle was destined for the Church. Such had been his mother's prayer. He took his arts course in Edinburgh. In the university, he says, ' there was much talk about progress of the species, dark ages, and the like, but the hungry young looked to their spiritual nurses and were bidden to eat the east wind.' He entered Divinity Hall, but already, in 1816, prohibitive doubts had arisen in his mind. Irving sought to help him. Irving was not the man for the task. The Christianity of the Church had become intellectually incredible to Carlyle. For a time he was acutely miserable, bordering upon despair. He has described his spiritual deliverance : ' Precisely that befel me which the Methodists call their conversion, the deliverance of their souls from the devil and the pit. There burst forth a sacred flame of joy in me.' With *Sartor Resartus* his message to the world began. It was printed in *Fraser's Magazine* in 1833, but not published separately until 1838. His difficulty in finding a publisher embittered him. Style had something to do with this, the newness of his message had more. Then for twenty years he poured forth his message. Never did a man carry such a pair of eyes into the great world of London or set a more peremptory mark upon its notabilities. His best work was done before 1851. His later years were darkened with much misery of body. No one can allege that he ever had a happy mind.

He was a true prophet, but, Elijah-like, he seemed to himself to be alone.   His derision of the current religion seems
sometimes needless.   Yet even that has the grand note of
sincerity.   What he desired he in no small measure achieved
—that his readers should be arrested and feel themselves face
to face with reality.   His startling intuition, his intellectual
uprightness, his grasp upon things as they are, his passion for
what ought to be, made a great impression upon his age.
It was in itself a religious influence.   Here was a mind of
giant force, of sternest truthfulness.   His untruths were
those of exaggeration.   His injustices were those of prejudice.
He invested many questions of a social and moral, of a political
and religious sort with a nobler meaning than they had had
before.   His *French Revolution*, his papers on *Chartism*, his
unceasing comment on the troubled life of the years from
1830 to 1865, are of highest moment for our understanding
of the growth of that social feeling in the midst of which we
live and work.   In his brooding sympathy with the down-
trodden he was a great inaugurator of the social movement.
He felt the curse of an aristocratic society, yet no one has
told us with more drastic truthfulness the evils of our democratic institutions.   His word was a great corrective for
much ' rose-water ' optimism which prevailed in his day.
The note of hope is, however, often lacking.   The mythology
of an absentee God had faded from him.   Yet the God who
was clear to his mature consciousness, clear as the sun in the
heavens, was a God over the world, to judge it inexorably.
Again, it is not difficult to accumulate evidence in his words
which looks toward pantheism ; but what one may call the
religious benefit of pantheism, the sense that God is in his
world, Carlyle often loses.

Materialism is to-day so deeply discredited that we find it
difficult to realise that sixty years ago the problem wore a
different look.   Carlyle was never weary of pouring out the
vials of his contempt on ' mud-philosophies ' and exalting
the spirit as against matter.   Never was a man more opposed
to the idea of a godless world, in which man is his own chief
end and his sensual pleasures the main aims of his existence.

His insight into the consequences of our commercialism and luxury and absorption in the outward never fails. Man is God's son, but the effort to realise that sonship in the joy and trust of a devout heart and in the humble round of daily life sometimes seems to him cant or superstition. The humble life of godliness made an unspeakable appeal to him. He had known those who lived that life. His love for them was imperishable. Yet he had so recoiled from the superstitions and hypocrisies of others, the Eternal in his majesty was so ineffable, all effort to approach him so unworthy, that almost instinctively he would call upon the man who made the effort, to desist. So magnificent, all his life long, had been his protest against the credulity and stupidity of men, against beliefs which assert the impossible and blink the facts, that, for himself, the great objects of faith were held fast to, so to say, in their naked verity, with a giant's strength. They were half-querulously denied all garment and embodiment, lest he also should be found credulous and self-deceived. From this titan labouring at the foundations of the world, this Samson pulling down temples of the Philistines on his head, this cyclops heaving hills at ships as they pass by, it seems a long way to Emerson. Yet Emerson was Carlyle's friend.

EMERSON

Arnold said in one of his American addresses : ' Besides these voices—Newman, Carlyle, Goethe—there came to us in the Oxford of my youth a voice also from this side of the Atlantic, a clear and pure voice which, for my ear at any rate, brought a strain as new and moving and unforgetable as those others. Lowell has described the apparition of Emerson to your young generation here. He was your Newman, your man of soul and genius, speaking to your bodily ears, a present object for your heart and imagination.' Then he quotes as one of the most memorable passages in English speech : ' Trust thyself. Accept the place which the divine providence has found for you, the society of your contemporaries, the connection of events. Great men have always done so, confiding themselves childlike to the genius of their age, betraying a perception which was stirring in their hearts, working through their hands, dominating their whole being.' Arnold speaks of Carlyle's grim insistence upon labour and righteousness but of his scorn of happiness, and then says : ' But Emerson taught happiness in labour, in righteousness and veracity. In all the life of the spirit, happiness and eternal hope, that was Emerson's gospel. By his conviction that in the life of the spirit is happiness, by his hope and expectation that this life of the spirit will more and more be understood and will prevail, by this Emerson was great.'

Seven of Emerson's ancestors were ministers of New England churches. He inherited qualities of self-reliance, love of liberty, strenuous virtue, sincerity, sobriety and fearless loyalty to ideals. The form of his ideals was modified by the glow of transcendentalism which passed over parts of New England in the second quarter of the nineteenth century, but the spirit in which Emerson conceived the laws of life, reverenced them and lived them, was the Puritan spirit, only elevated, enlarged and beautified by the poetic temperament. Taking his degree from Harvard in 1821, despising school teaching, stirred by the passion for spiritual leadership, the ministry seemed to offer the fairest field for its satisfaction. In 1825 he entered the Divinity School in Harvard to prepare himself for the Unitarian ministry. In 1829 he became associate minister of the Second Unitarian Church in Boston. He arrived at the conviction that the Lord's Supper was not intended by Jesus to be a permanent sacrament. He found his congregation, not unnaturally, reluctant to agree with him. He therefore retired from the pastoral office. He was always a preacher, though of a singular order. His task was to befriend and guide the inner life of man. The influences of this period in his life have been enumerated as the liberating philosophy of Coleridge, the mystical vision of Swedenborg, the intimate poetry of Words-worth, the stimulating essays of Carlyle. His address before the graduating class of the Divinity School at Cambridge in 1838 was an impassioned protest against what he called the defects of historical Christianity, its undue reliance upon the personal authority of Jesus, its failure to explore the moral nature of man. He made a daring plea for absolute self-reliance and new inspiration in religion : ' In the soul let redemption be sought. Refuse the good models, even those which are sacred in the imagination of men. Cast conformity behind you. Acquaint men at first hand with deity.' He never could have been the power he was by the force of his negations. His power lay in the wealth, the variety, the beauty and insight with which he set forth the positive side of his doctrine of the greatness of man, of the presence of God in man, of the divineness of life, of God's judgment and mercy in the order of the world. One sees both the power and the limitation of Emerson's religious teaching. At the root of it lay a real philosophy. He could not philosophise. He was always passing from the principle to its application. He could not systematise. He speaks of his ' formidable tendency to the lapidary style.' Granting that one finds his philosophy in fragments, just as one finds his interpretation of religion in flashes of marvellous insight, both are worth searching for, and either, in Coleridge's phrase, finds us, whether we search for it or not.

ARNOLD

What shall we say of Matthew Arnold himself ? Without doubt the twenty years by which Arnold was Newman's junior at Oxford made a great difference in the intellectual atmosphere of that place, and of the English world of letters, at the time when Arnold's mind was maturing. He was not too late to feel the spell of Newman. His mind was hardly one to appreciate the whole force of that spell. He was at Oxford too early for the full understanding of the limits within which alone the scientific conception of the world can be said to be true. Arnold often boasted that he was no metaphysician. He really need never have mentioned the fact. The assumption that whatever is true can be verified in the sense of the precise kind of verification which science implies is a very serious mistake. Yet his whole intellectual strength was devoted to the sustaining, one cannot say exactly the cause of religion, but certainly that of noble conduct, and to the assertion of the elation of duty and the joy of righteousness. With all the scorn that Arnold pours upon the trust which we place in God's love, he yet holds to the conviction that 'the power without ourselves which makes for righteousness' is one upon which we may in rapture rely.

Arnold had convinced himself that in an age such as ours, which will take nothing for granted, but must verify everything, Christianity, in the old form of authoritative belief in supernatural beings and miraculous events, is no longer tenable. We must confine ourselves to such ethical truths as can be verified by experience. We must reject everything which goes beyond these. Religion has no more to do with supernatural dogma than with metaphysical philosophy. It has nothing to do with either. It has to do with conduct. It is folly to make religion depend upon the conviction of the existence of an intelligent and moral governor of the universe, as the theologians have done. For the object of faith in the ethical sense Arnold coined the phrase : ' The Eternal not ourselves which makes for righteousness.' So soon as we go beyond this, we enter upon the region of fanciful anthropomorphism, of extra belief, *aberglaube*, which always revenges itself. These are the main contentions of his book, *Literature and Dogma*, 1875.

One feels the value of Arnold's recall to the sense of the literary character of the Scriptural documents, as urged in his book, *Saint Paul and Protestantism*, 1870, and again to the sense of the influence which the imagination of mankind has had upon religion. One feels the truth of his assertion of our ignorance. One feels Arnold's own deep earnestness. It was his concern that reason and the will of God should prevail. Though he was primarily a literary man, yet his great interest was in religion. One feels so sincerely that his main conclusion is sound, that it is the more trying that his statement of it should be often so perverse and his method of sustaining it so precarious. It is quite certain that the idea of the Eternal not ourselves which makes for righteousness is far from being the clear idea which Arnold claims. It is far from being an idea derived from experience or verifiable in experience, in the sense which he asserts. It seems positively incredible that Arnold did not know that with this conception he passed the boundary of the realm of science and entered the realm of metaphysics, which he so abhorred.

He was the eldest son of Thomas Arnold of Rugby. He was educated at Winchester and Rugby and at Balliol College. He was Professor of Poetry in Oxford from 1857 to 1867. He was an inspector of schools. The years of his best literary labour were much taken up in ways which were wasteful of his rare powers. He came by literary intuition to an idea of Scripture which others had built up from the point of view of a theory of knowledge and by investigation of the facts. He is the helpless personification of a view of the relation of science and religion which has absolutely passed away. Yet Arnold died only in 1888. How much a distinguished inheritance may mean is gathered from the fact that a granddaughter of Thomas Arnold and niece of Matthew Arnold, Mrs. Humphry Ward, in her novels, has dealt largely with problems of religious life, and more particularly of religious thoughtfulness. She has done for her generation, in her measure, that which George Eliot did for hers.

MARTINEAU

As the chapter and the book draw to their close we can think of no man whose life more nearly spanned the century, or whose work touched more fruitfully almost every aspect of Christian thoughtfulness than did that of James Martineau. We can think of no man who gathered into himself more fully the significant theological tendencies of the age, or whose utterance entitles him to be listened to more reverently as seer and saint. He was born in 1805. He was bred as an engineer. He fulfilled for years the calling of minister and preacher. He gradually exchanged this for the activity of a professor. He was a religious philosopher in the old sense, but he was also a critic and historian. His position with reference to the New Testament was partly antiquated before his *Seat of Authority in Religion*, 1890, made its appearance. Evolutionism never became with him a coherent and consistent assumption. Ethics never altogether got rid of the innate ideas. The social movement left him almost untouched. Yet, despite all this, he was in some sense a representative progressive theologian of the century.

There is a parallel between Newman and Martineau. Both busied themselves with the problem of authority. Criticism had been fatal to the apprehension which both had inherited concerning the authority of Scripture. From that point onward they took divergent courses. The arguments which touched the infallible and oracular authority of Scripture, for Newman established that of the Church ; for Martineau they had destroyed that of the Church four hundred years ago. Martineau's sense, even of the authority of Jesus, reverent as it is, is yet no pietistic and mystical view. The authority of Jesus is that of the truth which he speaks, of the goodness which dwells in him, of God himself and God alone. A real interest in the sciences and true learning in some of them made Martineau able to write that wonderful chapter in his *Seat of Authority*, which he entitled ' God in Nature.' Newman could see in nature, at most a sacramental suggestion, a symbol of transcendental truth.

The Martineaus came of old Huguenot stock, which in England belonged to the liberal Presbyterianism out of which much of British Unitarianism came. The righteousness of a persecuted race had left an austere impress upon their domestic and social life. Intellectually they inherited the advanced liberalism of their day. Harriet Martineau's earlier piety had been of the most fervent sort. She reacted violently against it in later years. She had little of the poetic temper and gentleness of her brother. She described one of her own later works as the last word of philosophic atheism. James was, and always remained, of deepest sensitiveness and reverence and of a gentleness which stood in high contrast with his powers of conflict, if necessity arose. Out of Martineau's years as preacher in Liverpool and London came two books of rare devotional quality, *Endeavours after the Christian Life*, 1843 and 1847, and *Hours of Thought on Sacred Things*, 1873 and 1879. Almost all his life he was identified with Manchester College, as a student when the college was located at York, as a teacher when it returned to Manchester and again when it was removed to London. With its removal to Oxford, accomplished in 1889, he had not fully sympathised. He believed that the university itself must some day do justice to the education of men for the ministry in other churches than the Anglican. He was eighty years old when he published his *Types of Ethical Theory*, eighty-two when he gave to the world his *Study of Religion*, eighty-five when his *Seat of Authority* saw the light. The effect of this postponement of publication was not wholly good. The books represented marvellous learning and ripeness of reflection. But they belong to a period anterior to the dates they bear upon their title-pages. Martineau's education and his early professional experience put him in touch with the advancing sciences. In the days when most men of progressive spirit were carried off their feet, when materialism was flaunted in men's faces and the defence of religion was largely in the hands of those who knew nothing of the sciences, Martineau was not moved. He saw the end from the beginning. There is nothing finer in his latest work than his early essays—'Nature and God,' 'Science, Nescience and Faith,' and 'Religion as affected by Modern Materialism.' He died in 1900 in his ninety-fifth year.

It is difficult to speak of the living in these pages. Personal relations enforce reserve and brevity. Nevertheless, no one can think of Manchester College and Martineau without being reminded of Mansfield College and of Fairbairn, a Scotchman, but of the Independent Church. He also was both teacher and preacher all his days, leader of the movement which brought Mansfield College from Birmingham to Oxford, by the confession both of Anglicans and of Non-conformists the most learned man in his subjects in the Oxford of his time, an historian, touched by the social enthusiasm, but a religious philosopher, *par excellence.* His *Religion and Modern Life,* 1894, his *Catholicism, Roman and Anglican,* 1899, his *Place of Christ in Modern Theology,* 1893, his *Philosophy of the Christian Religion,* 1902, and his *Studies in Religion and Theology,* 1910, indicate the wideness of his sympathies and the scope of the application of his powers. If imitation is homage, grateful acknowledgment is here made of rich spoil taken from his books.

Philosophy took a new turn in Britain after the middle of the decade of the sixties. It began to be conceded that Locke and Hume were dead. Had Mill really appreciated that fact he might have been a philosopher more fruitful and influential than he was. Sir William Hamilton was dead. Mansel's endeavour, out of agnosticism to conjure the most absurdly positivistic faith, had left thinking men more exposed to scepticism, if possible, than they had been before. When Hegel was thought in Germany to be obsolete, and everywhere the cry was ' back to Kant,' some Scotch and English scholars, the two Cairds and Seth Pringle-Pattison, with Thomas Hill Green, made a modified Hegelianism current in Great Britain. They led by this path in the introduction of their countrymen to later German idealism. By this introduction philosophy in both Britain and America has greatly gained. Despite these facts, John Caird's *Introduction to the Philosophy of Religion,* 1880, is still only a religious philosophy. It is not a philosophy of religion. His *Fundamental Ideas of Christianity,* 1896, hardly escapes the old antitheses among which theological discussion moved, say, thirty years ago. Edward Caird's *Critical Philosophy of Kant,* 1889, and especially his *Evolution of Religion,* 1892, marked the coming change more definitely than did any of the labours of his brother. Thomas Hill Green gave great promise in his *Introduction to Hume,* 1885, his *Prolegomena to Ethics,* 1883, and still more in essays and papers scattered through the volumes edited by Nettleship after Green's death. His contribution to religious discussion was such as to make his untimely end to be deeply deplored. Seth

Pringle-Pattison's early work, *The Development from Kant to Hegel*, 1881, still has great worth. His *Hegelianism and Personality*, 1893, deals with one aspect of the topic which needs ever again to be explored, because of the psychological basis which in religious discussion is now assumed.

JAMES

The greatest contribution of America to religious discussion in recent years is surely William James's *Varieties of Religious Experience*, 1902. The book is unreservedly acknowledged in Britain, and in Germany as well, to be the best which we yet have upon the psychology of religion. Not only so, it gives a new intimation as to what psychology of religion means. It blazes a path along which investigators are eagerly following. Royce, in his Phi Beta Kappa address at Harvard in 1911, declared James to be the third representative philosopher whom America has produced. He had the form of philosophy as Emerson never had. He could realise whither he was going, as Emerson in his intuitiveness never did. He criticised the dominant monism in most pregnant way. He recurred to the problems which dualism owned but could not solve. We cannot call the new scheme dualism. The world does not go back. Yet James made an over-confident generation feel that the centuries to which dualism had seemed reasonable were not so completely without intelligence as has been supposed by some. No philosophy may claim completeness as an interpretation of the universe. No more conclusive proof of this judgment could be asked than is given quite unintentionally in Haeckel's *Welträthsel*.

At no point is this recall more earnest than in James's dealing with the antithesis of good and evil. The reaction of the mind of the race, and primarily of individuals, upon the fact of evil, men's consciousness of evil in themselves, their desire to be rid of it, their belief that there is a deliverance from it and that they have found that deliverance, is for James the point of departure for the study of the actual phenomena and the active principle of religion. The truest

psychological and philosophical instinct of the age thus sets
the experience of conversion in the centre of discussion.
Apparently most men have, at some time and in some way,
the consciousness of a capacity for God which is unfulfilled,
of a relation to God unrealised, which is broken and resumed,
or yet to be resumed. They have the sense that their own
effort must contribute to this recovery. They have the sense
also that something without themselves empowers them to
attempt this recovery and to persevere in the attempt.
The psychology of religion is thus put in the forefront. The
vast masses of material of this sort which the religious world,
both past and present, possesses, have been either actually
unexplored, or else set forth in ways which distorted and
obscured the facts. The experience is the fact. The best
science the world knows is now to deal with it as it would
deal with any other fact. This is the epoch-making thing,
the contribution to method in James's book. James was
born in New York in 1842, the son of a Swedenborgian theologian. He took his medical degree at Harvard in 1870.
He began to lecture there in anatomy in 1872 and became
Professor of Philosophy in 1885. He was a Gifford and a
Hibbert Lecturer. He died in 1910.

When James's thesis shall have been fully worked out,
much supposed investigation of primitive religions, which is
really nothing but imagination concerning primitive religions,
will be shown in its true worthlessness. We know very
little about primitive man. What we learn as to primitive
man, on the side of his religion, we must learn in part from
the psychology of the matured and civilised, the present
living, thinking, feeling man in contact with his religion.
Matured religion is not to be judged by the primitive, but
the reverse. The real study of the history of religions, the
study of the objective phenomena, from earliest to latest
times, has its place. But the history of religions is perverted when it takes for fact in the life of primitive man
that which never existed save in the imagination of twentieth century students. Early Christianity, on its inner and
spiritual side, is to be judged by later Christianity, by present

Christianity, by the Christian experience which we see and know to-day, and not conversely, as men have always claimed. The modern man is not to be converted after the pattern which it is alleged that his grandfather followed. For, first, there is the question as to whether his grandfather did conform to this pattern. And beyond that, it is safer to try to understand the experience of the grandfather, whom we do not know, by the psychology and experience of the grandson, whom we do know, with, of course, a judicious admixture of knowledge of the history of the nineteenth century, which would occasion characteristic differences. The modern saint is not asked to be a saint like Francis. In the first place, how do we know what Francis was like ? In the second place, the experience of Francis may be most easily understood by the aid of modern experience of true revolt from worldliness and of consecration to self-sacrifice, as these exist among us, with, of course, the proper background furnished by the history of the thirteenth century. Souls are one. Our souls may be, at least in some measure, known to ourselves. Even the souls of some of our fellows may be measurably known to us. What are the facts of the religious experience ? How do souls react in face of the eternal ? The experience of religion, the experience of the fatherhood of God, of the sonship of man, of the moving of the spirit, is surely one experience. How did even Christ's great soul react, experience, work, will, and suffer ? By what possible means can we ever know how he reacted, worked, willed, suffered ? In the literature we learn only how men thought that he reacted. We must inquire of our own souls. To be sure, Christ belonged to the first century, and we live in the twentieth. It is possible for us to learn something of the first century and of the concrete outward conditions which caused his life to take the shape which it did. We learn this by strict historical research. Assuredly the supreme measure in which the spirit of all truth and goodness once took possession of the Nazarene, remains to us a mystery unfathomed and unfathomable. Dwelling in Jesus, that spirit made through him a revelation of the divine such as the world has never seen.   Yet that mystery leads forth along the path of that which is intelligible.   And, in another sense, even such religious experience as we ourselves may have, poor though it be and sadly limited, leads back into the same mystery.

It was with this contention that religion is a fact of the inner life of man, that it is to be understood through consciousness, that it is essentially and absolutely reasonable and yet belongs to the transcendental world, it was with this contention that, in the person of Immanuel Kant, the history of modern religious thought began.   It is with this contention, in one of its newest and most far-reaching applications in the work of William James, that this history continues.   For no one can think of the number of questions which recent years have raised, without realising that this history is by no means concluded.   It is conceivable that the changes which the twentieth century will bring may be as noteworthy as those which the nineteenth century has seen.   At least we may be grateful that so great and sure a foundation has been laid.

BIBLIOGRAPHY

CHAPTER I

WERNLE, PAUL. *Einführung in das theologische Studium.* Tübingen, 2. Aufl., 1911.

DIE KULTUR DER GEGENWART. Th. I., Abth. iv. 1. *Geschichte der Christlichen Religion,* v. Wellhausen, Jülicher, Harnack u. A., 2. Aufl. Berlin, 1909.

DIE KULTUR DER GEGENWART. Th. I., Abth. iv. 2. *Systematische Christliche Religion,* v. Troeltsch, Herrmann, Holtzmann u. A., 2. Aufl. Berlin, 1909.

PFLEIDERER, OTTO. *The Development of Theology in Germany since Kant, and its Progress in Great Britain since 1825.* Transl., J. FREDERICK SMITH. London, 1893.

LICHTENBERGER, F. *Histoire des Idées Religieuses en Allemagne depuis le milieu du XVIII*ᵉ* siècle à nos jours.* Paris, 1873. Transl., with notes, W. HASTIE. Edinburgh, 1889.

ADENEY, W. F. *A Century of Progress in Religious Life and Thought.* London, 1901.

HARNACK, ADOLF. *Das Wesen des Christenthums.* Berlin, 1900. Transl., *What is Christianity?* T. B. SAUNDERS. London, 1901.

STEPHEN, LESLIE. *History of English Thought in the Eighteenth Century.* 2 vols. London, 3rd ed., 1902.

TROELTSCH, ERNST. Art. 'Deismus' in Herzog-Hauck, *Realencyclopädie für Protestantische Theologie und Kirche.* 3. Aufl. Leipzig, 4. Bd., 1898, s. 532 f. : art. 'Aufklärung,' 2. Bd., 1897, s. 225 f. : art. 'Idealismus, deutscher,' 8. Bd., 1900, s. 612 f.

MIRBT, CARL. Art. 'Pietismus' in Herzog-Hauck, *Realencyclopädie,* 15. Bd., 1904, s. 774 f.

RITSCHL, ALBRECHT. *Geschichte des Pietismus,* 3 Bde. Bonn, 1880-1886.

CHAPTER II

WINDELBAND, W. *Die Geschichte der neueren Philosophie in ihrem Zusammenhang mit der allgemeinen Kultur und den besonderen Wissenschaften.* 2 Bde. Leipzig, 1899.

HÖFFDING, HAROLD. *Geschichte der neueren Philosophie.* Uebersetzt v. Bendixen. 2 Bde. Leipzig, 1896.

EUCKEN, RUDOLF. *Die Lebensanschauungen der grossen Denker*. 8. Aufl. Leipzig, 1909. Transl., *The Problem of Human Life as viewed by the Great Thinkers*, by W. S. HOUGH and W. R. BOYCE GIBSON. New York, 1910.

PRINGLE-PATTISON, A. SETH. *The Development from Kant to Hegel*. London, 1881.

DREWS, ARTHUR. *Die Deutsche Spekulation seit Kant*. 2 Bde. Berlin, 1893.

ROYCE, JOSIAH. *The Spirit of Modern Philosophy*. Boston, 1893. *The Religious Aspect of Philosophy*. Boston, 1885. *The World and the Individual*. 2 vols. New York, 1901 and 1904.

PAULSEN, FRIEDRICH. *Immanuel Kant, sein Leben und seine Lehre*. Stuttgart, 3. Aufl., 1899. Transl., CREIGHTON and LEFEVER. New York, 1902.

CAIRD, EDWARD. *A Critical Account of the Philosophy of Kant:* with an Historical Introduction. Glasgow, 1877.

FISCHER, KUNO. *Hegels Leben, Werke und Lehre*. 2 Bde. Heidelberg, 1901.

SIEBECK, HERMANN. *Lehrbuch der Religionsphilosophie*. Freiburg, 1893.

EUCKEN, RUDOLF. *Der Wahrheitsgehalt der Religion*. Leipzig, 4. Aufl., 1906. Transl., JONES. London, 1911.

TIELE, C. P. *Compendium der Religionsgeschichte*. Uebersetzt v. Weber. 3. Aufl. umgearbeitet v. Söderblom. Breslau, 1903.

CHAPTER III

VON FRANK, H. R. *Geschichte und Kritik der neueren Theologie insbesondere der systematischen seit Schleiermacher*. Hrsg. v. Schaarschmidt. Erlangen, 1898.

SCHWARZ, CARL. *Zur Geschichte der neusten Theologie*. Leipzig, 4. Aufl., 1869.

KATTENBUSCH, FERDINAND. *Von Schleiermacher zu Ritschl*. Giessen, 1892.

BROWN, WILLIAM ADAMS. *The Essence of Christianity: a Study in the History of Definition*. New York, 1902.

DILTHEY, WILHELM. *Leben Schleiermachers*, 1. Bd. Berlin, 1870.

GASS, WILHELM. *Geschichte der Protestantischen Dogmatik*, 4 Bde. Leipzig, 1854-67.

GARVIE, ALFRED. *The Ritschlian Theology*, 2nd ed. Edinburgh, 1902.

HERRMANN, W. *Der evangelische Glaube und die Theologie Albrecht Ritschls*. Marburg, 1896.

PFLEIDERER, OTTO. *Die Ritschlsche Theologie kritisch beleuchtet*. Braunschweig, 1891.

KAFTAN, JULIUS. *Dogmatik*. Tübingen, 4. Aufl., 1901.

STEVENS, GEORGE B. *The Christian Doctrine of Salvation*. New York, 1905.

CHAPTER IV

CARPENTER, J. ESTLIN. *The Bible in the Nineteenth Century.* London, 1903.
GARDNER, PERCY. *A Historic View of the New Testament.* London, 1901.
JÜLICHER, ADOLF. *Einleitung in das Neue Testament.* Freiburg, 6. Aufl. 1906. Transl., Miss JANET WARD. 1904.
MOORE, EDWARD CALDWELL. *The New Testament in the Christian Church.* New York, 1904.
LIETZMANN, HANS. *Wie wurden die Bücher des neuen Testaments heilige Schrift?* Tübingen, 1907.
LOISY, A. *L'Évangile et l'Église.* Paris, 2nd ed., 1903. Transl., London, 1904.
WERNLE, PAUL. *Die Anfänge unserer Religion.* Tübingen, 1901.
SCHWEITZER, ALBERT. *Von Reimarus zu Wrede, eine Geschichte der Leben-Jesu-Forschung.* Tübingen, 1906.
SANDAY, WILLIAM. *The Life of Christ in Recent Research.* Oxford, 1907.
HOLTZMANN, OSKAR. *Neu-Testamentliche Zeitgeschichte.* Freiburg, 2. Aufl., 1906.
DRIVER, SAMUEL R. *Introduction to the Literature of the Old Testament.* Edinburgh, 2nd ed., 1909.
WELLHAUSEN, JULIUS. *Prolegomena zur Geschichte Israels.* Berlin, 5. Aufl., 1899.
BUDDE, KARL. *The Religion of Israel to the Exile.* New York, 1899.
KAUTSCH, E. *Abriss der Geschichte des alt-testamentlichen Schriftthums in seiner 'Heilige Schrift des Alten Testaments.'* Freiburg, 1894. Transl., J. J. TAYLOR, and published separately, New York, 1899.
SMITH, W. ROBERTSON. *The Old Testament in the Jewish Church.* Glasgow, 2nd ed., 1892. *The Prophets of Israel,* 2nd ed., 1892.

CHAPTER V

MERZ, JOHN. *A History of European Thought in the Nineteenth Century.* Vols. 1 and 2, Edinburgh, 1904 and 1903.
WHITE, ANDREW D. *The History of the Warfare of Science with Theology in Christendom.* 2 vols. New York, 1896.
OTTO, RUDOLF. *Naturalistische und religiöse Weltansicht.* Tübingen, 2. Aufl., 1909.
WARD, JAMES. *Naturalism and Agnosticism.* 2 vols. London, 1899.
FLINT, ROBERT. *Agnosticism.* Edinburgh, 1903.
TULLOCH, JOHN. *Modern Theories in Philosophy and Religion.* Edinburgh, 1884.
MARTINEAU, JAMES. *Essays, Reviews and Addresses.* Vols. 1 and 3 London, 1890.

BOUTROUX, ÉMILE. *Science et Religion dans la Philosophie contemporaine.* Paris, 1908. Transl., NIELD. London, 1909.
FLINT, ROBERT. *Socialism.* London, 1895.
PEABODY, FRANCIS G. *Jesus Christ and the Social Question.* New York, 1905.

CHAPTER VI

HUNT, JOHN. *Religious Thought in England in the Nineteenth Century.* London, 1896.
TULLOCH, JOHN. *Movements of Religious Thought in Britain during the Nineteenth Century.* London, 1885.
BENN, ALFRED WILLIAM. *The History of English Rationalism in the Nineteenth Century.* 2 vols. London, 1906.
HUTTON, RICHARD H. *Essays on some of the Modern Guides to English Thought in Matters of Faith.* London, 1900.
MELLONE, SIDNEY H. *Leaders of Religious Thought in the Nineteenth Century.* Edinburgh, 1902.
BROOKE, STOPFORD A. *Theology in the English Poets.* London, 1896.
SCUDDER, VIDA D. *The Life of the Spirit in the Modern English Poets.* Boston, 1899.
CHURCH, R. W. *The Oxford Movement: Twelve Years, 1833-1845.* London, 1904.
FAIRBAIRN, ANDREW M. *Catholicism, Roman and Anglican.* New York, 1899.
WARD, WILFRID. *Life and Times of Cardinal Wiseman.* 2 vols. 5th ed. London, 1900.
WARD, WILFRID. *Life of John Henry, Cardinal Newman.* 2 vols. London, 1912.
DÖLLINGER, J. J. IGNAZ VON. *Das Papstthum: Neubearbeitung von Janus: Der Papst und das Concil, von J. Friedrich.* München, 1892.
GOUT, RAOUL. *L'Affaire Tyrrell.* Paris, 1910.
SABATIER, PAUL. *Modernism.* Transl., MILES. New York, 1908.
STANLEY, ARTHUR P. *The Life and Correspondence of Thomas Arnold.* 2 vols. London, 13th ed., 1882.
BROOKE, STOPFORD A. *Life and Letters of Frederick W. Robertson.* 2 vols. London, 1891.
ABBOTT, EVELYN and CAMPBELL, LEWIS. *Life and Letters of Benjamin Jowett.* 2 vols. London, 1897.
DRUMMOND, JAMES, and UPTON, C. B. *Life and Letters of James Martineau.* 2 vols. London, 1902.
ALLEN, ALEXANDER V. G. *Life and Letters of Phillips Brooks.* 2 vols. New York, 1900.
MUNGER, THEODORE T. *Horace Bushnell, Preacher and Theologian.* Boston, 1899.

INDEX